A Note on Pronunciation, Place Names, and Dates

To aid pronunciation, diacritic marks have been used for Sanskrit words, names, and places up until the Mughal period.

ā	car	ṛ	rig
ṣ (retroflex)	dish	ṇ (retroflex)	renown
ī	queen	ṃ	like the n in uncle
ṅ (velar)	sung	ṭ	tub
ū	boot	ś (palatal)	shame
ñ (palatal)	canyon	ḷ	able

In recent decades, many cities in India have ditched their colonial names, thus Calcutta became Kolkata and Bombay is now officially Mumbai. The following text reverts to names in use during the periods that are being discussed. To aid the reader, the modern equivalents of ancient names are given, thus Kāñcī is now Kanchipuram and Kashi is today's Varanasi. Dates for births, deaths, and reigns of prominent historical figures up to the Mughal period are also given.

Chronology

ANCIENT INDIA	**c. 1.5 million BCE**	Earliest humans in India
	c. 65,000 BCE	Out-of-Africa migration reaches India
	c. 7000 BCE	Earliest evidence of agriculture
	c. 3300–2600 BCE	Early Harappān civilization
	c. 2600–1900 BCE	Mature Harappān
	c. 2000–1500 BCE	Āryan migration from Central Asia
	c. 1900–1300 BCE	Late Harappān
	c. 1200–1100 BCE	*Ṛig Veda* compiled
	c. 800–300 BCE	*Upaniṣhads* composed
	c. 599–527 BCE	Mahāvīra, founder of Jainism
	c. 563–483 BCE	Siddhārtha Gautama, founder of Buddhism
	c. 400 BCE–300 CE	*Mahābhārata* and *Ramayana* composed
	326 BCE	Alexander the Great invades northern India
AGE OF EMPIRES	**c. 322–185 BCE**	Mauryan Empire
	c. 100–240 BCE	First Indian Buddhist missions to China
	135 BCE–150 CE	Kuśāṇa Empire
	c. 100–500	Gandharan art flourishes in North India and Afghanistan
	c. 320–550	Gupta Empire
	c. 200–400	*Kāmasūtra* composed
AGE OF INVASIONS	**c. 455**	First Hūṇa invasion
	c. 606–47	Reign of Harṣa
	c. 712	Arabs occupy Sindh
	c. 300–888	Pallavas of Kāñcī
	c. 871–907	Rise of the Cholan Empire
	1004–30	Mahmud of Ghazni raids India
	1192	Prithviraj Chauhan defeated at battle of Tarain
	1206–1526	Delhi Sultanate
	1336–1565	Vijayanagara Empire

THE
SHORTEST
HISTORY
OF
INDIA

**From the World's Oldest Civilization
to Its Largest Democracy—
A Retelling for Our Times**

JOHN ZUBRZYCKI

THE EXPERIMENT
NEW YORK

To April

Originally published in Australia by Black Inc. in 2022. First published in North America in revised form by The Experiment, LLC, in 2023.

The Experiment, LLC
220 East 23rd Street, Suite 600
New York, NY 10010-4658
theexperimentpublishing.com

The Experiment's books are available at special discounts when purchased in bulk for premiums and sales promotions as well as for fundraising or educational use. For details, contact us at info@theexperimentpublishing.com.

Library of Congress Cataloging-in-Publication Data

Names: Zubrzycki, John, author.
Title: The shortest history of India : from the world's oldest civilization
  to its largest democracy - a retelling for our times / John Zubrzycki.
Description: [Revised edition]. | New York : The Experiment, 2023. |
  Series: The shortest history series | Originally published: Australia :
  Black Inc., 2022.
Identifiers: LCCN 2023024238 (print) | LCCN 2023024239 (ebook) | ISBN
  9781615199976 (paperback) | ISBN 9781615199983 (ebook)
Subjects: LCSH: India--History.
Classification: LCC DS436 .Z835 2023 (print) | LCC DS436 (ebook) | DDC
  954--dc23/eng/20230520
LC record available at https://lccn.loc.gov/2023024238
LC ebook record available at https://lccn.loc.gov/2023024239

ISBN 978-1-61519-997-6
Ebook ISBN 978-1-61519-998-3

Cover and text design by Jack Dunnington

Manufactured in the United States of America

First printing November 2023
10 9 8 7 6 5 4 3 2 1

Contents

GREAT MUGHALS	1526–1530	Reign of Babur
	1530–40, 1555–56	Reign of Humayun
	1556–1605	Reign of Akbar
	1605–27	Reign of Jahangir
	1627–58	Reign of Shah Jahan
	1632–54	Taj Mahal constructed
	1658–1707	Reign of Aurangzeb
COLONIALISM	1600	British East India Company (EIC) founded
	1739	Delhi sacked by Persian Nadir Shah
	1756	Black Hole of Calcutta
	1757	Battle of Plassey
	1765	EIC gains rights to revenue collection in Bengal
	1773	Regulating Act establishes a governor general and supervising council
	1799	Tipu Sultan defeated at Srirangapatnam
	1813	Charter Act allows Christian missionaries into India
	1817–18	Third Anglo-Maratha War and British conquest of India
	1856	Lord Dalhousie orders annexation of Awadh
	1857	Indian Uprising or Mutiny
	1858	India comes under the Crown
BRITISH RAJ	1876	Queen Victoria becomes Empress of India
	1885	Indian National Congress founded
	1905	Partition of Bengal
	1906	Muslim League founded
	1918	Mahatma Gandhi holds first *satyagraha* in Bihar
	1919	Amritsar Massacre
	1930	Indian National Congress calls for self-rule
	1931	Gandhi attends Round Table Conference in London
	1942	"Quit India" resolution, Congress leadership jailed
	August 16, 1946	Jinnah proclaims Direct Action Day
	August 14–15, 1947	Pakistan and India gain independence from Britain

October 1947	India and Pakistan war in Kashmir
January 30, 1948	Gandhi assassinated
January 26, 1950	India officially becomes a republic
1952	First general election
1962	India-China border war
May 27, 1964	Jawaharlal Nehru dies
September 1965	India and Pakistan war over Kashmir
January 1966	Indira Gandhi becomes prime minister
December 1971	India and Pakistan war over East Pakistan
June 1984	Indian troops storm the Sikh Golden Temple
October 31, 1984	Indira Gandhi assassinated; Rajiv Gandhi becomes prime minister
May 21, 1991	Rajiv Gandhi assassinated
1991	Congress launches sweeping economic reforms
December 6, 1992	Hindu zealots tear down the Babri mosque, Ayodhya
1998	Bharatiya Janata Party forms a coalition government
May 1998	India and Pakistan conduct nuclear tests
May 1999	Kargil conflict
May 2004	Manmohan Singh becomes prime minister
November 2008	Mumbai terror attack
May 2014	Narendra Modi becomes prime minister
November 2016	Demonetization
May 2019	BJP wins second term
March–June 2021	Devastating second COVID-19 wave kills thousands
April 2023	India's population overtakes China's to become largest in the world

INDEPENDENT INDIA

Introduction

Whatever you can rightly say about India, the opposite is also true.

—British economist Joan Robinson

Early on the morning of August 9, 1942, the leader of the Indian National Congress Jawaharlal Nehru and nine of his colleagues were bundled into a train at Bombay's Victoria Terminus. Their destination was Ahmadnagar Fort in the sweltering hills of modern-day Maharashtra. In 1707, the last of the Great Mughals, Aurangzeb, had died in the fort—the moment of his passing coinciding with a whirlwind "so fierce that it blew down all the tents standing in the encampment . . . villages were destroyed and trees overthrown." Under the British, Ahmadnagar had been turned into a high-security jail. Nehru's incarceration would last two years and nine months—the longest of his nine stints as a prisoner of the Raj. His crime was to launch the Quit India movement, a desperate bid by Congress to pressure Britain into granting immediate independence if it were to count on India's full support for the war effort. The war would be almost over by the time he was released.

India's future prime minister described Ahmadnagar as a kind of "Plato's cave"—a prison whose inmates can only see shadows of what is going on around them. Yet he took solace in the sky over his prison yard with its "fleecy and colourful clouds in the daytime, and . . . brilliant star-lit nights." Inside the fort's walls was a firmament of a different kind: Nehru's small cohort of fellow prisoners represented a cross-section of Indian politics, scholarship, and society. Between them, they spoke four of India's classical languages—Sanskrit, Pali, Arabic, and Persian—as well as more than half a dozen of its modern ones, including Hindi, Urdu, Bengali, Gujarati, Marathi, and Telugu. "I had all this wealth to draw upon and the only limitation was my own capacity to profit by it," Nehru mused. There was plenty of time to cultivate a garden, hold impromptu seminars, and speculate on what was going on in the rest of the country. As he had done during his earlier jail terms, Nehru took the opportunity to satisfy his voracious appetite for reading classic works on history and politics, and to translate those ideas into his own writings.

Compiled during many long, hot days, *The Discovery of India* (1946) would become his best-known work. Nehru dismissed it as a "jumble of ideas"—a journey through the past that also "peeped into the future." Much of the work is just that—a skein of unconnected thoughts. But he begins the book with a fundamental question: "What is this India, apart from her physical and geographical aspects?" In the last chapter, he feels confident enough to offer an answer, writing that India is "a cultural unity amidst diversity, a bundle of contradictions held together by strong but invisible threads . . . She is a myth and an idea, a dream and a vision, and yet very real and present and pervasive."

Nehru's conclusion might appear frustratingly vague and contradictory to aspiring students of India's history. Yet India as both an idea and an entity has endured for thousands of years, accommodating a diversity of religions, cultures, languages, ethnicities, and castes. "India has had that past tradition of synthesis," Nehru pointed out in a speech in 1953, adding: "Currents came to it, rivers of humanity flowed into it, and got mixed up with the ocean of India, making changes there no doubt, and affecting it and being affected by it."

Nehru took for granted the importance of "discovering India." But for many outsiders, making the "passage to India," to borrow the title from E. M. Forster's book, is challenging. The country's cultural and linguistic complexity, its extremes of wealth and poverty, its mosaic of religions and rituals, and its convoluted and increasingly contested history might deter all but the most committed. It may seem impossible to meld overlapping cultural, political, and social currents into a coherent and comprehensive narrative. As the Bengali author and scholar Nirad Chaudhuri (1897–1999) wrote back in the 1950s, India is "so vast and so populous, the individuals who form the exceptions may well run into millions."

Whatever the hurdles India's complexity puts in the path of students and historians, it would be a folly to ignore the wider lessons of the country's past and present. India is the world's oldest continuous civilization and its largest democracy. It is the fulcrum between the eastern and western parts of Asia and an assertive Indian Ocean power. It is also changing rapidly, ditching the last remnants of the socialist experiment that guided its economy for decades and adapting to a new world order where its rhetoric of nonalignment—its refusal to side with one superpower or another—has less and less relevance.

India has yet to replicate China's shiny bullet trains, its glittering megalopolises, or its giant factories producing laptops and smartphones for tech-hungry consumers around the world. It has also been poorly served by its democratically elected leaders, who have consistently failed to harness the country's full potential. Rich in natural resources and with an immense pool of highly educated, globally literate workers, India holds huge promise. India's population overtook China's in 2023, as both countries broke through the 1.4 billion mark. India's five largest cities have economies of comparable size to middle-income countries such as Serbia and Bulgaria today. By 2025, one fifth of the world's working-age population will be Indian, and a billion Indians will be connected to one another and the world through smartphones. According to the brokerage house Morgan Stanley, India will become the world's third-largest economy by 2027, thanks to global trends in outsourcing, key investments it has made in technology and energy, and policy changes that favor job creation.

Unlike China's history, which can be divided neatly into dynastic periods such as those of the Yuan, the Ming, or the Qing, India's past is untidy, with disparate and competing centers of power. Even at the height of its imperial expansion, India's three great empires—Mauryan, Gupta, and Mughal—did not control the entire subcontinent. It was not until the defeat of the Marathas in 1818 that Britain could make that claim. Even then, the princely states, which covered two fifths of India's landmass and were home to one third of India's population, retained some nominal independence.

To include here the reign of every ruler on the subcontinent, the fortunes of all its major and minor dynasties, and the outcome of every battle for territory and wealth—not to mention India's contribution to the world in fields such as science, literature, and art—would be self-defeating, a jumbled mass of names, dates, and declarations devoid of texture and depth. It is challenging to condense five thousand years of Indian history into a couple of hundred pages while trying to convey these subtleties, but it is necessary.

What's in a Name?

For traders and invaders who made the long trek over the Hindu Kush and arrived on the plains of what is now Pakistan's Punjab province, the first significant geographical barrier was the Sindhu River. Unable to pronounce the *S*, the Persians called the river the Hindu. When the Greeks arrived in the fourth century BCE, the *H* was dropped and it became the Indus, as it is known today, and the lands beyond it, Ἰνδία, the root of the word India. In the same way that America and Australia are inventions that bear no relation to how the precolonial inhabitants referred to their lands, the name India never really took hold until the European trader encounter of the sixteenth and seventeenth centuries brought to India's shores Portugal's Estado da Índia, the Dutch Vereenigde Oost Indische Compagnie, France's Compagnie des Indes, and, finally, Britain's East India Company. A more common name was Hindustan, which referred to "land of the Indus" rather than "land of the Hindus." The generic term "Hindustanee" was commonly used to refer to anyone who came from what was then British India until the early twentieth century.

The Sanskrit name for India is *Bharata*, which was defined in the third century text the *Viṣṇupurāṇa*: "The country that lies north of the ocean, and south of the snowy mountains, is called Bhārata, for there dwelt the descendants of [King] Bhārata. It is nine thousand leagues in extent, and is the land of works, in consequence of which men go to heaven, or obtain emancipation." The opening article of the Indian Constitution states: "India, that is Bharat, shall be a Union of States."

Geographically, it is relatively simple to define the parameters of India and Indian civilization over the millennia. Approximately 180 million years ago, the supercontinent of

Gondwana began to break up, with the Indian Plate drifting in a northeast direction at the rate of around six inches a year until it collided with the Eurasian Plate nearly fifty-five million years ago to create the world's highest mountain range, the Himalayas. The approximately 1,550-mile-long range marks the northern boundary of what is referred to today as the Indian subcontinent. Quadrilateral in shape, its eastern extremities are hemmed by the jungle-clad ranges that form the Indo-Myanmar border. In the west lies the Hindu Kush, where the Bolan and Khyber passes became the pathways for waves of invading armies. The subcontinent's southern boundary is a massive peninsula that protrudes like a spearhead into the Indian Ocean.

Today, the subcontinent is divided into five nations. India is the largest of these, with an area of just under 1.27 million square miles, if all of contested Kashmir is included; it measures almost 2,000 miles from north to south and about 1,800 miles from east to west. It is also the most populous, home to approximately 1.4 billion people. It shares land borders with the other four countries of the subcontinent—Pakistan, Nepal, Bhutan, and Bangladesh—as well as with China and Myanmar. India is also one of the most densely populated countries in the world, with around 1,200 people per square mile—more than three times that of China.

As with Egypt and Mesopotamia, which flourished on the Nile, Tigris, and Euphrates rivers, India's earliest civilizations grew up around the fertile floodplains of the Ganges and Indus. From its source at Gangotri, in the northeast, the Ganges cuts through the Himalayas, before it flows eastward and merges with the Brahmaputra River to form one of the agriculturally richest deltas in the world, encompassing the modern Indian

state of West Bengal and the independent nation of Bangladesh. South of the Vindhya mountain range, which divides the subcontinent neatly in half, is the Deccan plateau, bounded on either side by the Eastern and Western Ghats. The major rivers of the Deccan and southern India include the Narmada, the Godavari, the Krishna, and the Kaveri.

One of the most anticipated announcements in India is the annual monsoon forecast. The southwest monsoon, which begins in June and lasts until September, dumps approximately 80 percent of the country's annual rainfall. Parts of northeastern India receive up to 464 inches a year, while the western Thar Desert of Rajasthan can get as little as 4 inches. The monsoon is crucial to agricultural output in a country where only half of the farmland is irrigated. By raising food prices and cutting rural incomes, a poor monsoon can topple a government.

The subcontinent's rivers, mountains, and coastline define its sacred geography. Varanasi, also known as Kashi or the City of Light, is located on the Ganges. Sacred to the god Śiva, the city is as holy to Hindus as Mecca is to Muslims, the Vatican is to Roman Catholics, and Jerusalem is to Jews. For Hindus it is a place of spiritual liberation. To die here is to achieve *moksha*, or freedom from the endless cycle of rebirth. Upstream at the confluence of the Ganges, Yamuna, and mythical Saraswatī rivers is Prayagraj, formerly known as Allahabad, the site of the greatest gathering of humanity anywhere in the world—the Kumbh Mela—which occurs on four occasions every twelve years. Devout pilgrims carry jars of sacred Ganges water to the dozens of holy places scattered around mountain ranges, rivers, and coastlines. When Sufi mystics, practicing a more devotional form of Islam, began arriving in India early in the last millennium, they, too, established networks of *dargahs* or shrines, such as that of Nizamuddin Auliya in Delhi and Mu'inuddin Chishti in Ajmer, one of the holiest places of Islam aside from Mecca and Medina. The web of pilgrimage routes crisscrossing India includes places sacred to Sikhs, Jains, Buddhists, and Christians.

Though formidable, the subcontinent's geographical boundaries have always been porous, allowing new cultures, agricultural practices, languages, religions, and even methods of warfare to take root. The nomadic Āryans, who spread into northern India from the steppes of Central Asia, were followed by the armies of Alexander the Great. From western China came the Kuśāṇas and from the Central Asian steppes the Hūṇas, a tribe related to the Huns. Chinese pilgrims seeking scholarship and enlightenment made their way to centers of learning such as Nalanda, considered the first university in the world, where the subjects taught ranged from Buddhist theology to alchemy and astronomy. The rise of Islam in the seventh century made its presence felt through trade and then conquest, culminating with the establishment of the Delhi Sultanate and the Mughal Empire. Even at the height of Mughal supremacy in the seventeenth century, European powers including the Portuguese, Dutch, French, and British had footholds in India.

Over the millennia, the influence of Indian religion, thought, and science would spread well beyond its borders, giving the world everything from the decimal system to yoga, from Bollywood movies to vegetarianism. The legacy of British colonial rule inculcated the English language with a masala of Indian words: *bungalow*, *polo*, *gymkhana*, *loot*, *mogul*, *jungle*, and *thug*, to name just a few. Indian soft power predates the

Raj by two millennia. In c. 240 BCE, the Third Buddhist Council—held in Pāṭaliputra, in the country's north—was instructed by the Emperor Aśoka (r. c. 268–c. 232 BCE) to send emissaries to nine countries to spread Buddha's teachings. As early as the first century CE, Hinduism was making its presence felt as far away as the islands of Java and Bali in the Indonesian archipelago. By the 1960s and 1970s, gurus such as Maharishi Mahesh Yogi had become household names in the West for preaching the benefits of Transcendental Meditation to the Beatles, and thousands of Westerners were making their way along the hippie trail.

India's other outstanding gift to the world has been its diaspora. Numbering around eighteen million, it is the largest in the world. Zubin Mehta is a name synonymous with conductors of Western classical music. M. Night Shyamalan's films inducted the genre of "scary movies with a twist." CEOs of Indian heritage head major companies, including Google, Twitter, and Microsoft. The diaspora's reach was symbolized in January 2021 by the swearing in of Kamala Harris as the first American vice president of South Asian heritage. As the ceremony was beamed in live to their smartphones, residents of her ancestral village of Thulasendrapuram, about 210 miles from Chennai, lit firecrackers, distributed sweets and flowers as a religious offering, and prayed at the local temple for her welfare.

Nehru once compared India's ability to absorb and conserve ideas from abroad to a palimpsest: an ancient manuscript that is written over again and again without completely obliterating the layer before. The following pages of this short history aim to bring those layers to life.

CHAPTER 1

Lost Civilizations

In 1856, a contractor named William Brunton, working on the Multan-to-Lahore railway, found the perfect source for track ballast to construct embankments. At the small village of Harappā, he discovered thousands of uniformly shaped kiln-fired bricks buried in a series of mounds that locals had been excavating to obtain building material for their houses. The news eventually reached Alexander Cunningham (1814–1893), the founder of the Archaeological Survey of India, who, in 1873, surveyed an extensive series of ruins about half a mile long running along the banks of the Ravi River. He assumed they were the remains of a Greek settlement left behind by Alexander the Great's army in the fourth century BCE. So much of the rubble had been cleared away that he decided there was little worth preserving, leaving the most significant discoveries for future archaeologists.

Among the artifacts Cunningham did collect was a small seal, not much bigger than a postage stamp, made of smooth, black soapstone and bearing the image of a bull with six characters above it. Because the bull had no hump and the characters did not resemble the letters of any known Indian language, he believed the seal came from elsewhere. Other seals were gradually uncovered featuring animals such as elephants, oxen, and rhinoceroses—and mysterious characters.

Some of the seals made their way to the British Museum, where one, depicting a cow with a unicorn-like horn, features in Neil MacGregor's 2010 book, *A History of the World in 100 Objects*. As the museum's former director notes, the tiny seal would lead to the rewriting of world history and take Indian civilization thousands of years further back than anyone had previously thought.

It was Cunningham's successor, Sir John Marshall (1876–1958), who recognized the significance of the seals. In the 1920s, he ordered further excavations at Harappā and a site that came to be known as Mohenjo-daro, or "Mound of the Dead Men," several hundred miles to the south in what was then British India and is now the province of Sindh, in Pakistan. Marshall realized immediately there was a link between the two sites. At both places there were numerous artificial mounds covering the remains of once-flourishing cities. As dozens of similar sites came to light over an area stretching from the Yamuna River in the east to present-day Afghanistan in the west, it became clear that between roughly 3300 BCE and 1300 BCE, it had been home to the world's largest civilization (by area).

Until Marshall's discoveries, there was no material evidence of any Indian civilization that predated Alexander the Great (356–323 BCE), whose conquering armies reached the shores of the Indus River in 326 BCE. Almost all of the archaeological remains from around this date were Buddhist, with much of the statutory bearing Grecian influences.

As Marshall continued his excavations, he was stunned by the uniqueness of the finds. To begin with, those prized bricks turned out to be remarkably uniform across all the excavated sites. The settlements were built on similar grid layouts, with street widths conforming to set ratios depending on their importance. There were imposing communal buildings, what appeared to be public baths, and a sophisticated sanitation system—triumphs of town planning, far in advance of anything known in the ancient world and not to be repeated in India until Maharaja Jai Singh I laid out plans for Jaipur in the early eighteenth century. Even the weights and measures used in trade were remarkably uniform.

Originally thought to be a unicorn, the animal on this seal is now believed to be a bull. The seals of the Harappān civilization contain the oldest writing in South Asia. It has yet to be deciphered.

Toys and figurines made of clay and bronze, jewelry and cooking aids, rudimentary agricultural tools, fragments of painted pottery, whistles made in the form of hollow birds, and even terra-cotta mousetraps were found at dozens of sites. Then there were those seals—almost five thousand have been discovered so far—some with anthropomorphic figures, others with animals, including that mysterious unicorn-like bovine in the British Museum. "Not often has it been to archaeologists, as it was given to Schliemann at Tiryns and Mycenae, or to Stein in the deserts of Turkestan, to light upon the remains of a long-forgotten civilization. It looks, however, at this moment, as if we were on the threshold of such a discovery in the plains of the Indus," Marshall announced triumphantly in September 1924.

We now know that at its peak in 2500 BCE, around the time the Great Pyramid of Giza was completed and a century

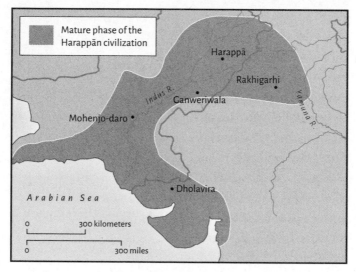

Map showing Mature phase of the Harappān civilization, also known as the Indus Valley civilization. The former, named after the first discovered site, is now preferred because the civilization extended beyond the Indus River.

or so before Stonehenge rose from the fields of Wiltshire, the Harappān civilization covered an area of about 385,000 square miles, making it bigger than the civilizations of Egypt and Mesopotamia combined. But unlike our knowledge of its better-known contemporaries, what we know of this momentous civilization is scanty. No Rosetta Stone has been discovered to crack the code of those ubiquitous markings on the seals.

Over the past century and a half, attempts to identify the characters by linking them to scripts or languages as diverse as Brāhmī (the ancestor to most modern South Asian scripts), Sumerian, Egyptian, Old Slavic, and even Easter Island rongorongo have proven futile. Citing the brevity of most inscriptions (fewer than one in a hundred objects with "writing" have more than ten characters), some historians and linguists have speculated that the seals do not contain script at all but are devices that denote ownership—a primitive form of a barcode.

If this was a form of writing, it would make the Harappān civilization the largest literate society of the ancient world, and arguably its most advanced. It would not be until the reign of Emperor Aśoka in the third century BCE that evidence of writing emerged on the Indian subcontinent. Unless archaeologists stumble upon a buried library or archives, the mystery of the script, if indeed that is what it is, will remain just that.

In their attempt to establish a chronology of the Harappān civilization, archaeologists have made little headway in determining how the society was governed and functioned. None of the structures appeared to be palaces or places of worship. Fortifications weren't added until the later phase of the civilization, and few weapons have been unearthed. The lack of elaborate burial places suggests a degree of social equality found nowhere else in the ancient world. Evidence of a ruling class with kings or queens has yet to be established.

Based on the discovery of seals as far afield as Iraq, Oman, and Central Asia, it is clear that this was also a significant trading empire. Copper, gold, tin, ivory, and possibly cotton were traded with Mesopotamia, while bronze, silver, and precious stones such as lapis lazuli were imported. Yet after a century of excavations, considerable uncertainty remains over how this prosperous and sophisticated civilization was founded and what caused it to vanish.

In the absence of definitive evidence, numerous theories have filled the vacuum. The race to decipher the script has led to forgeries, including the doctoring of an image on a seal to make it look like a horse, an animal of considerable importance in Vedic ritual. Most of these forgeries have been constructed around the need to provide a continuous line to the foundation of the modern Indian state. In recent decades, Hindu nationalist historians have sought to incorporate the Harappān civilization with the beginnings of Hinduism, which they argue dates back to the third or fourth millennium BCE, thereby making it the oldest religion in South Asia.

The Earliest Indians

If the archaeological discoveries of the early 1920s were a watershed in pushing back the beginnings of Indian civilization by thousands of years, the 2010s will be remembered for the astonishing advances in our understanding of the ancestry of the earliest Indians. The ability to analyze the genetic DNA of skeletal remains has enabled scientists to map migration routes into India, identify the first agriculturalists and even date the beginnings of social stratification known as the caste system.

Based on archaeological finds, such as beach middens in Eritrea, we can confidently date the migration of modern humans, or *Homo sapiens*, out of Africa to around seventy thousand years ago. Their route took them through the Arabian Peninsula and across modern-day Iraq and Iran, until they reached the Indian subcontinent some sixty-five thousand years ago. There, they encountered groups of what are termed "archaic humans." In the absence of any fossil evidence other than a cranium discovered on the banks of the Narmada River and dated to approximately 250,000 years ago, we do not know who these people were. The discovery of Paleolithic tools in South India pushes back the timeline for these archaic people to 1.5 million years ago, making them one of the earliest populations outside Africa. As modern humans settled in the more fecund areas of the subcontinent, their population increased rapidly until India became the epicenter of the world's population during the period from approximately forty-five thousand to twenty thousand years ago.

DNA dating points to a second wave of migrants who made their way eastward from the southern or central Zagros region in modern-day Iran around 8000 BCE. The precursor to what became the Harappān civilization can be found in a village so remote and obscure that even people living in the area don't know of its existence. Mehrgarh is located in the Pakistani province of Baluchistan, a lawless tribal area on the western edge of the Indian subcontinent. Archaeologists digging at the site in the late 1970s found the earliest evidence of agriculture outside the Fertile Crescent. Crops such as barley were cultivated, and animals, including cattle, zebu, and possibly goats, were domesticated. Buildings ranged in size from four- to ten-roomed dwellings, with the larger ones probably used for grain storage. Buried alongside the dead were ornaments made from seashells, lapis lazuli, and other semiprecious stones. Archaeologists discovered the world's first examples of cotton being woven into fabric.

By the time it was abandoned in favor of a larger town nearby sometime between 2600 and 2000 BCE, Mehrgarh had grown to become an important center for innovation, not only in agriculture but also in pottery, stone tools, and the use of copper. The agricultural revolution it sparked would become the basis of the Harappān civilization.

The World's First Secular State?

Historians divide the Harappān civilization into three phases. The Early Harappān, dating from around 3300 to 2600 BCE, was proto-urban. Pottery was made on wheels, barley and legumes were cultivated, and cattle, sheep, goats, buffalo, deer, and pigs were domesticated. The civilization was extensive—remains from this period have been found as far west as the Indo-Gangetic Plain, and south to the Rann of Kutch, in the modern Gujarat state. However, there is much about this phase that is unknown. At sites such as Mohenjo-daro, the ruins extend several meters below the current excavation depth, but with preservation taking precedence over excavation it may take many years before a more definitive picture of this period emerges.

The Mature Harappān phase, dating from 2600 to 1900 BCE, is considered the peak of urbanization, though villages still outnumbered urban centers. The positioning of citadels, granaries, and public and private buildings varied across the settlements, but all, from the biggest to the smallest, had some degree of planning. Irrigation works were sophisticated enough to allow a succession of crops to be grown; ploughs were used to cultivate the fields. Skeletal remains of dogs suggest their domestication. The population estimate for the Mature phase ranges from four hundred thousand to one million people.

While the absence of any evidence of large royal tombs, palaces, temples, standing armies, or slaves makes it difficult to picture a centralized empire, some form of state structure likely existed. The uniformity in crafts such as pottery and brickmaking down to the village level suggests specialized hereditary groups or guilds, and a well-developed system of internal trade. By the Mature phase, the symbols that were found on seals became standardized. Gambling was widespread, as evidenced by dozens of cubical terra-cotta dice discovered at Mohenjo-daro and other sites. Cotton was cultivated for clothes and possibly traded with West Asia.

Although no structures that can be definitively classified as temples have been discovered, some kind of religious ideology almost certainly existed—the links between what is known of Harappān systems of belief and the development of Hinduism are too numerous to ignore. Images of what could be deities in peepul trees with worshippers kneeling in front of them were common (the tree is considered sacred in both Hinduism and Buddhism). Bathing, an important part of Harappān civilization, is a centerpiece of Hindu ritual. The existence of what appear to be fire altars, evidence of animal sacrifices, and the use of the swastika symbol recall Hindu ceremonies.

The most compelling evidence of a link is a seal depicting a figure seated in a yogic position wearing a horned headdress and surrounded by a tiger, elephant, buffalo, and rhinoceros. The figure on the inch-high seal was named Pashupati, or "Lord of the Beasts," and was described by Marshall as a "proto-Śiva," or early model of Śiva—a key deity in the Hindu pantheon, considered the god of creation and destruction.

The description of the Lord of the Beasts seal as a proto-Śiva was eagerly embraced by Jawaharlāl Nehru and subsequently by Hindu nationalist historians.

But as the American Indologist Wendy Doniger points out, the Śiva connection is just one of more than a dozen explanations for the figure "inspired or constrained by the particular historical circumstances and agenda of the interpreter." Similarly, small terra-cotta statuettes of buxom women could be prototypes of Hindu goddesses or mere expressions of admiration for the female form. What we do know is that the migrating tribes from Central Asia drew on existing deities and belief systems. If these alleged deity prototypes were not evidence of a coherent religious system, they open up the tantalizing possibility that the Harappān civilization may have been the world's first secular state, predating the European Enlightenment by four millennia.

What caused the decline of the Harappān civilization in the lead-up to its demise in 1300 BCE is still open to interpretation. Later religious texts suggest that invading war-like pastoralists who had mastered horse-drawn chariots laid waste to the civilization's cities. Sir Mortimer Wheeler, director-general of the Archaeological Survey of India from 1944 to 1948, was a proponent of this theory, declaring famously: "On circumstantial evidence, Indra stands accused!"—a reference to the Āryan god of war.

But the archaeological record no longer supports this theory. Skeletal remains give no evidence of an assault on any of the major cities. Excavations at several sites point to a series of floods, possibly exacerbated by tectonic movements that raised the ground level. Other possible causes for the demise of the Harappān civilization include changing river courses, deforestation, rising salinity, and diseases carried by waves of new migrants. A large-scale study by a team of scientists from the Woods Hole Oceanographic Institution published in 2012 suggests a prolonged drought that caused rivers to dry up or become seasonal as the most probable culprit. There is currency to this theory: in 2018, scientists classified a new age in geological time, the Meghalayan, which began around 2200 BCE with a prolonged drought that triggered the end of civilizations not only in India, but also in Egypt, Mesopotamia, and China.

The Vedas

If our inability to decipher those Harappān characters leaves us bereft of stories, historical figures, and a reliable chronology of events for the period up to 1300 BCE, our knowledge of the following millennium and a half remains obscure for different reasons. The next chapter in the story of Indian civilization would be shaped by multiple waves of migration by nomadic pastoralists who left behind few clues aside from tools, weapons, and fragments of pottery. The paucity of archaeological remains, however, is more than made up for by a vast corpus of elaborate, sacred poetry known as the Vedas.

Composed in Sanskrit and initially transmitted orally through priests known as Brahmins, the Vedas form the basis of Hinduism. The mantras recited to waken the gods every morning and the prayers offered when a dead person's body is placed on a funeral pyre have been passed down verbatim through the centuries. So precise was the transmission that when the Vedas began to be recorded in text form, versions from Kashmir, in the north, were found to be virtually identical to ones from Tamil Nadu, at the southernmost tip of the subcontinent. They have been studied by Europeans since the sixteenth century, but it wasn't until the late eighteenth century that the mystery of the authorship of these hymns would be solved. It was linguistics, rather than archaeology, that filled in the missing pieces of what we now know about India's early history.

William Jones was a polymath who published his first book in 1770 at the age of twenty-four, a translation from Persian into French of the history of Persian king Nader Shah. It was followed a year later by *A Grammar of the Persian Language*, which remained a standard work for decades. Even before landing at Chandpal Ghat, on the banks of the Hooghly River in Calcutta, in September 1783, Jones had made it his ambition "to know India better than any other European ever knew it." A year after his arrival, he founded the Asiatic Society.

Jones's passage to India was to take up an appointment as a judge on the Bengal Supreme Court. He believed that to dispense justice fairly, judges needed access to the sources of Hindu law, and that required the understanding of Sanskrit texts. His first hurdle was to find a teacher. The high-caste Brahmins he approached refused to teach the sacred language to a foreigner but, fortunately for us, he found a medical doctor well-versed in Sanskrit who agreed to make him his pupil. While studying the grammar, Jones noticed a remarkable similarity between it and certain European languages. He compiled his findings in a paper, "On the orthography of Asiatik words," which was published in the first volume of *Asiatik Researches*. In it he identified the Indo-European family of languages. Sanskrit scholar Thomas Trautmann has dubbed the article a major contribution to "the project of finding India's place."

William Jones: "The Sanscrit language, whatever be its antiquity, is of a wonderful structure; more perfect than the Greek, more copious than the Latin, and more exquisitely refined than either, yet bearing to both of them a stronger affinity, both in the roots of verbs and the forms of grammar, than could possibly have been produced by accident; so strong indeed, that no philologer could examine them all three, without believing them to have sprung from some common source, which, perhaps, no longer exists; there is a similar reason, though not quite so forcible, for supposing that both the Gothic and the Celtic, though blended with a very different idiom, had the same origin with the Sanscrit; and the old Persian might be added to the same family."

Jones went on to study the similarities between Hindu and European gods, leading him to conclude that there was not only a family of languages, but also a family of religions. The Roman god Janus becomes the elephant-headed Ganeśa; Jupiter corresponds to Indra. The Dionysian Kṛṣṇa is equated with Apollo. Saturn, Noah, and Manu are all players in the same creation myth. For Jones, Hinduism was a living representation of the ancient paganism of Greece and Rome.

The only explanation for this remarkable linguistic and religious confluence, he surmised, was migration: those who spoke Indo-European languages had once shared a common homeland in the vast steppe that stretched from Poland to the Trans-Ural. Historians have traced some of the earliest usages of this Indo-European language to northern Syria. A peace treaty signed between a Mitanni and Hittite king in c. 1380 BCE calls upon certain gods as witnesses. At least four of them—Uruvanass, Mitras, Indara, and Nasatia—correspond to the Hindu gods Varuṇa, Mitra, Indra, and Nasatya. The treaty suggests that although the Mitanni people spoke the local Hurrian language, their rulers had Indo-Āryan-sounding names and invoked Indo-Āryan gods.

The nomadic pastoralists who set off from these steppes referred to themselves as the Ārya: the name used by ancient Persians and the origin of the word "Iran." "Ārya" also forms the root of "Eire," the most westerly of the lands colonized in this great migration. (The term "Aryan" and the swastika symbol which first appeared in the early Harappān period would be co-opted by the Nazis to denote a pure master race and more recently by white supremacists to differentiate themselves from minorities.) The Āryans who settled in India tamed the horse and used light chariots capable of carrying three men. They bred cattle, melted bronze to make tools and weapons, and, like their Harappān counterparts, gambled.

Vedic texts tell of a sudden invasion that decimated the Harappān civilization. With their fleets of horse-drawn chariots and egged on by their warrior gods such as Indra—variously described as the Mars, Zeus, or Thor of the Āryan pantheon—the Āryans destroyed the remnants of the Harappān civilization and subdued the Dāsa, the descendants of the first wave of migration to India sixty millennia earlier.

The invasion theory took root during the British period, when scholars were looking for convenient ways to justify their military conquest of India. The problem with the theory is twofold: there is no archaeological evidence to support the invasion hypothesis, and it does not account for the two-century-long gap in the archaeological record between the demise of Harappā and the arrival of the Āryans.

DNA testing of ancient burial sites now confirms what archaeologists had long surmised: rather than a single Āryan invasion, there were waves of migrations, which interacted with a variety of cultures coexisting in India, steadily bringing various diverse indigenous cultures into the Āryan fold.

Perhaps the most important book to tackle this question is Tony Joseph's *Early Indians: The Story of Our Ancestors and Where We Came From* (2018). His sweeping appraisal of recent genetic DNA testing and studies leads him to conclude that today's Indians "draw their genes from several migrations to India; there is no such thing as a pure group, race or caste that has existed since time immemorial." Hindu nationalist historians see this as heretical. As Joseph explains:

For many in the right wing the idea that they came to India from elsewhere is unacceptable because it would dethrone Sanskrit and the Vedas as the singular and fundamental source of Indian culture, as it would mean that the mighty Harappān civilisation that has left an indelible impression on Indian history and culture would have preceded their arrival.

Because of the gaps in the historical record, even DNA evidence has been unable to satisfy those who cling to the belief that Vedic civilization preceded the Harappān. It is hard to see how this debate will ever be settled conclusively. The corpus of literature composed between 1100 and 600 BCE is vast but open to interpretation. Like so much in India's early history, little is definitive.

Vedic India and the Rise of the Raja

Of the four Vedas, the *Ṛig Veda* is the oldest and most important. The emerging consensus among historians is that it was first compiled around 1100 BCE, or possibly a century earlier. It comprises 1,028 hymns to the gods, arranged in ten books, or mandalas, of varying lengths and composed over several hundred years. There is no evidence that the Āryans made effigies of their gods. Mantras, not statues, were the means of communicating with the sacred. They were meant to be chanted at sacrifices accompanied by the consumption of *soma*, a hallucinogenic drink. The Bengali Nobel laureate Rabindranath Tagore (1861–1941) described them as "a poetic testament of a people's collective reaction to the wonder and awe of existence."

The *Sama Veda* consists of stanzas mostly taken from the *Ṛig Veda* and arranged for chanting, while the *Yajur Veda* is a series of prose poems or mantras for conducting rituals. The fourth Veda, the *Atharva Veda*, was associated with the rites, superstitions, and spells of the inhabitants of pre-Āryan India. Some may have been the ancestors of the Stone Age inhabitants of India; others were the Dāsa or tribal communities that had arrived with the out-of-Africa migration. Common to them was the practice of sorcery and witchcraft and the belief in the efficacy of charms and incantations through which men could achieve powers greater than the gods. Rather than trying to suppress these beliefs, the Āryans absorbed them.

The Brahmins, who transmitted the Vedas, used their knowledge to monopolize the performance of important rituals. Indra, the god of war and rain, is mentioned in almost a quarter of the hymns in the *Ṛig Veda*, followed by Agni, the god of fire, and Surya, the sun god.

Place names mentioned in the Vedic texts reveal that the first Āryan migrants settled in an area known as the Sapta Sindhu, or Seven Rivers. The name "Sindhu" refers to the Indus River; the five others were its tributaries, and the seventh was the Saraswatī, which has since dried up. Vedic society was based around tribes and clans—around thirty are mentioned in the texts. Numerous battles are described, and it is almost impossible to distinguish between real and mythical foes. Nowhere is this expressed more clearly than in the Battle of the Ten Kings, which is akin to an ancient Indian version of *Game of Thrones*. The battle was fought on the banks of the Ravi River between the Āryan king Sudās and a vaguely defined alliance of ten chiefs, who may have been "fallen Āryans" or Dāsas. It was won not by superior weaponry or tactics, but through the recitation of prayer.

As an agricultural society, the early Āryans were dependent on horses and cows. Grazing lands were prized. They were notorious as cattle rustlers—historian of comparative religion Karen Armstrong even likens them to cowboys from the American Wild West. The sacred status of cows—almost a cliché in today's India, where the consumption of beef is banned in most states—did not hold as strongly in Vedic India. Although one verse of the *Ṛig Veda* forbids the consumption of cow meat, another permits it at weddings as long as it had been ritually and humanely slaughtered.

In the early phase of Vedic civilization, societies were based on tribes. At the apex of the social structure were warrior chieftains, who are referred to in the *Ṛig Veda* as rajas, a word that is related to the Latin *rex*. The raja was not an absolute monarch; various tribes were governed by councils known as *sabhās* and *samitis*. The former were committees of elders that presided over courts and councils and were arranged in a type of con-federacy or republic, while the latter comprised all free tribes-men. Although the post was hereditary, a raja generally needed the approval of both to accede to the throne. When riding into battle, the raja would be accompanied by the royal priest, who chanted prayers and performed the rituals necessary for victory.

Despite their focus on religion, the Vedas and later texts such as the *Mahābhārata* do enable us to piece together a picture of this ancient society, though scholars such as the historian A. L. Basham caution that "It is as futile to try to reconstruct the political and social history of India in the tenth century BC from the *Mahābhārata* as it would be to write the history of Britain immediately after the evacuation of the Romans from Malory's *Morte d'Arthur*." Basham allows one significant exception—the *Mahābhārata*'s references to the Battle of Kurukshetra. In this battle, the Pāṇḍavas, led by five brothers and aided by their cousin and charioteer the god Kṛṣṇa, defeat their cousins, the Kauravas, at a site near today's New Delhi. Archaeological remains confirm that a battle did take place, but date it to the beginning of the ninth century BCE, rather than in 3102 BCE, as the *Mahābhārata* suggests. Whether it was the great war described in the text or a small-scale skirmish that was transformed on the page into an epic battle is unlikely to ever be resolved, particularly in the politi-cally charged atmosphere that prevails in India.

Composed between the fourth century BCE and the third century CE, the *Mahābhārata* is the most renowned of the Hindu epics, and the longest—roughly ten times the length of the *Iliad* and the *Odyssey* combined. Scenes from the *Mahābhārata* describing the battle between the rival clans of the Kuru tribe can be found wherever Hinduism spread, the sculptural reliefs of Angkor Wat in Cambodia and the wayang puppet theater of Java being just two examples. In the late 1990s, the epic was serialized as ninety-four weekly episodes on the state-run Indian television network Doordarshan, bringing the country to a virtual standstill every time it was broadcast.

The most famous section of the *Mahābhārata* is the *Bhagavad Gītā*, or *Song of the Lord*—a discourse between the god Kṛṣṇa and the Pāṇḍava prince Arjuna, who is questioning why he should fight his cousins. Kṛṣṇa tells Arjuna that killing his cousins is his duty: "To die in one's duty is life: to live in another's is death." Circumstances, rather than personal interests or sentiments, must guide one's actions, whatever the cost. Today the text is as well known among Hindus as the New Testament is among Christians. J. Robert Oppenheimer, the father of the atomic bomb, would reach for a verse from the *Gītā* to describe his feelings after watching the first testing of the weapon in New Mexico in 1945: "Now I have become Death, the destroyer of worlds."

The Bhagavad Gītā *is a dialogue between Kṛṣṇa (standing) and Arjuna (kneeling) before the start of the climactic Kurukshetra War in the* Mahābhārata.

From the reading of texts such as the *Śatapatha Brāhmaṇa*, which details Vedic rituals, we know that the heartland of Āryan culture and society began shifting eastward to the Doab, the land between the Ganges and the Yamuna rivers, from around the tenth century BCE. What is now a patchwork of cultivated fields being encroached upon by some of India's fastest-growing urban conflagrations was once, as the English historian John Keay describes it, a "moist green wilderness of forest and swamp, a tropical taiga of near-Siberian extent."

The jungles, though more productive than the drier lands of western India, were hard to clear. Ultimately, however, they would support far greater population densities, which in turn led to the establishment in around 800 BCE of the first cities, such as Kashi (today's Varanasi) and Hastināpura. What can be loosely thought of as republics based on geographical entities began to appear, made possible through more advanced technology. The use of iron dates to around this period, but its quality was poor. It would not be until the middle of the millennium that more sophisticated furnaces enabled the use of iron-tipped ploughs, which in turn led to the widespread cultivation of crops and the creation of a labor force. Another feature of this eastward expansion was the appearance of more sophisticated pottery known as painted grayware. By studying the remains of this grayware, we can trace the gradual migration of the Āryans to the borders of present-day Bihar and south to the Narmada River.

While evidence of social stratification in the Indian subcontinent dates back to the Harappān civilization, it took on a deeper meaning as the light-skinned, Sanskrit-speaking Āryans mixed increasingly with the darker Dāsas. Purity of blood became important. By the middle of the first millennium BCE, the social division between Āryans and Dāsas had widened into a system of classes, or *varṇas*—its basis codified like so many aspects of Hinduism today by a verse from the *Ṛig Veda*.

The "Poem of the Primeval Man" postulates a social order created at the beginning of time, one that is meant to last forever.

It describes how the Primeval Man's body was dismembered into the four varnas, or colors. From the man's mouth came the Brahmins, whose power derived from their monopoly over rituals such as the fire sacrifice (*yajna*). Like an ancient algorithm, the sacred words of Vedic hymns needed to be intoned perfectly or else they would be rendered valueless. So powerful were these hymns they could sway the gods to do good or evil. Through their knowledge of these hymns and rituals, Brahmin priests, known as *purohitas*, led prayers to ensure an abundant harvest, the birth of a son, or victory in war.

From the arms came the *ksatriya*, comprising rulers and the warrior classes. The *vaisya*, who loosely encompassed peasants, merchants, traders, and farmers, comprised the trunk. The lowest of the varnas, emanating from the feet, were the *śūdras*, the servants: non-Āryans and intermarried Dāsa Āryans. Below them were the Untouchables, or those without caste, who did the most menial and degrading work, such as sweeping streets and removing night soil.

The first three varnas were designated as the *dvija*, or twice-born; the second birth was an initiation into ritual status. That left the śūdras outside the caste system, perpetually locked into their lower status without any means of entering the ranks of the twice-born. The varnas were the precursor to the caste system that became enshrined from the first century CE. Despite discrimination on the basis of caste being illegal under the Constitution, it remains a defining feature of Indian society.

The basic contours of Āryan society during the Later Vedic period (1100–500 BCE) can thus be characterized as the use of Sanskrit, though still as an oral language; a system of social stratification that placed the priesthood above kings; an economy based mainly on cattle herding; a pantheon of gods, most of whom shared a similarity with Western deities; and the reliance on the Vedas for rituals governing every aspect of life, from gambling to marriage and death.

The rise in urban populations led to an increase in trade, but the predominantly agrarian nature of society meant links were rudimentary. There is no evidence of money being used or of the existence of a merchant class until the sixth century BCE. Nor is there any mention in the Vedas of writing, though its omission may have been due to it being seen as an objectionable innovation by the priesthood. The practice of cremation took precedence over burial, probably because of the association between fire and ritual purity. The concept of reincarnation, in which souls would be born into happiness or sorrow depending on their actions in their previous lives, would not become entrenched until after the composition of the corpus of literature known as the *Upaniṣhads*.

For all that can be gleaned from thousands of stanzas in the Vedas and epic texts such as the *Mahābhārata*, the history of India up to the middle of the first millennium BCE remains, as Basham laments, "a jigsaw puzzle with many missing pieces . . . lacking in the interesting anecdotes and interesting personalities which enliven the study of the past for professional and amateur historians alike." The picture is further muddied by disagreements, some based on interpretations of historical evidence, others motivated by purely ideological aims.

But the late Vedic period was also the cusp of a new historical epoch. For the first time, the era of myth and legend was about to be transformed into an age of kingdoms and visionary leaders. Foremost among them was Gautama Buddha, whom Tagore would later call "the greatest man ever born on earth."

CHAPTER 2

Religious Revolutionaries

On October 14, 1956, B. R. Ambedkar (1891–1956)—the author of India's Constitution and, importantly, the leader of the country's Untouchables—stood before a crowd of almost half a million people in the city of Nagpur, renounced Hinduism, the religion of his birth, and converted to Buddhism. The majority of those in attendance followed Ambedkar's example, making it the single-largest religious conversion in history. Over the following months and years, more than three million Untouchables fast-tracked their escape from the caste-based order that placed them on the lowest rung of Hindu society by embracing Buddhism. When the 1961 census was counted, the number of Buddhists in India had risen by 1,671 percent in the space of a decade.

In the country that gave the world the Buddha (c. 563–483 BCE), his followers had almost become extinct by the mid-twentieth century, aside from the remote Buddhist kingdom of Ladakh and a smattering of communities in northeastern India. Ambedkar's revival of Buddhism in India was as much a social phenomenon as a religious and ethical one. Before converting, he had developed a new doctrine called Navayana Buddhism that did away with concepts such as renunciation, rebirth, and the monkhood, but retained notions of compassion and equality, which he harnessed into a form of social activism.

Ambedkar's fine-tuning was not as radical as it sounds. When Buddhism first emerged in India, it was a reaction against the strict orthodoxy of Vedic Brahmanism. All creeds and social classes, men and women, were free to follow the Buddha.

Siddhārtha Gautama, as the Buddha was known, was born to royal parents in southern Nepal between 566 and 563 BCE and died some eighty years later. Buddhist lore ascribes the Buddha's birth to divine intervention: his mother, Māhāmāya, dreamt of a great white elephant, the symbol of royal majesty and authority, entering her womb; Siddhārtha then emerged painlessly from her side and was caught in a golden net held by demigods known as *devas*. As he surveyed his surroundings, he proclaimed, "I am the chief of the world." Asked to interpret such a marvel, sages discovered the imprints of wheels on the child's hands and feet and predicted he would grow up to be a mighty king or a great religious teacher.

The middle of the first millennium BCE was a period of ferment—not just in India, but also in other parts of the civilized world. In China, Confucius was articulating his teachings; early philosophers of Greece, such as Socrates, were exploring the notion of truth, and in the Near East, Hebrew prophets were spreading the word of the Old Testament.

In India, the mainly pastoral, seminomadic tribal culture of the Āryans was giving way to agriculture-based societies living in urban centers. Birth rates soared. Writing in the fifth century BCE, the Greek historian Herodotus described India as the most populous country on earth. Republics built around tribal groupings began to appear, as well as regional kingdoms. The largest of these were Kosala, in the eastern part of the modern state of Uttar Pradesh, and Magadha, in what is now Bihar. By taxing their docile populations, the rulers of these kingdoms were able to amass huge armies and create efficient state structures. A ruler's strength no longer relied on the supernatural aid of his Vedic Brahmin adviser but on his political skills and the strength of his military.

New forms of heterodoxy that rejected the Vedas and the Brahmanical social dominance were also taking root. For non-Brahmins, much of the Hindu religion was incomprehensible. The hymns of the Vedas were complex, and their teachings had little relevance to everyday life. Vedic gods could not compete with the local nature and fertility deities that had long been worshipped in small wayside shrines. Sacrificial rituals, particularly those involving animal slaughter, were being sidelined, and with them the basis of Brahmanical authority. The role of caste in spiritual life was being questioned, with the less privileged flocking to new sects that rejected the rigid hierarchy of the Vedic period.

The *Upanishads*, a set of Vedic texts composed from around 800 to 300 BCE, introduced the concept of *saṃsāra*, the cycle of birth, death, and rebirth. The *Upanishads* preached that the form of the reincarnated soul depends upon the individual's actions. Virtue is rewarded and evil punished. Salvation (*nirvāṇa*) enables a permanent release from the cycle of rebirth. Such ideas spawned the inevitable quest for a path to salvation. Renunciation would become the basis of a new set of religions that would have far-reaching implications for both India and much of Asia.

In the vast forests of the Gangetic Plains, the quest for salvation and resistance against Brahmin ritualism and exclusiveness manifested in the form of wandering ascetics and

The stereotypical image of the near-naked ascetic reclining on a bed of nails probably has its origins during the period around 800 to 300 BCE, when renunciation became a central premise of the Upaniṣhads.

mendicants. Often naked and with matted hair, they tried to outdo one another with their feats of endurance, while disputing each other's religious credentials in the quest for new converts. This metaphysical culture of protest and resistance would underpin the emergence of new faiths that cast aside Brahmanical teachings and claims to divine authority.

Paths to Enlightenment

Siddhārtha Gautama's father was the ruler of the Shakya tribe, which was under the hegemony of the Kosala kingdom. He was raised in his father's palace in Kapilavastu, now the town of Lumbini in the lowland Terai region of Nepal. Siddhārtha's life was one of privilege, sheltered from the realities of the outside world with "some new delight provided every hour." One day, aged about eighteen and curious to see what lay beyond the palace walls, he entered a garden, where he confronted human suffering for the first time in the form of an old man, a sick man, a corpse, and a wandering ascetic. The first three sights—representing aging, illness, and death—brought home to Siddhārtha the inevitability of suffering and the transience of existence, regardless of one's wealth or background. The ascetic offered a solution by revealing a way that transcended the temporal.

Vowing to follow the ascetic's example, Siddhārtha renounced his wife and son, his palace, his wealth and royal robes, and withdrew from the world. For the next six years he joined the wandering mendicants of the Gangetic Plains, practicing their severe austerities and experimenting with different paths to salvation.

In the end it was not austerity but meditation that revealed the path to enlightenment. As a child, Siddhārtha would free himself from sensual desires and evil thoughts by sitting in the shade of a rose-apple tree. Remembering these earlier revelations, he started meditating under a sacred peepul tree, vowing to remain there until he re-created that state of blissful peace. After several days of meditation, he finally realized the true nature of suffering and transience, formulated a scheme for overcoming it, and so became the Buddha—the Awakened One. Today, the place where the Buddha achieved enlightenment is known as Bodh Gayā.

The Buddha then set out for a royal deer park at Sarnath, near the holy city of Kashi. Before a gathering of five of his former associates, he preached a sermon known as "Turning of the Wheel of the Law." He began by advocating "the middle way": both asceticism and

In the legend of the Four Passing Sights, the Buddha recounts that he ate so little during one of his austerities—just six grains of rice a day—that "my body became extremely lean . . . When I thought I would touch the skin of my stomach, I actually took hold of my spine."

worldly indulgence were to be avoided, as was hatred, envy, and anger. He then announced the Four Noble Truths on the nature, origin, and cessation of suffering. To end suffering, one had to embrace the Noble Eightfold Path, namely right views, right resolve, right speech, right conduct, right livelihood, right effort, right mindfulness, and right meditation.

The sermon laid out the basis of the Buddhist worldview, a set of interlinked propositions that held that ignorance was the cause of human misery. This ignorance was born of our failure to understand the nature of the world, namely the inevitability that sorrow will permeate every aspect of life and that the universe is transient. Our ignorance of this lack of permanence leads to sorrow.

Finally, he preached that the universe was soulless. The essence of transmigration was that nothing passed over from one life to another. By curbing indulgence and mastering desire, the human condition could become bearable. If enough merit was accumulated in a person's lifetime, he or she could achieve a state of nirvana or extinction and free oneself from the endless cycle of rebirth.

There was no mention of a creator or redeemer. The Buddha claimed no spiritual authority and forbade the worship of imagery. As such, Buddhism complemented existing religions rather than supplanted them. The debate over whether Buddhism is a religion or a philosophy is still ongoing.

The Buddha's teachings became known as the *dharma*, a word that encompasses multiple related meanings such as law, duty, righteousness, morality, piety, and so on. In Buddha's teachings, dharma referred to a set of principles to be followed in conducting one's life, rooted firmly in a philosophical plane. It was his followers who would later elevate the Buddha to the status of a deity.

Early representations of the Buddha were in the form of symbols such as the cakra or great wheel, the peepul tree, an upturned hand, or a footprint.

The five disciples at Sarnath became the core of the Buddhist monastic community, the *sangha*. The monastic orders spread quickly throughout northern India and were open to everyone regardless of their sex or social standing. Because spiritual credit could be accrued by donating money and worldly goods, monasteries grew rich, enabling them to fund more missionary activity.

The Buddha was not the only spiritual teacher whose legacy would spawn religious revolution. Jainism's principles of *ahiṃsā* (nonviolence) and *satya* (truth) were appropriated by Mahatma Gandhi during India's struggle for independence. Like the Buddha, Jainism's founder, Vardhamāna (c. 599–527 BCE), was a descendant of a kṣatriya martial clan. His period as a wandering mendicant started at the age of thirty, roughly the same time as Buddha's, but lasted twelve years, or twice as long. His penances, which included a six-month-long fast, were also more severe, and when he found enlightenment it was not while sitting comfortably under the shade of a tree

MAIN RELIGIONS OF INDIA, 2011 CENSUS

Hindus	827,578,868	80.5%
Muslims	138,188,240	13.4%
Christians	24,080,016	2.3%
Sikhs	19,215,730	1.9%
Buddhists	7,955,207	0.8%
Jains	4,225,053	0.4%
Others/not stated	7,367,214	0.7%

but while squatting on his heels for two and a half days in the blazing sun. He became a possessor of absolute knowledge (*kevalin*) and a conqueror (*jina*), the latter title being the derivative of the name for the Jain religion.

Mahāvīra, as he was now known, would spend the next three decades traveling in northern India with a band of followers. But Jainism spread more slowly than Buddhism due to its rigid ascetic practices and lesser emphasis on missionary activity. After his death in c. 527 BCE, Mahāvīra was followed by a series of eminent teachers who received patronage from royal emperors, such as Candragupta Maurya (r. 321–297 BCE).

Like Buddhism, Jainism was a protest against aspects of Brahmanism. The basis of Jainism is the belief that all forms of existence, from humans down to the tiniest insects, have a soul or life force. This life force, or *jiva*, was at the root of *ahimsā*, or noninjury to other beings. The Digambara sect of Jainism takes this to its extreme. Its monks go about naked with no possessions other than a water pot made of gourd, a bunch of peacock feathers to clean the ground, and a gauze mask across their faces to prevent accidentally inhaling an insect. Candles cannot be burned at night in case a moth flies into the flame. According to the strictest Jaina traditions, it is only these "sky-clad" monks who can attain enlightenment.

Because tilling the soil can kill insects, Jains eschewed farming in favor of commerce. Today they are one of India's richest communities, playing leading roles in banking and the jewelry trade. One extended network of Jains from the small town of Palanpur, in Gujarat, controls around 90 percent of the world's diamond cutting and polishing trade.

As Buddhism and Jainism flourished, so did the states where they were first established. By the early part of the fifth century BCE, Magadha, under the rule of Ajātaśatru (r. 492–461 BCE), would emerge as the foremost kingdom on the subcontinent at the time. Ajātaśatru came to the throne after murdering his father, Bimbisara (r. 544–492), an enlightened leader and a fervent admirer of the Buddha. He vanquished the rival kingdoms of Kosala and Videha, subduing a vast swathe of territory from the Nepal Himalayas to the Bay of Bengal. Most importantly, he shifted his capital to Pāṭaliputra, on the Ganges River, a hub for northern India's lucrative riverine trade. Ajātaśatru's successors, most of whom came to the throne by murdering their fathers, went on to establish the powerful Nanda dynasty in the early fourth century BCE.

India's "Julius Caesar"

Though the extent of the Nanda territory was unprecedented in Indian history, it was dwarfed in size by the rapidly expanding empire of Alexander the Great (356–323 BCE). Since setting out from Athens, his army had taken control of much of West Asia. In 331 BCE, he marched into Persia, defeating Darius III, the last of the Achaemenids. His army then swept across the Hindu Kush and occupied the area around Kabul before crossing the Indus River in 326 BCE. But this was no longer an invincible conquering force. Years of forced marches and tough campaigning, coupled with the fears of what lay beyond, had broken his soldiers both physically and mentally. When he reached the Beas River, Alexander was forced to turn back on the advice of his generals, who feared their troops would mutiny.

The significance of Alexander's conquest is debatable. As the first "Westerner" to invade India, he was lionized by nineteenth-century British colonizers as a precursor—a grand imperial hero who opened up Asia to Western civilization. Although his superior military tactics and sometimes reckless bravado were also an inspiration for later Indian rulers, Alexander lacked both a strategic plan and an effective

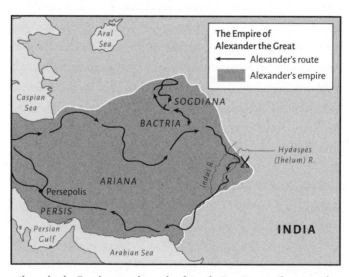

Alexander the Great's army advanced as far as the Beas River in the present-day Indian state of Punjab, before being forced to retreat.

administration. As the Irish Indologist Vincent Smith points out, "India was not Hellenised. She continued to live her life of 'splendid isolation' and soon forgot the passing of the Macedonian storm."

As Alexander retreated down the Indus, sailing past the mysterious remains of Harappān cities, he left behind a scattering of garrisons and appointed satraps to govern conquered territories. But for all the romance of Alexander's advance, he left so little impression that there is no reference to him in surviving ancient Indian literature. Within a year of his death in Babylon in 323 BCE, local uprisings had snuffed out most of his remaining outposts.

One of those hoping that Alexander had continued his eastward march into India was an Indian general known in ancient Greek texts as Sandrokottos. The identity of this semi-mythical figure would remain a mystery until William Jones, translating a Sanskrit play from the first century CE, stumbled across references to an Indian ruler named Candragupta Maurya (r. c. 322–297 BCE), who seized a rival's throne and made his capital at Pāṭaliputra, where he received envoys from distant lands. Sandrokottos and Candragupta, he concluded, were one and the same. The significance of Jones's discovery went beyond connecting the two. By fixing the dates of Candragupta's reign, the reconstruction of much of ancient India's history was possible at last.

Candragupta was in his mid-twenties when he was sent into exile by the ruler of Magadha. Stories of the strength of the Magadhan army was one of the reasons why Alexander halted his march into India. Candragupta, however, urged Alexander to cross the Beas, insisting that conquering Magadha would be easy because the people would rise up against their king, "hated and despised on account of his baseness and low birth."

Snubbed by Alexander, Candragupta started to amass his own army, composed primarily of soldiers from disparate tribes from the northwest frontier of India. His forces made short work of the remaining Greek garrisons and defeated Nanda, the Magadhan ruler, in 321 BCE, occupying his capital, Pāṭaliputra, and taking control of his army, which consisted of eighty thousand horses, two hundred thousand infantry, and six thousand war elephants.

In his drive westward, Candragupta also inflicted a humiliating defeat on one of Alexander's generals, Seleucus Nicator (c. 358–281 BCE), who was attempting to recover his leader's lost territories. The Greek general was forced to trade a large chunk of what is now southern and eastern Afghanistan in exchange for a mere five hundred elephants. The two leaders then arrived at some sort of accommodation, possibly sealed by a matrimonial alliance.

As a goodwill gesture, Seleucus sent his ambassador, Megasthenes (c. 350–290 BCE), to Pāṭaliputra. As he journeyed across India, Megasthenes compiled the first detailed description of the country written by a foreign traveler. The original of his *Indica* has been lost, but fragments were preserved in the writings of Strabo, Pliny, Arrian, and others. His descriptions of "this mystical and magical land" were not always accurate. What Megasthenes didn't observe firsthand he borrowed from earlier legends, which described men without mouths who could survive on nothing but the smell of roasted meat and the perfume of fruit and flowers, of Hyperboreans who lived for a thousand years, and of races with ears so large they wrapped themselves in them as if they were blankets.

More valuable to historians are his descriptions of the imperial court of "Sandrokottos," which he wrote was "maintained with barbaric and luxurious ostentation." Even allowing for hyperbole, it is clear from his writings that Pāṭaliputra was one of the greatest cities of the ancient world. It contained lakes and gardens brimming with lotus flowers, jasmine, and hibiscus, and cooled by fountains—a far cry from the chaotic and crowded modern city of Patna that stands on its ruins. Candragupta's palace was made entirely of wood and featured "basins and goblets of gold, some measuring six feet in width, richly carved tables and chairs of state, vessels of Indian copper set with precious stones, and gorgeous embroidered robes were to be seen in profusion, and contributed to the brilliancy of the public ceremonies." Amusements included gladiatorial contests, ox races, and royal hunts.

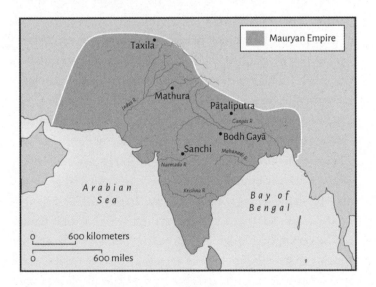

Megasthenes describes a well-organized civil service run by a ruler who was so preoccupied with the administration of his state and his own security that he slept little more than four hours a night. Guards accompanied him wherever he went—his preferred mode of transport being a gold palanquin carried by elephants and shaded from the sun by female umbrella bearers. Although he ruled for only twenty-four years, Candragupta came to be known as India's "Julius Caesar," its "man of blood and iron." After expelling the Greek garrisons in the northwest, he expanded his territories to include most of northern India, from the Arabian Sea to the Bay of Bengal. By embracing such a large territory, the Mauryan Empire became the first multiethnic kingdom in India. Under his grandson Aśoka, it would grow to encompass almost the entire subcontinent by the third century BCE, the closest India would come to its modern boundaries until the reign of the Mughal emperor Aurangzeb in the late 1600s.

Greek writers such as Megasthenes and the occasional Indian playwright had the last word on the Mauryas until the early 1900s, when a Brahmin scholar from Tanjore arrived at the Mysore government Oriental Library carrying a manuscript of dried palm leaves. This turned out to be the *Arthaśāstra*, variously translated as the "Science of Polity" or "Treatise on Success." One of the most important sources of information on administration, law, trade, war, and peace in ancient India, its authorship was attributed to Candragupta's Brahmin adviser, Kauṭilya (375–282 BCE), whose name can be variously translated as meaning "crooked," "bent," or "devious." Recent scholarship suggests it was revised extensively in the second or third century CE by multiple authors.

The *Arthaśāstra*'s clearest message, the Nobel Prize–winning Indian economist Amartya Sen states, is "might is right." Others have compared it to Sun Tzu's *The Art of War* as a manual for aspiring entrepreneurs "seeking to amass wealth in a competitive and globalising country." Trust in another prince was a recipe for death. Morality should never be allowed to influence statecraft. Skill in intrigue was a far better qualification for kingship than either power or enthusiasm. Intrigue was so fundamental to statecraft that Kauṭilya recommended courtesans be employed as spies or informers. Spies could also be used to spread misinformation, to cause panic among enemy troops, or to inspire confidence among one's own soldiers by fabricating victories, or by pretending astrologers had proclaimed a king's omniscience.

To the German sociologist Max Weber, the *Arthaśāstra*'s radicalism made Machiavelli's *The Prince* look "harmless." Nowhere was this clearer than in Kauṭilya's advice on the pursuit of power. His name for a king is *vijigīṣu*, meaning one who is yearning for conquest. But while an expansionary policy is key to Kauṭilya's vision, the king was always faced with the dilemma of how to combine his power with the religious authority claimed by the Brahmin priestly order. As the political scientist Sunil Khilnani writes, "To acquire legitimacy, a ruler has to show his disinterest in worldly power for its own sake and to manifest a renunciatory streak—but never so much as to hobble his pursuit of power. The never-ending struggle to achieve that balance continues to challenge India's rulers today."

> Kauṭilya on corruption: "Just as it is impossible to know when fish, moving about in water, are drinking water, so it is impossible to know when officers appointed to carry out tasks are embezzling money."
>
> Kauṭilya on power: "A ruler should win over his people by seduction: a king should know how to perform magic tricks to give him an aura of miraculous powers and should make liberal use of manipulation."

According to legend, Candragupta abdicated in c. 297 BCE. Accounts of why he did so at the height of his power vary, with one Jaina legend referring to a prophecy by his spiritual adviser that his kingdom would be beset by a twelve-year famine as retribution for the violence inflicted during his reign. According to this legend, he converted to Jainism and, together with a congregation of monks, traveled to southern India. They finally stopped at Śravaṇa Beḷagoḷa, where, it is said, he undertook the ultimate act of renunciation and fasted to death.

Aśoka: The "Greatest of Kings"

What we know of the next chapter of Indian history owes much to the forensic work of William Jones's successors at the Asiatic Society. In 1837, while examining inscriptions on the stone railings of the Buddhist stupa at Sanchi, James Prinsep (1799–1840) deciphered two letters of the alphabet. They were enough to identify the language as Pāli. He then began to decipher other inscriptions scattered all over the subcontinent. Some were on boulders, others on cliff faces. But the most impressive were those inscribed on massive cylindrical pillars. Theories on the meanings of the inscriptions ranged from obscure Vedic incantations to peculiarly Indian versions of the Ten Commandments. It soon became clear to Prinsep that they were edicts announcing the directives of a single sovereign. Most began with the words "Thus speaks Devanāmpiya Piyādassi." Buddhist chronicles of Ceylon referred to a Sri Lankan king called Piyādassi, who shared his name with an Indian sovereign who had championed Buddhism and ruled over an immense kingdom. But it would not be until the early twentieth century that Devanāmpiya Piyādassi, "beloved of the gods and gracious of men," was identified as the emperor Aśoka.

In his *A Short History of the World*, H. G. Wells calls Aśoka the "greatest of kings" for his renunciation of war, his adoption of Buddhism, and his declaration that all his conquests "would be conquests of religion." For the historian A. L. Basham, Aśoka "towers above the other kings of ancient India, if for no other reason than that he is the only one among them whose personality can be reconstructed with any degree of certainty." Describing Aśoka's character, Basham discerns a man who was "a little naive, often rather self-righteous and pompous, but indefatigable, strong-willed and imperious."

When Aśoka came to the throne in c. 268 BCE, he inherited an empire with an estimated population of fifty million socially, religiously, and ethnically diverse people. The area around Magadha and the Western Gangetic Plains was largely under the influence of Āryan culture. Those areas further to the west and north were in contact with the Hellenized culture of Afghanistan, while the south had its unique pre-Āryan Dravidian civilization. The empire's size and diversity required a strong emphasis on government machinery and authority. Roads were constructed, shaded by trees, with wells and rest houses a day's walk apart. Aśoka also ordered the planting of medicinal herbs. To administer so vast an empire he appointed *dhamma-mahāmāttas*, or "overseers of the law," to tour his kingdom and ensure that local officials were performing their duties. The edicts were integral to his imperial project. Placed in or near important population centers, their messages were meant to endure "as long as my sons and great-grandsons reign, [and] as long as the sun and the moon endure."

Although Aśoka is most often remembered for his policies of persuasion over coercion, his reign began in violence. A rock edict at Girnar, in western India, describes how a hundred thousand people were slaughtered in his conquest of the Kalinga kingdom. Many more probably died from famine and disease, a calamity that awakened in Aśoka feelings of "remorse, profound sorrow and regret," the edict stated.

Most of the thirty-three edicts that have been discovered are in Prākrit, a collection of vernacular dialects that were much more widely understood than the literary Sanskrit or the Pāli used in Ceylonese Buddhist texts. Those in the western part of India are in Greek and Aramaic, the lingua franca of the Persian Empire. The Aśokan pillars are remarkable for their artistic beauty, crowned with life-like images of lions and bulls, probably carved by skilled stonemasons who migrated to India from Persia after the fall of the Achaemenid Empire. Carved out of a single stone, some pillars are forty to fifty feet high. After being quarried at Chunar, near Varanasi, the pillars, which weighed up to fifty tonnes, were transported hundreds of miles to geographically important sites.

While the pillars and rock-cut edicts were probably derived from the monumental inscriptions of Darius I of Persia, they do not extol the emperor and his greatness, but rather explain his policy of dharma. The most important principle of dharma was tolerance, both of people and of their beliefs and ideas. As Aśoka explained, this meant "consideration towards slaves and servants, obedience to mother and father, generosity towards friends, acquaintances and relatives, and towards priests and monks." Another principle was nonviolence. Wherever possible, conquest should be conducted with clemency. By setting an example of enlightened govern-

The most famous Aśokan pillar is the lion capital discovered at Sarnath. It shows four lions looking out, one in each direction, standing on a dharma cakra (wheel of law). The image would become the official emblem of independent India, gracing coins, banknotes, stamps, and seals. The cakra also appears on the Indian flag.

ment, Aśoka believed that he would convince neighboring kingdoms of the merits of his policies and they would seek to join his empire, forming a kind of enlightened confederacy.

Indian statecraft, which until now had been based on the expansion of empire through violent conquest, was overturned. Influenced by Buddhist ideas, Aśoka came to believe that conquest could be based on the law of piety. He abolished animal sacrifices and restricted the consumption of meat. Royal hunts were ended. Parakeets, pigeons, bats, ants, tortoises, squirrels, cows, rhinoceroses, and nanny goats were among the animals protected from slaughter. Thanks to his adherence to *ahimsā* (nonviolence), many of his subjects became vegetarians.

Second Minor Rock Edict: "Father and mother must be obeyed; respect for living creatures must be enforced; truth must be spoken. These are the virtues of the Law of Duty which must be practised. Similarly, the teacher must be reverenced by the pupil, and proper courtesy must be shown to relations. This is the ancient standard of duty that leads to length of days and according to this men must act."

Aśoka's most lasting legacy was to transform Buddhism from a localized Indian sect into a world religion. He ordered the opening up of eight stupas where Buddha's ashes had been buried in the region of Bihar. These were distributed throughout his kingdom, with many ending up in Taxila, which was linked to Pāṭaliputra by a royal highway constructed during Candragupta's reign. He also directed caves be dug as meditation retreats for Buddhist and Jaina monks at several sites scattered around his empire. Those in the Barabar Hills near Bodh Gayā would be later immortalized as the Marabar Hills in E. M. Forster's *A Passage to India* (1924). In c. 250 BCE, Aśoka convened a major conclave at Pāṭaliputra at which the Pāli canon was codified. Members of the saṇgha were ordered to disseminate Buddhism throughout India and beyond.

The spread of Buddhism during this period is evidenced by the existence of a vibrant Buddhist colony set up by Indian merchants in Alexandria in the second century BCE. The colony prompted the city's governor to complain that "the Greeks stole their philosophy from the barbarians." Recent scholarship points to startling similarities between the Buddhist Jātaka tales and Christian parables and miracles. In one

Jātaka tale, a pious Buddhist disciple walks on water only to sink when his faith abandons him. In another, the Buddha feeds five hundred of his followers with a single piece of bread from his begging bowl. Another Buddhist work bears a close resemblance to the Old Testament tale of the prodigal son. As Vincent Smith writes: "Nascent Christianity met full-grown Buddhism in the Academies and markets of Asia and Egypt, while both religions were exposed to the influences of surrounding Paganism in many forms, and of the countless works of art which gave expression to the forms of polytheism."

The peace and prosperity of Aśoka's reign were fleeting. Despite deploying "Officers of Righteousness" to spread the Buddha's teachings, the ingrained stratification of Indian society gradually began to undermine his message. By the time Aśoka died in c. 232 BCE, the Mauryan Empire was beginning to fracture. His sons fought over succession. Aśoka's renunciation of further conquest was forgotten, and war once again became the norm. "In general, the history of post-Mauryan India is one of struggles of one dynasty with another for regional dominance, and the political, though not the cultural, unity of India was lost for nearly two thousand years," A. L. Basham glumly notes.

The reasons for the decline of the Mauryan Empire are still disputed. Some historians argue that Aśoka's pro-Buddhist sympathies were resisted by the Brahmin priestly caste. Others claim that his policies of nonviolence weakened the military strength of his state, leaving it vulnerable to invaders from the West. The difficulty of forging a sense of nationhood over such a large area is cited as another cause. Ultimately, it may well have come down to basic economics, with historians pointing to the debasement of silver coins in the later Mauryan period as proof that financing an army and the massive bureaucracy he inherited from Candragupta based on a largely agricultural economy became unviable.

The Age of Intruders

The period that followed the Mauryan civilization is often described as India's "Dark Age." This descriptor is rather harsh. Although waves of nomadic warriors from Central Asia and Greek adventurers laid waste to India's cities and towns, the period was not bereft of enlightened rulers. Buddhism grew in the land of its birth and spread to neighboring countries, and Greco-Bactrian kings brought with them Western theories of astrology and medicine. Trade between India and West Asia and the Mediterranean flourished to such an extent that senators in ancient Rome complained that women were wasting their money on Indian luxuries such as silks and jewelry. India had become "the sink of the world's gold," Pliny the Elder lamented in 77 CE. Much of this gold came from the fabled mines of Kolar in southern India, where from the days of the Harappān civilization it had made its way to much of Asia, Europe, and Africa.

Events taking place thousands of miles to the northeast of India were now about to intrude on the history of the subcontinent. In China, the first phase of the Great Wall had been erected to repel a succession of marauding tribes. In c. 165 BCE, one of the tribes forced to turn back was the Yüeh-chih. As they made their way westward, they displaced other tribes in an "ethnic knock-on effect" until they settled in Bactria, where a tribe known as the Shakas had earlier driven out the remnants of Greek settlers who had stayed on in the region after Alexander's retreat.

Forced out of their strongholds in Bactria, the Greek settlers had no choice but to make an accommodation with the mainly Buddhist inhabitants of Gandhāra, the region in northern Pakistan around the city of Taxila. Buddhist scholars were appointed as advisers to the Greek rulers. It was an advantageous arrangement that ensured the spiritual, social, economic, and cultural needs of the Buddhist community were taken care of. The Greek language began to be used in official documentation and Greek coinage was introduced. A unique school of sculpture that blended Greco-Roman aesthetics with distinctively Indian subject matter began to flourish.

By the late first century, one of the Yüeh-chih clans, the Kuśāṇa, moved into Gandhāra and then into northwest India, giving them control of two important trade routes into Asia. Like the Āryans a millennium and half earlier, they were excellent horse riders. Whether they came as invaders, as allies to one of the existing rulers, or even as refugees is open to debate due to the paucity of historical sources.

The Kuśāṇa kings called themselves "sons of heaven," adopting the title from Chinese rulers of the period. Their most illustrious ruler, Kaniṣka (r. 127–150 CE), came to power in c. 127 CE and governed an empire that stretched from Kashgar to the Gangetic Basin. His twin capitals were Purushapura, the site of today's city of Peshawar, and Mathura, on the Yamuna River in northern India.

Like Aśoka, Kaniṣka converted to Buddhism. He convened a major Buddhist conclave in Kashmir attended by more than five hundred monks, who undertook a thorough reexamination of the Buddhist canon. Monasteries became large economic enterprises engaged in everything from trade to brewing and distilling alcohol, enabling them to fund missionary activity that saw the spread of Buddha's teaching throughout Central Asia and China. In the latter part of his reign, coins bearing the image of Buddha inscribed in Greek lettering started to appear, as did images of deities from Persia, Rome, and Greece, as well as Brahmanical India.

Kaniṣka's other contribution to Indian civilization was his patronage of Gandhāran art and Buddhist architecture. Standing figures of the Buddha in flowing toga-like robes and displaying distinctly Medi-

In 1911, archaeologists uncovered a statue of Kaniṣka wearing a Kuśāṇa kaftan, ceremonial staff and broadsword, and riding boots, but missing a head. An almost identical statue that stood in the Kabul Museum was destroyed by the Taliban in 2001.

terranean hairstyles and facial features bear testimony to the influence of Greco-Roman art. They were probably executed by Roman sculptors who migrated along the Silk Routes that converged on northwestern India. The region around Taxila became the heartland of Buddhism. Hundreds of stupas dotted the landscape, ranging from small devotional shrines to what was the ancient world's tallest building, a tower some 560 feet high and crowned with thirteen gilded and bejeweled umbrellas that greeted visitors to Purushapura.

Beyond this patronage of Buddhism, Indian civilization borrowed little from these nomadic invaders aside from the use of horse-mounted cavalry in warfare. Almost nothing is known about Kaniṣka's immediate successors, and the empire he founded eventually disintegrated. The Gandhāran school of art, however, continued to flourish in Afghanistan and Kashmir. Situated on the caravan route between Bactria and Taxila was the Buddhist monastic center of Bamiyan, established in the second century. The sacred grottos dug into the cliff faces of Bamiyan's narrow valley as monastic retreats still exist, but the three colossal Buddha statues, the tallest of which reached a height of 174 feet, fell victim to Taliban iconoclasts and were blown up in March 2001—an event that marked the nadir of an even darker age than India had endured in the early part of the first millennium.

CHAPTER 3

The Classical Age

"Perfection has been achieved," reads a fifth-century inscription engraved on the railing of a Buddhist stupa at Sanchi in central India. The inscription was written at the height of what is nostalgically referred to today as India's Golden Age (320–550 CE). Also known as the Classical Age, it was a time of unprecedented economic prosperity. Science flowered, trade flourished, and crime was minimal. An enlightened citizenry funded free hospitals for the poor. A person's duty or dharma was laid out in the *Manu Smriti* or Laws of Manu. Once duty was fulfilled, the pathway to pleasure was mapped out in texts such as the *Kāmasūtra*. Spiritual guidance could be found in more accessible Hindu texts such as the *Purāṇas*, a collection of legends and moral precepts, as well as in epic poems, namely the *Mahābhārata* and the *Rāmāyaṇa*.

The foundations for this utopian age were laid by Candra Gupta I (r. 319–350 CE; referred to this way to differentiate him from the Mauryan ruler Candragupta), who ascended to the throne of Magadha in 319 CE. The origins of the Gupta dynasty, the first pan-Indian empire since the Mauryas, are obscure. What few sources there are suggest that Candra Gupta came from a rich land-owning family, married a princess from the well-connected Lichchavi tribe, and became the ruler of

Magadha, where Pāṭaliputra was still the capital. This marriage of convenience was marked by the issuing of coins featuring the new king and his queen, something unprecedented in the annals of Indian numismatics.

It was his son and successor Samudra Gupta (r. 350–375) who extended the empire and established the government machinery for it to thrive. Much of the information about his conquests comes from a lengthy inscription on a stone column discovered in Allahabad in the early 1800s. The inscription lists wars of conquest that extended his rule north to the Himalayan foothills and as far south as Kanchipuram in southern India, the capital of the Pallava kingdom. Demographers estimate the population of the subcontinent at the time to have been around seventy-five million, and one of his epithets describes him as "conqueror of the four quarters of the earth," a reference to rulers in Nepal, Sri Lanka, and possibly Southeast Asia who acknowledged his sovereignty. Based on coins minted during his reign, we know that Samudra Gupta saw himself as a living manifestation of the god Viṣṇu. Other coins showing him slaying a lion, warrior-like with a bow and arrow, or playing a lute. Court chroniclers, usually selected for their hagiographic skills, praised his poetry and knowledge of Hindu scriptures. His support for Hinduism and his pursuit of dharma make him popular with today's Hindu nationalists, who see him as epitomizing the classical ideal of kingship. The reach of his empire is presented as proof that foreigners weren't the only ones who could conquer India.

Samudra Gupta was succeeded by Candra Gupta Vikrama-ditya (r. 375–415). Like his father, he was a patron of the arts and sciences. The Buddhist university at Nalanda was founded during his reign and he supported playwrights such as Kālidāsa. Candra Gupta II, as he is often known, ruled for approximately thirty-five years and extended the kingdom's boundaries westward toward Sindh and the Konkan coast. He also moved his capital to Ayodhya, the legendary birthplace of the Hindu god Ram.

Candra Gupta II's administration was far more decentralized than that of the Mauryas, with considerable powers devolved to officials at regional and local levels. Once a territory came under Gupta control, its old rulers were generally reinstated and left alone as long as they paid a tribute to the emperor and swore their continued allegiance. Trade boomed, with spices, textiles, ivory, precious stones, perfumes, and medicinal herbs being transported by sea to ports in Southeast Asia, the coast of East Africa and the Gulf, and over land along the interconnected branches of the Silk Road.

With trade came exchanges in the scientific sphere. Indian mathematicians were responsible for the notation of numerals from one to nine and the concept of zero—among the most significant of India's contributions to the world. Āryabhata (476–550) posited the theory that the Earth was a sphere that rotates on its axis, calculated the length of the day to within less than a second of its actual value, and suggested that eclipses were caused by the alignment of the sun, the moon, and the Earth, not by the mythological demon Rahu. He also correctly ascribed the luminosity of the moon and planets to reflected sunlight and calculated pi to four decimal places. When India joined the space race in 1975 by launching a satellite into the Earth's orbit, it named the craft after Āryabhata. Brahmagupta (598–665), another Gupta-period mathematician, defined zero as the result of subtracting a number from itself, but the rigidities of the caste system meant that this knowledge never circulated beyond a small section of society.

The Gupta Gambit

Historians date the invention of chess to the Gupta period. Its first iteration was as a four-player war game called *chaturanga*, a Sanskrit word meaning "four limbs" and the name of a quadripartite battle formation mentioned in the *Mahābhārata* (as well as the flow sequence in yoga). By the seventh century, *chaturanga* had evolved into a two-player game recognizable as today's chess—pieces had differing levels of power based on their importance in society, and victory was achieved by eliminating the king. In the original Indian version, the bishop was an elephant and the queen a royal counselor.

The growing power of the Brahmins was reflected in the increasing use of Sanskrit in coinage and in literature. The epitome of this linguist revival was the playwright and poet Kālidāsa, who probably lived in the late fourth century. Dubbed India's Shakespeare, his most famous drama, *Śakuntalā*, was based on part of the *Mahābhārata*. It was translated from the Sanskrit by William Jones in the late eighteenth century, revealing to the outside world the richness of the Indian literary canon. Sanskrit became the language of scholarship wherever Indian influence spread. As the Indologist Sheldon Pollock notes: "There was nothing unusual about finding a Chinese traveller studying Sanskrit grammar in Sumatra in the seventh century, an intellectual from Sri Lanka writing Sanskrit literary theory in the northern Deccan in the tenth, or Khmer princes composing Sanskrit political poetry for the magnificent pillars of Mebon and Pre Rup in Angkor in the twelfth."

The best-known text of this period is the *Kāmasūtra*, or *Treatise on the Art of Love*. Not much is known about the author, Vātsyāyana—though it has been established that his real name was Mallanaga and he lived in the late second or early third century CE, probably in Pāṭaliputra. Written while he was practicing celibacy and deep meditation, the *Kāmasūtra* describes an idealized world where pleasure was a legitimate indulgence. Although just one out of the seven books of the *Kāmasūtra* details sexual positions, its eroticism captured the public's imagination when it was first presented to the West. The British explorer Richard Burton's 1883 translation became the most pirated book of the Victorian era.

The bulk of the *Kāmasūtra* is about the arts of finding a partner, maintaining a marriage, living with a courtesan, and committing adultery without being discovered—though cheating on one's partner is discouraged. Its audience was the rich urban elite, who had time and money to indulge in pleasure. In the text's ideal world, a wealthy man would buy a home in a decent neighborhood, preferably enclosed in a leafy garden and close to a river. His bedroom would be perfumed and his bed strewn with fresh flowers. Every morning he would apply sandalwood oil to his forehead and temples and outline his eyes with collyrium. His days would be spent teaching parrots to talk, attending cock fights, and visiting inns or pleasure houses to talk about art and poetry, and to listen to singers. Later, he would light incense in his house to welcome his lover. If she had been caught in a shower of rain and smudged her makeup, he would reapply it. If her skirt was wet, he would dry her with a towel.

While the *Kāmasūtra* stresses the tenderness of lovemaking, the intensity of sexual acts is depicted by scratches and teeth marks on the skin. As well as describing numerous sexual positions, it lists no fewer than twenty-six ways of kissing. Homosexuality is mentioned only briefly and somewhat unenthusiastically.

Kāma was only one of the forms of conduct and knowledge necessary for pleasure. Vātsyāyana insisted that *artha*, the acquisition of wealth—one of the three fundamental goals of life together with dharma (religious duty)—should come before pleasure. The courtly citizen was also expected to achieve religious merit in his or her old age.

The Hindu Renaissance

Indian historians look back on the Gupta age as the "Hindu renaissance." Buddhism in India had peaked, though rates were still growing in parts of Kashmir and Afghanistan. An emphasis on sacrificial acts was giving way to new forms of

Among the most dramatic examples of Gupta art is a relief on an early fifth-century rock-cut shrine at Udayagiri, near Bhopal, showing Viṣṇu as the Cosmic Boar, Varāha, rescuing the earth goddess from the serpent who tried to drown her in the cosmic ocean at the moment of creation.

devotion known as bhakti that emphasized an emotional attachment to and love for a personal god. The most popular gods became Brahmā, the god of creation; Viṣṇu and his ten incarnations; and Śiva, in his aspects as creator and destroyer. Known as the *Trimūrti* (cosmic triad), these gods are still central to Hinduism today. From the vast pantheon of Vedic deities, only one—Surya, the sun god—would find a place in the new iconography. Having honed their skills at portraying the figure of the Buddha and

Describing the cave paintings of Ajanta, the Dutch art historian Alex Jarl wrote: "Everything in these pictures, from the composition as a whole to the smallest pearl or flower, testifies to depth of insight coupled with the greatest technical skills."

female figures known as *yakshas*, Gupta stonemasons turned their attention to sculpting what are arguably the most sublime images of Hindu gods ever produced.

The earliest surviving freestanding Hindu temples, built to demonstrate the piety of a ruler or a noble, date from the Gupta era. But it would not be until late in the first millennium that the rate of Hindu temple construction matched that of Buddhist stupas. Even today, Hindus are often most comfortable making offerings at small shrines in the courtyard of a house, under the spreading branches of a peepul tree, or on the banks of sacred rivers or tanks.

Despite this Hindu revival, tolerance toward other religions such as Buddhism and Jainism never waned. In 1817, a group of British soldiers hunting tigers in the northwest Deccan were led by a village boy into a horseshoe-shaped ravine. Hidden by thick undergrowth were a series of twenty-eight caves that contained some of the earliest surviving examples of Indian painting. Executed over the course of several centuries, those dating from the late fifth century are considered the finest. Illustrating episodes of the life of Buddha based on the Jātaka tales, they reflect the ample patronage enjoyed by the artists who executed them.

Much of the Gupta Empire's reputation as India's Golden Age is based on writings of the Chinese Buddhist pilgrim Fa-hsien (337–422), who spent six years traveling around the territories controlled by Candra Gupta II. He depicts a peaceful and prosperous society with little, if any, crime. He speaks approvingly of the numerous charitable institutions in Pāṭaliputra. The Gupta capital has an excellent hospital free to all patients, its running costs met by benevolent citizens, he observes. Vegetarianism is almost universal, and the eating of onions and garlic is frowned upon. Wine is off the menu. Unlike in China, regulations are few and no passports are needed to travel from one part of the Gupta territories to the other: "Those who want to go away, may go; those who want to stop, may stop." Justice, when dispensed, is mild, with the amputation of a hand the most severe form and carried out rarely. Criminal and civil laws are demarcated for the first time. Government interference in daily life is kept to a minimum, with citizens left to go about their business and prosper.

> ### *Fa-hsien*, A Record of Buddhist Kingdoms
> "No man among his subjects falls away from *Dharma*; there is no one who is distressed, in poverty, in misery, avaricious, or who, worthy of punishment, is over much put to torture."

Fa-hsien's religious prejudices come to the fore when he describes a society guided by the teachings of Buddhism. While there were numerous Buddhist monasteries in the kingdom, including two in the capital that catered to hundreds of students from around the Buddhist world, there are also signs that Buddhism was in decline. Bodh Gayā, an important place of pilgrimage where the Buddha achieved enlightenment, had been left to the jungle. Other holy places associated with the Buddha, such as Kapilavastu and Kuśinagara, were deserted aside from a few monks begging for alms from the occasional pilgrim. Fa-hsien's writings also contain the first descriptions of untouchability in the caste system. Members of the lowest caste, he noted, had to beat a piece of wood to announce their arrival to prevent others from being ritually contaminated by them.

By the early part of the millennium, the four varṇas had taken on new layers of complexity and society split into specialized groups, or *jātis*, based on occupations. Just as English names such as Baker, Smith, and Potter relate to occupation, Indian surnames are generally a clue to caste—for instance, Bhat traditionally referred to a scholar, while Yadav was a cattle herder. Individuals were forced to regulate their behavior on the basis of caste. Food could only be shared with other caste members. Sexual relations and intermarriage between castes was forbidden. Untouchables generally lived at a distance from the higher castes. Even the shadow of an Untouchable was considered to be polluting. Temple entry was banned to them, and they had separate wells.

Despite this emphasis on ritual purity, the system was not rigid, and, over time, castes could move up the hierarchy by giving up customs such as eating meat or adopting more orthodox religious practices. The frequent wars that accompanied Muslim invasions of the eleventh century onward made it possible for lower castes to upgrade their status by offering themselves as soldiers in local armies. More recently, the opening up of livelihood choices, greater mobility, and the drift from villages to urban areas have meant that people are not always bound to follow their caste occupations. Today, however, the stigma of untouchability extends even to expatriate Indian communities, leading to calls for anti-caste discrimination legislation to be passed in the United Kingdom.

The Age of the Invaders

India's Golden Age was short-lived. During the reign of Candra Gupta's son and successor, Kumāra Gupta (r. 415–455), a new threat emerged. As usual, it came from the mountain passes of the northwest. The Hūṇas were related to the barbarian hordes of Attila the Hun. As they moved out of the Central Asian steppes, they split into two groups, one heading for the Volga River and one for the Oxus. The former invaded Eastern Europe in 375 and pushed the Goths south of the Danube River. The branch that settled on the Oxus was known as the White Huns. Early in the fifth century, they captured Kabul and swept down through the Khyber

Pass. Although Kumāra Gupta's son and successor, Skanda Gupta (r. 455–467), was able to repel the first wave of attackers in 455, his death twelve years later saw the collapse of central authority. The Gupta Empire split into numerous smaller kingdoms, with some rulers switching their allegiance to the invaders rather than submit their people to Hūṇa barbarity.

Indian historians rarely dwell on the seventy-five years that the Hūṇas executed their reign of brutal repression. The invaders paid no heed to the rules of caste, defiling sacred places and not differentiating between Brahmins and Untouchables. The most ruthless of all was Mihirakula, the "Atilla of India," who took morbid pleasure in rolling elephants down mountainsides. The Hūṇas had a particular dislike of Buddhism. As they conquered new territory, monks were among the first to be slaughtered, dealing a deathblow to the religion in northern India from which it never recovered. Buddhist texts assert that, as punishment for his atrocities, Mihirakula met a ghastly death—the moment of his "descent into Hell of unceasing torment" marked by the day turning to night, a fierce wind, and an earthquake.

Eventually, a central Indian ruler, Yaśodharman, formed a confederation that defeated Mihirakula in c. 528. Remnants of the Hūṇas were integrated into militarized warrior tribes known as the Rajputs.

Much of the rest of the sixth century is a historical blank, with a clearer picture of the various rulers competing for prominence not emerging until the middle of the seventh. Once again, the writings of a Chinese Buddhist pilgrim provide an invaluable snapshot of the era. Hsuan-tsang (c.

602–664) traveled extensively throughout northern India from 640 to 644 before returning to China with twenty horses loaded with Buddhist relics and texts. At the time, much of the north was ruled by Harṣa (r. 606–647), who came to the throne at the age of fifteen in 606. Despite possessing a relatively small army of five thousand war elephants and twenty thousand cavalry, he quickly subdued his enemies, coming to rule over a swathe of territory from the Punjab border in the west to Bengal in the east. Like Aśoka, he then proclaimed his opposition to conquest and the rest of his three-decade-long reign was mostly peaceful. He dispensed alms to both Hindus and Buddhists, though in his final years favored the latter. On his order, thousands of stupas were constructed along the Ganges, made mostly from bamboo and wood—none of which remain today. Hsuan-tsang notes Harṣa's interest in alchemy: while at his court he met a sage named Nāgārjuna, a man so skilled in the art of compounding medicines that he produced a pill which allegedly extended his life and that of his companions by hundreds of years. When Harṣa ran out of funds to build a monastery for Nāgārjuna, one of the monks "scattered some drops of numinous and wonderful pharmakon over certain large stones, whereupon they all turned to gold."

Another chronicler of Harṣa's reign was the bohemian Banā, "a rakish brahman" with an "ill-spent youth and varied circle of friends." His *Harṣacarita* is the first authentic biography of an Indian ruler. Under Harṣa, we find Buddhists and Brahmins of every sect, "all diligently following their own tenets, pondering, urging objections, raising doubts and resolving them." Banā's description of Harṣa takes hagiography to new heights:

His eyes are not stained by the deadly poison of pride; his voice is not choked by the convulsive effects of the baneful drug of conceit; his postures do not lose their natural dignity through any sudden epileptic fit of forgetfulness caused by the heat of arrogance; his changes of feeling are not exaggerated by the fevered outbursts of ungovernable self-will; his gait is not agitated by the unnatural movements of an access of self-conceit; his voice is not rendered harsh by the words being uttered under a tetanus of hauteur which distorts his lips.

Little is known about how Harṣa died, though Hsuan-tsang records a botched assassination attempt toward the end of his reign plotted by disaffected Brahmins. His death marked the end of the last Hindu empire of note in northern India before the Islamic conquests of the eleventh century. For much of the next five hundred years, India would fall back to the default position of much of its ancient past: disparate centers of power vying for dominance, with numerous minor kingdoms constantly switching allegiances depending on where they could get a better deal. However, patterns do emerge from this messy patchwork.

India divides itself more or less neatly into four main geographical and political regions: the north, stretching from the Indus River to the Gangetic Plains; the east, encompassing Bengal and Assam; the center, comprising the agriculturally rich and geologically ancient central plateau known as the Deccan plateau; and the southern peninsula. The dominant power in each of these regions was never quite strong enough to control any of the other three for more than short periods of time. Interregional conflict, however, was often severe, particularly in the northern and central regions.

Empires of the South

South India presents a more cohesive picture. Although Hinduism had its roots in the Āryanized north, much of its growth from the seventh century onward would take place in the southern peninsula. The richest religious and devotional literature would be composed in Dravidian languages, predominantly Tamil. Some of the most sublime temple architecture, as well as bronze and stone sculpture, would be executed during this period.

The most important southern kingdoms were the Pāṇḍyas, Ceras, Pallavas, and Cholas. The Pāṇḍyas were first mentioned in Greek writings in the fourth century BCE; their capital was at Madurai. The Ceras date to the first century CE and ruled over much of what is now the state of Kerala. The first empire to encompass a substantial portion of the Indian peninsula and

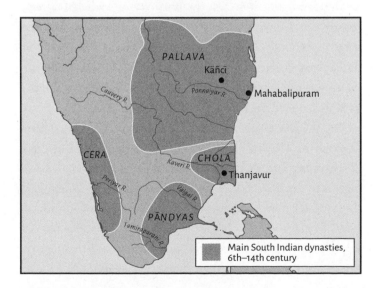

to impact other regions of India and Southeast Asia were the Pallavas. Established in 275 CE with its capital at Kāñcī, now Kanchipuram, the Pallava kingdom at its peak stretched from the northern part of present-day Andhra Pradesh to the Kaveri River in the south. From Kāñcī, merchants and colonizers spread Hinduism into Southeast Asia. Evidence for this comes from the earliest Khmer rulers of Cambodia who, like the Pallavas, almost always bore names ending in -varman. The names of Cambodia and Khmer can be traced to a common ancestor, Kambu, who is mentioned in the *Purāṇas*.

The Pallavas were a significant trading empire, sending Indian goods to ports in Persia, Rome, Sumatra, and Malaya. They were tolerant of all faiths, with one of their kings converting from Jainism to Hinduism. Music, painting, and literature were patronized. Having worked on sites such as the Ajanta caves, sculptors and painters migrated southward to meet the growing demand for Hindu art and architecture in the Tamil kingdoms. At the port city of Mahabalipuram, the dynasty's founder, King Simhavishnu, commissioned the huge relief of the Descent of Ganga that depicts the descent of India's holiest river from the Himalayas to the sea, while one of his successors was responsible for the Kailasānāthar temple in Kāñcī, one of the oldest Śiva temples in India.

By the ninth century, the balance of power had shifted toward the Cholas. They were first mentioned in Aśoka's inscriptions, and their ancestors had probably occupied the region of the Kaveri delta since prehistoric times. During the Pallavas' reign they were relegated to the status of subsidiary state. When the Pallavas were looking the other way, preoccupied with settling scores with their traditional enemies the Cālukyas, a Hindu kingdom based at Bādāmi, the Cholas made a bid for power, intervening in a Pallava succession crisis and taking control of Kāñcī, as well as Mahabalipuram.

The most celebrated Chola ruler, Rājarāja (r. 985–1014), whose name means "king of kings," was an administrative genius who laid the foundation for the most stable, best administered, and longest lived of all early South Indian polities.

Rājarāja has been compared to Aśoka as an illustrious empire builder who patronized the arts, was accepting of other religions, and ordered the construction of some of India's most magnificent monuments, notably the Rājarājeshvara temple in Thanjavur—its sacred architecture placing it at the center of the Hindu universe. Consecrated in 1010 and rising two hundred feet above the flat plains of Tamil Nadu, it was three to four times higher and larger than any other building in the south. Its dominical capstone weighs eighty tonnes and was probably put in place using an earth ramp. The temple was built to mark Rājarāja's victory over the Cālukyas and dedicated to Śiva, whose massive liṅgam is the object of worship. Rājarāja donated five hundred pounds of gold and even more silver, mostly war booty, to the temple, and villagers in the surrounding area were taxed to support its maintenance. Wealthy pilgrims added to its coffers and the temple functioned like a bank, making investments and loaning funds to the same villagers it taxed. The endowments also paid the wages of four hundred dancing girls and hundreds more attendants, artisans, tailors, and administrators.

A portrait of Rājarāja offering flowers to Lord Śiva on one of the temple's murals is the earliest identifiable portrait of any king in Indian art. The veneration of Rājarāja as well as his reputation as a boon-dispensing leader have parallels with the cult of leadership that thrives in South India today. Sunil Khilnani draws comparisons between Rājarāja and the former

The UNESCO-listed Rājarājeshvara temple in Thanjavur (also known as the Brihadishwara temple) is one of the largest temples in South India. Its distinctive steep pyramidical temple tower reflects the predominant architectural style in the south.

chief minister of Tamil Nadu state, Jayalalitha, who successfully cultivated an image of magnanimous bounty, distributing gifts to her followers such as televisions, motorbikes, and school fees for girls. When she was imprisoned for corruption in 2014, more than 150 people are believed to have died either of shock or by taking their own lives.

After vanquishing the Cālukyas, Pāṇḍyas, and Ceras, Rājarāja conquered most of Sri Lanka and sacked the old capital, Anuradhapura, in 993. He then seized the Maldives, which controlled many of the trade routes with the Arab world. Following Rājarāja's death in 1014, his son Rājendra I (r. 1014–1044) pushed the Chola realm northward. His generals stuck mainly to the coast, where elephants were lined up in the rivers to form bridges for the infantry to cross. After subduing the Buddhist Pālas of Bengal, Rājendra's army reached the banks of the Ganges in 1023. Great jars of its holy waters were transported southward, where they were emptied into a massive ceremonial tank in his new capital, Gaṅgaikoṇḍacoḷapuram, literally "the city of the Chola who conquered the Ganga." The temple Rājendra commissioned to mark his victory still stands there, but of the city he established nothing remains.

Having subdued all the kingdoms of South India, Rājendra picked off the last remnants of the Buddhist kingdom of Mahinda V (982–1029) in Sri Lanka and made Polonnaruwa the island's new capital. He then became the only Indian ruler to launch a navy. After a millennium of cordial relations with the states of Southeast Asia that saw trade flourish and India's cultural influence spread, Rājendra decided to "add lustre to his crown," as one historian put it, and conquered parts of Burma, Malaya, and Sumatra. In 1025, Chola forces invaded the Sumatran kingdom of Srivijaya, which controlled the Malacca Straits. It was an ambitious raid. A contemporary Arab geographer reported that even the fastest ship would take more than two years to visit all the islands controlled by Rājendra's kingdom, and described its ruler as the richest man in the world.

The Cholas would ultimately conquer fourteen ports, but the effects of the raids were transitory. There are many theories as to what prompted this uncharacteristic pattern of conquest. Suppressing piracy that was rampant in the area, breaking China's control over lucrative trade routes, or the old-fashioned lure of plunder have all been put forward as theories to explain the eastward push.

If measured by the longevity of their empire—around three centuries—and the refinement of architecture, literature and the arts, the importance of religion, and the sophistication of their administration, the Cholas can be said to represent South India's Golden Age. Hundreds of Chola temples with their majestic pyramidical towers still rise above the rice paddies of

Tamil Nadu and Kerala. More than places of worship, they functioned like parallel courts, and were often designed like palaces, with high walls enclosing voluminous courtyards where religious ceremonies could take place. "Temples were central to the imperial projects of the upwardly mobile dynasties; every conquering monarch felt it incumbent upon him to build a temple as a way of publicizing his achievement," notes Wendy Doniger. Private worship became public, with temples increasingly becoming not just the centers for pilgrimage and religious activity, but also meeting places and markets where devotional paraphernalia was sold.

Their immense wealth also made them prime targets for Hindu armies from the north long before plundering Muslim invaders carried their riches back to their strongholds in Afghanistan. Possibly the richest of these depositories is said to be buried in a series of vaults beneath the Sri Padmanabhaswamy Temple in Trivandrum, the former seat of the royal family of Travancore and now the capital of the southern state of Kerala. Even conservative estimates put the value of gold, silver, bejeweled ornaments, and coins in the vaults at more than seven hundred billion dollars—a hoard that has been accumulating since 800 CE. Years of legal wrangling over whether the Travancore royals or the Indian government were the rightful administrators of the temple kept some of the chambers sealed, as did rumors that giant cobras protected the innermost hidden chamber, known as Vault B.

The Cholas are also remembered for their school of bronze sculpture, which the art historian J. C. Harle describes as "the finest unsurpassed in any place or age." The most recognizable of the bronzes show the figure of Śiva as Lord of the Dance, creating and destroying the universe, posing with one knee bent in an aureole of flame as he dances, transfixed by the rhythm of the small hourglass-shaped drum held in his upper right hand. In another sense, the figure of the dancing Śiva can also be seen as an allegory for the upheavals that were about to beset India and would make their presence felt even in the deep south. As John Keay writes:

> The historian who looks for a classic example of mātsyanyāya, that "big fish eats little fish" state of anarchy so dreaded in the *Purāṇas*, need look no further than India in the eleventh and twelfth centuries. *Dharma*'s cosmic order appeared utterly confounded and the geometry of the mandala hopelessly subverted. Lesser feudatories nibbled at greater feudatories, kingdoms swallowed kingdoms, and dynasties devoured dynasties, all with a voracious abandon that woefully disregarded the shark-like presence lurking in the Punjab.

"The King of the Dance is all rhythm and exaltation," writes the French art historian René Grousset. "[He] wears a broad smile. He smiles at death and at life, at pain and at joy alike, or rather, if we be allowed to express it, his smile is both death and life, both joy and pain."

That presence would change the face of India forever, and not even geography would save the kingdoms of the south.

CHAPTER 4

The Coming of Islam

It must have seemed like a good idea at the time. After the disastrous First Anglo-Afghan War that started in 1839, the East India Company decided it needed to be on a firmer footing in India. In 1842, an army of retribution had successfully retaken the citadel of Ghazni, where they found two huge gates believed to have been carved from sandalwood and plundered from the Somnath temple in Gujarat in the early eleventh century. Sensing an opportunity to cast the British as rectifiers of the historical harm the Muslims had inflicted on India, the governor of the East India Company, Lord Ellenborough (1790–1871), issued a proclamation that the gates would be returned. The "insult of 800 years is at last avenged . . . the gates of the temple of Somnath, so long the memorial of your humiliation, are [to] become the proudest record of your national glory." Unfortunately, the gates were not from Somnath. They were not made of sandalwood but deodar and were carved by local craftsmen. Nor was there any reference to the gates being plundered in earlier Muslim chronicles.

A century and a half later, Somnath was in the spotlight again when the president of the Bharatiya Janata Party, L. K. Advani (b. 1927), began his so-called Rath Yatra at the temple. Setting out on September 25, 1990, in a truck made to look like a Hindu chariot, he crisscrossed northern India until he reached Ayodhya in Uttar Pradesh. The aim of the *yatra* was to erect a temple of the god Ram on the site of a mosque built by the Mughal emperor Babur. Advani would live to see the mosque demolished by fanatical Hindu volunteers known as *kar sevaks* in 1992, but had retired from politics before India's Supreme Court ruled that a temple could be built on the site in late 2019.

That Somnath's symbolism is strong enough to unite a rapacious multinational trading corporation and an avowedly nationalist Hindu political party revolves around the controversial figure of Mahmud of Ghazni—the eleventh-century Turkic ruler who launched more than a dozen raids into India. Portrayed by Hindu nationalists and some Indian historians as the devil incarnate, he looms large over the historical narrative of the coming of Islam to the subcontinent and what has happened since.

Sacred to Śiva, the temple of Somnath is located on the shores of the Arabian Sea. Situated inside a fort and surrounded on three sides by water, it was defended only by Brahmins and devout Hindus and fell easily to Mahmud's forces in 1026. Such was the scale of the carnage that even Muslim chroniclers betrayed a sense of unease when describing it. After stripping the temple of its gold, Mahmud is said to have personally destroyed the giant lingam, a representation of Śiva's phallus, and said to be "the greatest idol of al-Hind." Its fragments were allegedly taken back to Ghazni and incorporated into the steps of its mosque, where they would be defiled daily by the feet of Muslim devotees.

Historians are now starting to question whether Mahmud would occupy the space he now does had it not been for

Ellenborough's ill-advised "proclamation." Over the course of twenty-six years, Mahmud made seventeen raids on India, his objective being plunder, not territorial control. As the Indian historian Romila Thapar points out, there are no references to the raids in contemporary sources aside from a passing mention in a Jaina text. Two centuries later, an Arab merchant who asked to build a mosque in the town was warmly welcomed by the local administration and Somnath's priests. An inscription in Sanskrit describes the mosque in Hindu terms as a site "where people did puja in order to gain merit" and uses the same wording to denote both Śiva and Allah.

Mahmud's incursions do raise deeper questions regarding why India was so unprepared to meet the Islamic challenge from the eleventh century onward. Its wealth, based on a rich agrarian society, should have provided its rulers with ample resources to defend their land militarily. Despite centuries of invasions through the passes leading out of Afghanistan dating back to the time of Alexander, there had never been a collective drive to build defensive fortifications along the border.

So what went wrong? The potential culprits are many and varied: rapacious rulers who taxed peasantry and diverted resources to secular and religious beneficiaries; local chieftains preoccupied with their own internal squabbles and lulled into a false sense of security by perceiving their Muslim foes as raiders rather than potential conquerors; a fragmented political landscape of dozens of regional kingdoms more interested in waging self-destructive wars against one another than forging a national consciousness.

In his prodigious study of the world's civilizations, British historian Arnold Toynbee adds into the mix the caste system and its effect on disrupting social unity. Sanctioned by the Hindu religion, the caste system "is bound to grow to monstrous proportions," Toynbee wrote. The self-stultified Hindu civilization "had lost its claim to the mimesis of the society at large; nevertheless, it insisted on imposing its will on the society." This "marked the most fateful occurrence" in ancient India's history.

Indian historians such as J. L. Gupta describe the Hindu population at the time as a house divided: "Their social and national vision had become so narrow that they did not consider themselves to be responsible for the defence of their own hearths and homes." India's internal weaknesses "had sapped its vitality": "Its fabulous wealth, weak political structure, and 'petrified society' extended an open invitation to the Muslim invaders to lay their hands on its poorly defended treasures."

While divisions in Indian society played a role, the Muslim invaders had certain military advantages, employing cavalries mounted on swift Central Asian horses and using superior military tactics that emphasized agility over strength of numbers. Their armies also tended to have a permanent core of professional soldiers who were accustomed to fighting together, whereas Indian forces tended to be composed of separate units under individual lords who came together only when required.

Commerce Before Conquest

India's contacts with the Arab world predated the rise of Islam by many centuries. Indian merchants employed Arab sailors. Arab cameleers carried merchandise along the Silk Road between the Mediterranean and the subcontinent. Arab trading communities were already well established along

India's west coast, and Indian goods such as cotton and silk, ivory and precious stones, spices and sugar could be found in the markets of Baghdad and Cairo. These links also enabled Indian culture, science, and philosophy to spread westward. The story-within-a-story technique of *One Thousand and One Nights* can be traced back to the interrelated animal fables found in the *Pañcatantra* literature of Vedic India and the Buddhist Jātaka tales.

The death of Prophet Muhammad in 623 triggered a campaign of conquest with few parallels in history. Within twenty years, Muslim armies had conquered much of the Byzantine Empire in Syria and Egypt and the Sassanid Empire in Iraq and Iran. After taking over most of Afghanistan, they reached Sindh in 712, but advanced no further. For the next three centuries, the border between India and its Islamic neighbors ran in a rough line from the Indus River to Kabul. It would not be until the late tenth century that Islamic armies would threaten India. The invaders came not from the existing Islamic outposts in Sindh, but from Central Asia. In around 986, a former slave turned Turkic general named Sabuktigin left his stronghold in the legendary city of Bukhara and conquered Kabul before marching into Punjab. The Shahi king, Jayapāla, put up a strong resistance, but when a massive storm pummeled the battlefield he took it to be an omen and sued for peace. Sabuktigin now controlled the strategic Khyber Pass, a valuable springboard for future raids. But instead of pressing further eastward, he returned to Bukhara, where he was made caliph, leaving future conquests in the hands of his son Mahmud.

By Mahmud's own account, he was "defective in external appearance": "The sight of a king should brighten the eyes of his beholders, but nature has been so capricious to me that my aspect seems the picture of misfortune," he said. Although he is best remembered for desecrating Hindu temples, his first campaign in 1004 was against the Ismailis of Multan in Pakistan. Belonging to the Shia branch of Islam, the Ismailis were considered heretics by Sunni Muslims. Multan was strategically located on the Indus Plain at the crossroads of important trade routes between the Gulf and western India. The city was sacked a second time by Mahmud in 1007. The following year he overran and destroyed the great citadel and temple of Kangra, returning to his capital with four hundred pounds of gold and two tons of silver as well as coinage worth the equivalent of seventy million dirhams. A similar fate befell the great temple of Mathura, a center of worship for followers of the god Kṛṣṇa in 1018. The following year, he raided Kanauj, capturing all seven forts that defended the city in a single day.

For all his ruthlessness, it is possible to salvage something positive from Mahmud's legacy. He used the booty of his conquests to erect one of the finest mosques of its day in Ghazni and to assemble a vast library. He cultivated the poet Firdausi, who wrote the *Shahnama*, an epic poem of the rulers of pre-Islamic Persia, and ordered the scholar Alberuni (also known as al-Biruni) to spend ten years in India, where he learned Sanskrit and translated Hindu texts. Alberuni's *Kitab al Hind* or *Book of India*, which drew largely on Sanskrit sources, is arguably the finest account of the country, its people, philosophies, and religions prior to the Mughal period.

Mahmud's death in 1030 prompted a power struggle sharpened by the unfortunate fact that two of his sons were born on the same day to separate mothers. After his eventual successor Ma'sud was killed in a palace coup, the Ghaznavid dynasty began to decline. In 1173, Ghazni fell to the Ghurids,

Indian elephants were used as a primary battle engine for over 2,000 years across the subcontinent and were valued by rulers far above horses.

who then set their sights on the Ghaznavid's capital of Lahore, which they captured in 1186.

Unlike Mahmud, the Ghurid leader Muhammad Ghuri wanted to expand his territories eastward. His dreams of easy victory were dashed when his army engaged the Rajput prince Prithviraj III at Tarain, north of Delhi, in 1191. Rajput chroniclers still celebrate this victorious battle that saw Ghuri's forces retreat in disarray after he was struck in the upper arm by a spear and whisked off the battlefield by one of his soldiers. To avenge this humiliation, he punished those soldiers who had fled by parading them in public wearing their horses' nosebags and eating chaff.

Ghuri wasn't willing to give up so easily. After reassembling his forces, he once again marched eastward. Despite heading the most formidable force of Rajputs ever gathered, including hundreds of war elephants, Prithviraj was no match for the invaders. According to one account, Ghuri tricked the

Rajputs into believing he had agreed to a truce. Lulled into a false sense of security, they spent the night in riotous revelry. Groggy from wine and opium, they were outmaneuvered by Ghuri's lightly armed cavalry and Prithviraj was hunted down and killed.

The 1192 rout of the Rajputs at Tarain has been described as "the most decisive battle in the history of India." The "key to the Delhi gate" and the whole of India was now in the hands of Ghuri and his victorious soldiers. Islam had well and truly arrived in South Asia.

The Delhi Sultanate

Ghuri didn't live to see his dreams of empire fulfilled. He was assassinated in 1206 by a member of a rival Islamic sect, leaving his trusted deputy, Qutb ud-din Aybak, to establish the Mamluk dynasty, the first of five successive dynasties that made up the Delhi Sultanate. They were followed by the Khalji, the Tughluq, the Sayyid, and the Lodi. The Lodi ruled until 1526, when their sultan, Ibrahim, was killed in a battle against Babur, the first of the Mughals. Each successive dynasty would also leave its mark on Delhi, creating new cities, mosques, and tombs that still dot the Indian capital today.

> *Dynasties of the Delhi Sultanate*
> Mamluk/Slave dynasty (1206–1290)
> Khalji dynasty (1290–1320)
> Tughluq dynasty (1320–1414)
> Sayyid dynasty (1414–1451)
> Lodi dynasty (1451–1526)

Three recurrent themes mark the history of the Delhi Sultanate: the bloodshed that almost inevitably accompanied successions to the throne; the ongoing resistance from Indian rulers; and the omnipresent military threats from the west. Their capital, Delhi, was a well-established city that had been inhabited since the sixth century BCE and was considered of strategic and symbolic importance. Under the sultanate, it became a center of Persian learning. Persianate institutions and practices such as a salaried bureaucracy and military slavery were established. A tradition of spiritually powerful holy men, or Sufis, who practiced a more mystical form of Islam gave the religion in India a distinctly softer edge.

The Mamluks were known as the Slave Dynasty because many of its rulers had once been captives of their Turkish overlords. The term "slave" was a loose one. After being purchased and converted to Islam (if they weren't Muslim already), they were trained to hold positions such as "keeper of the stables" and "keeper of the hunting leopards." Some rose to senior military and administrative posts. Their devotion to their masters eclipsed their loyalty to their own kin and ethnic groups. So strong was their loyalty that when engaged to go into battle against the Mongol marauders who periodically threatened India, the mainly Turkish slaves never flinched at fighting their own countrymen.

Qutb ud-din Aybak died in a polo accident in 1210. His successor, Iltutmish, reigned for twenty-six years, long enough to consolidate his power. He also threw open the doors of his kingdom to refugees fleeing the Mongol invasion of Persia. So large was the influx that he tripled the size of the Qutb mosque and added three more stories to its minaret. The refugees included the cream of Persian scholars, artists, and

The most enduring reminder of Qutb ud-din Aybak's reign is the Qutb Minar, which rises over the flat plains to the east of New Delhi. The minaret was constructed using the pillars, capitals, and lintels of Hindu and Jain temples. The Delhi sultans employed Hindu temple-building techniques and Hindu artisans to construct their mosques.

artisans, who filled the ranks of the bureaucracy and judiciary. Persian became the language of government and diplomacy. At the same time, Mongol expansion in the west isolated the Delhi Sultanate from its Islamic counterparts in Mesopotamia and northern Africa, ensuring it would remain an independent state.

It is at this point that the exclusively male story of kings, princes, and sultans takes an unexpected turn with the coming to power of Raziyya al-Din (1205–1240), the first female ruler of an Islamic dynasty in India. Declaring his sons incapable of leadership, Iltutmish on his death bed proclaimed his thirty-one-year-old daughter, raised as an equal, to be his successor. In 1983, Bollywood would immortalize Raziyya's story in the controversial film *Razia Sultan* starring the veteran actress Hema Malini (b. 1948). Released at a time when even kissing in Indian cinema was taboo, the film portrays Raziyya in a fictional lesbian relationship with Khakun (Parveen Babi), one of the women in her harem. In the film's most famous scene, Khakun draws a feather over her face and either kisses Raziyya or whispers in her ear (such opaqueness was necessary to get past the censors) as the empress is rebuffing the advances of one of her male admirers. Despite having to learn Urdu, walk across the

Popular with the masses, Raziyya appeared unveiled, wearing a cap and coat so she could "show herself among the people."

hot desert sands, ride elephants, and engage in sword fights while clad in oversized costumes, Malini had, critics agreed, pulled off one of her best performances.

In the film, Raziyya tosses off the "emperor's garb," which she considers a "shroud" because it is an impediment to finding true love. In real life her motivation for appearing in public unveiled was to be closer to the people. Initially this worked to endear herself to her subjects—but not the ulema or clergy of Delhi. Things took a turn for the worse when her liaison with an Abyssinian slave who supervised the royal horses earned her the ire of provincial governors. She was eventually incarcerated by Altunia, a Turkic slave, while she was putting down a rebellion in Lahore. Turning the tables on those opposed to her, she married Altunia and the two of them led an army of local clans to reclaim her throne.

Raziyya was killed in 1240 after their soldiers deserted them. Though her reign was short, her legacy was significant. After coming to power, she issued coins in her name, proclaiming herself to be the "pillar of women" and "Queen of the times," and established schools and libraries. As the scholar S. A. A. Rizvi notes: "[Raziyya] combated intrigues competently, displayed a remarkable insight into military tactics, resourcefully implemented her independent decisions, and diplomatically reconciled the recalcitrant *iqta* [land] holders. Her chief merit was to rise above the prejudices of her age."

Raziyya's eventual successor, after the usual jockeying for the throne, was Ghiyath al-Din Balban (r. 1266–1287), who had been bought by Iltutmish as a slave and risen through the ranks to become a trusted member of a junta of Turkish soldiers known as "The Forty." To compensate for his lowly background, he created a court renowned for its pomp and grandeur. His insistence that visitors prostrated and kissed his feet, the Indian historian Jaswant Lal Mehta writes, "left the nobility and visitors utterly humbled, terror-stricken and dumbfounded." According to the court chronicler Barani, not even his domestic servants ever saw him dressed in anything other than royal apparel, socks, and headgear. It was said he never laughed. Nor did he allow any courtier to smile in his presence.

Despite his reputation as a despot, Balban's reign was an oasis of stability in an otherwise tumultuous period. His benign rule created such an atmosphere of peace and contentment that it was said the god Viṣṇu could "sleep in peace on his ocean of milk." His prioritization of political stability over religious dictates was reflected in his tolerant attitude toward non-Muslims. This prompted outrage from Muslim nobles such as Barani, who were appalled that Hindus were allowed to practice idol worship and infidelity. Referring to Balban, he wrote: "Muslim kings not only allow but are pleased with the fact that infidels, polytheists, idol-worshippers and cow-dung worshippers [could] build houses like palaces, wear clothes of brocade and ride horses caparisoned with gold and silver ornaments."

Following Balban's death in 1287, his seventeen-year-old son tried unsuccessfully to negotiate the internecine power games that beset the court, opening the way for the army commander Jalal al-Din Khalji (c. 1220–1296) to seize power in a coup d'état and establish the Khalji dynasty. Originally from Afghanistan, the Khaljis had served as soldiers in the Ghurid armies. Following the Mongol invasion of Afghanistan in the twelfth century, they migrated en masse to northern India as soldiers and settlers, gradually rising to administrative and military posts. The dynasty's greatest ruler, Ala al-Din Khalji (r. 1296–1316), extended the boundaries of the sultanate south of the Vidhaya mountain range. Under the command of his African slave eunuch Malik Kafur, Ala al-Din Khalji's armies launched numerous raids into the Deccan, sacking its cities to finance a line of defenses to protect dominions from Mongol incursions. For the first time, Muslim invaders reached the deep south of India, plundering temples in Madurai, Srirangam, and Chidambaram and bringing back hundreds of tonnes of gold, silver, and precious stones. The Somnath temple was ransacked, its lingam was once again smashed, and its shards incorporated into the steps of a mosque in Delhi. After each raid, the defeated Hindu kings were reinstated on their thrones, provided they publicly acknowledged the overlordship of the Delhi Sultan and sent him a hefty annual tribute.

Ala al-Din Khalji's fanaticism was tempered by his reforms. He opened public office to commoners, including the non-privileged Muslim immigrants, Indian converts to Islam, and even Hindus. The sale of wine and liquor was banned. Harsh penalties helped curb bribery and corruption. He also introduced agrarian reforms that curbed the powers of Hindu middlemen to collect taxes and confiscated all landed properties of his courtiers and nobles to deprive them of the wealth they could use to start an insurrection. A ministry of commerce set prices; shopkeepers who charged above the fixed rates were publicly flogged. The result was an immediate drop in grain prices for consumers that was maintained even in years of drought.

Barani on Ala Al-din Khalji's rule: "A camel could be had for a dang [farthing], the price of a slave girl was fixed at 5 to 12 tankas and that of a concubine at 20 to 40 tankas. A handsome young lad could be had for 20 to 30 tankas whereas the price of slave labourers varied from 10 to 15 tankas each. With the consumers' goods and domestic labour so cheap, a man of moderate means could afford to enjoy a happy and comfortable life with one to four legally married wives, a number of concubines and a dozen of slave girls and slave labourers at his beck and call."

Peak Sultanate

Ibn Battuta (1304–1369) has been called the greatest Arab adventurer of all time—the Moroccan equivalent of Marco Polo (almost his exact contemporary). In 1325, the Tangier-born jurist set off on a pilgrimage to Mecca. Instead of returning home, he spent the next three decades traversing most of the known world, from northern Africa to eastern China. Ten of those years were spent in India, the bulk of them at the court of Muhammad bin Tughluq (1290–1351). Described as "the most controversial figure ever to rule India," bin Tughluq's various epithets included "Muhammad the Bloody," "Delhi's own Nero," and "India's Ivan the Terrible." Battuta, who served him for eight years, first as a judge and then as an ambassador, left behind a detailed description of the man—and his contradictions. He was more addicted than anyone Battuta knew to "the making of gifts and the shedding of blood. His gate is never without some poor man enriched or some living man executed . . . For all that, he is of all men the most humble and the readiest to show equity and to acknowledge the right."

Battuta arrived in Delhi in 1334, as the sultanate was in the throes of a particularly bloody succession crisis following the death of Ala al-Din Khalji in 1316. The most notorious ruler to occupy the throne during this period was the brutal transvestite Qutb al-Din Mubarak, who was assassinated by his catamite slave Khusrau Khan. He stayed on the throne for just four months—long enough to massacre all of al-Din Khalji's sons and to alienate the nobility, who transferred their allegiance to the sexagenarian army commander Ghiyath al-Din. His rule was also short-lived. In 1325, bin Tughluq disposed neatly of his father by constructing a flimsy timber reception pavilion at Afghanpur, on the banks of the Yamuna River. According to the official version, a lightning bolt hit the pavilion while father and son were dining, bringing down the roof, which killed Ghiyath al-Din. Battuta maintained that the pavilion was deliberately built to collapse easily. When

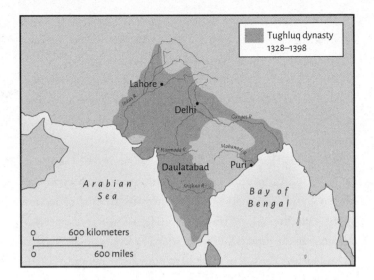

everyone else had gone to prayer, bin Tughluq had ordered elephants to stamp the ground, creating a mini earthquake that caused the structure to collapse.

While violence was no stranger to the Delhi sultans, bin Tughluq took the concept of revenge to new extremes. He ordered one of his enemies be flayed alive, his skin stuffed and put on display, his flesh minced, cooked with rice, and served to his family. His administration was no less controversial. He levied so much additional tax on farmers to pay for his vast army that many were forced from the land, leading to a devastating famine. Perhaps his most spectacular failure was the attempt to replicate China's system of paper money by introducing brass and copper coins that were assigned higher arbitrary value than their metallic content. These proved so easy to forge that the sultan was forced to withdraw them from circulation, buying back real and counterfeit coins in such quantities that "heaps of them rose up in Tughluqabad like mountains."

When it came to the treatment of non-Muslims, however, pragmatism triumphed over religious zeal. Funds were assigned for the repair of Hindu temples, and anyone who paid *jizya*, a poll tax imposed on non-Muslims, could build places of worship. The importance of the jizya to the revenues of the state neutralized the need for conversions. The fewer the number of Muslims, the more tax collected.

Under bin Tughluq, the Delhi Sultanate reached its greatest geographical extent, encompassing much of western and eastern India and extending deep into the Deccan. The shift in the epicenter of power prompted another controversy—transferring the capital 870 miles south to Daulatabad. According to Battuta, the sultan wanted to punish the people of Delhi for their habit of penning anonymous abusive letters to him. A deeper underlying motive may have been his suspicions that the ulema, or clergy, were planning a revolt. Moving his court and bureaucracy to Daulatabad (or the "city of government," as it had been renamed), a grueling forty-day journey from the current capital in the heat of summer, earned him few friends among Delhi's aristocracy, its Islamic clergy, traders, and businessmen. Although Battuta noted that so many trees had been planted along the route that walking along it was like "going through a garden," the presence of bandits and armed tribal groups made the journey a perilous one.

In what was a rare event for an Indian ruler, bin Tughluq died of natural causes in 1351 while pursuing rebels in the deserts of Sindh. He was succeeded by his cousin Firuz Shah Tughluq (1309–1388), who inherited a crumbling empire. Large areas that had been under the sultanate's control in Bengal rebelled and became independent of Delhi but retained their Muslim identities. A poor military strategist who showed no interest in empire-building, Firuz Shah Tughluq watched as further rebellions saw Gujarat slip into semiautonomy and much of the Deccan achieve complete independence under the Bahmani dynasty. Saddled with an inferiority complex because of his Hindu mother, he took his role as the sovereign of an Islamic state and leader of the faithful seriously. The great Jagannath temple in Puri was desecrated and Brahmins were no longer exempt from paying jizya. Following a well-established precedent, Firuz built a separate city named Firuzabad to the north of Tughluqabad to glorify his rule.

Firuz Shah Tughluq's death in 1388 sparked yet another succession crisis that left an enfeebled sultanate vulnerable to attacks from outsiders. When the Central Asian warlord Tamerlane (Timur) invaded India in 1398, the sultanate could muster only ten thousand troops and was unable to defend the capital. Tamerlane ordered his troops to spare the lives of Delhi's citizens, but the reprieve was short-lived. After some of the invaders were caught looting, scuffles broke out and several soldiers were killed. For the next three days, Tamerlane's forces went on a rampage, killing or enslaving Hindus and pillaging their belongings. As he later recorded in his autobiographical memoir, the *Tuzak-i-Timuri*:

The spoil was so great that each man secured from fifty to a hundred prisoners, men, women and children. There was no man who took less than twenty. The other booty was immense in rubies, diamonds, garnets, pearls and other gems, jewels of gold and silver, *ashrafis*, *tankas* of gold and silver, and brocades and silks of great value. Gold and silver ornaments of the Hindu women were obtained in such quantities as to exceed all account.

The immediate outcome of Tamerlane's raid was a further fragmentation of the sultanate. New semiautonomous power centers sprang up in the Punjab and in the Eastern Gangetic Plains, where one of Firuz Shah Tughluq's Ethiopian-born slaves established a sultanate at Jaunpur. The Sayyid dynasty, which had replaced the Tughluqs, saw its territories shrink to almost nothing. Sultan Alam Shah, one of its last monarchs, was mocked for calling himself "the king of the world" when his dominions extended only as far as the village of Palam, which today is near the city's international airport.

The arrival of the Lodis in 1451 gave the sultanate a flickering lease of life. Descendants of Afghan merchants and mercenaries, the Lodis were little more than a confederation of loosely aligned states. Their sultans did not build thrones for themselves but shared a carpet with their peers. Not all Afghans residing in the sultanate's territory were supporters of the regime, as Ibrahim Lodi (1480–1526), the last ruler, found out in 1526 when Babur launched a raid on Delhi. The founder of the Mughal Empire probably never would have succeeded had Afghan chieftains in Punjab laid out a welcoming carpet for him.

Promising freedom from caste and idolatry, Sufi orders flourished in cities such as Ajmer and parts of Sindh. Like the devotional bhakti traditions of Hinduism, they were a potentially disruptive force as they bypassed orthodox religious practices to achieve a personal relationship between an individual and God. Muslims, Christians, Jews, Zoroastrians, and Hindus, Sufis proclaimed, "all were striving toward the same goal and that the outward observances that kept them apart were false." Sufi shrines dedicated to saints sprung up all over northern India and were visited by Hindus and Muslims alike.

Nowhere is the confluence of Sufi and Hindu devotionalism more pronounced than in the works of the fifteenth-century poet Kabir. Born into a caste of Muslim weavers, he lived in Varanasi, where his shrine still attracts devotees of all faiths. Legend has it that when he died his body turned into flowers, ensuring that he could not receive either a Hindu cremation or a Muslim burial. Today he has two graves, each tended by the other faith. For Kabir, neither priest nor mullahs were of any consequence. Sincere avowals of faith, no matter how they were expressed, had more chance of reaching the ears of God than precise ritual.

> *Kabir*
> Listen carefully,
> Neither the Vedas
> Nor the Qur'an
> Will teach you this:
> Put the bit in its mouth,
> The saddle on its back,
> Your foot in the stirrup,
> And ride your wild runaway mind
> All the way to heaven.

The Muslim rulers of India from the time of the Delhi Sultanate until the early eighteenth century were mostly pragmatists who recognized they were a minority reigning over a large, mainly Hindu population scattered over a vast subcontinent. The armies they maintained were primarily to protect India from the constant threat of a Mongol invasion, rather than to pursue territorial conquest. From ruler to ruler, dynasty to dynasty, Islam swung between being inclusive and iconoclastic, but at no time was there any attempt at mass conversion.

When Hindu temples were destroyed, the aim was to seize their considerable treasures and undermine the political authority of local rulers. For the most part, Hindus, Jains, and religious minorities, such as the Jews and Parsis, were allowed to worship their gods without interference. The need to attract Hindus to bureaucratic posts and as soldiers into their armies overruled their desire for proselytizing. Hindus generally ran the economy, and Hindu bankers made huge profits by helping newly arrived Muslims from Central Asia buy slaves, brocades, jewels, and even horses.

Conquest was more about commerce than conversion. Beyond the Indus River lay a land rich in resources, with one of the most sophisticated economies in the world. It was a land of gold, silver, and precious stones, of spices and slaves. Roads were safe, ports efficient, tariffs low. The characterization of Muslim rulers as destructive and despotic was popularized by the British in the nineteenth century onward in order to justify their rule as just and benevolent. The communal friction that erupted between Hindus and Muslims around the time of Indian independence, and has simmered ever since, was largely absent during the period when Muslim dynasties were the most powerful force in India.

The City of Victory

Although the territorial gains of rulers such as Muhammad bin Tughluq in South India were generally fleeting, they precipitated the destruction of many existing kingdoms. The most significant outcome of the fluid political landscape that ensued was the establishment of the Vijayanagara Empire in

1336 by Harihara (r. 1336–1356) and his brother Bukka (r. 1356–1377), Hindu converts to Islam who served under and then rebelled against the Tughluqs. According to legend, a Hindu sage recognized Harihara as an embodiment of the god Virupaksha. He switched religions and was allowed to establish a kingdom based on Hindu principles. Named after its capital, Vijayanagara, or City of Victory, it lasted for three centuries and at the peak of its power was the largest state ever created in South India, ruling over a population of around twenty-five million at a time when the subcontinent had about 150 million people. On reaching the capital in the middle of the fifteenth century, the Timurid ambassador Abd Al-Razzaq (1413–1482) remarked, "The city is such that the pupil of the eye has never seen a place like it, and the ear of intelligence has never been informed that there existed anything to equal it in the world." The jewelry bazaar was stocked with pearls of such quality "that the field of the moon of the fourteenth

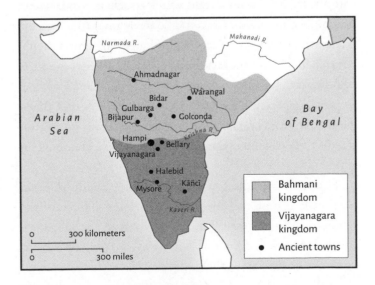

day caught fire simply by gazing on them." Its rulers claimed universal sovereignty—their aim was "to rule the vast world under a single umbrella."

Vijayanagara's main rivals were the Bahmani sultans who ruled from Gulbarga, and the Gajapatis, or Lords of the Elephant, who controlled much of what is now the state of Odisha. Vijayanagara's pragmatic ruler Deva Rayā II (r. 1432–1446) narrowed the military gap with the Bahmanis by enlisting them into his army, both as officers and foot soldiers. After coming to the throne in 1509, Kṛṣṇa Deva Rayā (1471–1579), considered the greatest of all the Vijayanagara kings, pushed the Gajapatis back to their capital, Cuttack.

Ruling an empire that stretched from the Malabar to the Coromandel coasts, Kṛṣṇa Deva Rayā was one of the first Indian leaders to welcome European traders to his kingdom and believed that trade was the key to universal sovereignty. A good ruler, he wrote, should oversee the development of harbors so that all important articles such as sandalwood, precious stones, and pearls could be freely imported. Foreign sailors who were shipwrecked on his kingdom's shores should be cared for: "Make the merchants of distant foreign countries who import elephants and good horses attached to yourself by providing them with daily audience, presents and allowing decent profits. Then those articles will never go to your enemies." Portuguese gunners formed the backbone of his army.

Historians have long seen Vijayanagar's Hindu rulers as a bulwark against the expansion of Muslim influence into southern India. However, an examination of the kingdom's culture, society, and architecture paints a different picture. From the beginning of their empire, they styled themselves "sultan among Indian kings" (*hindu-rayā-suratrana*) and absorbed Persianate ideas and practices. The precinct of the capital known as the royal center incorporated Islamic architectural styles such as domes, pointed arches, cross vaultings, and stucco reliefs. Turkish and Iranian soldiers were recruited into the army. Sculptures of Turkish soldiers even guarded some of the city's Hindu temples.

Abd Al-Razzaq noticed that the king wore a tunic of Chinese silk styled after the royal attire of twelfth-century Iran. Nobles wore brimless headgear that also derived from Persia for public events, switching to traditional South India dress for Hindu religious ceremonies. "For these elites, an important sign of the sophistication of the court was precisely its ability to participate in a larger Islamic civilisational sphere, while at the same time continuing to support and patronise what was becoming a distinctive pan-south Indian elite culture," writes the historian Rosalind O'Hanlon. The establishment of the Mughal Empire would see these interactions between the Hindu and Islamic spheres reach their zenith.

CHAPTER 5

The Magnificent Mughals

A visitor touring South Asia in 1500 would have found a land divided into dozens of rival kingdoms—a multiethnic tapestry of elites vying for power, prestige, and a share of India's vast resources. A century later, virtually all the northern half of the subcontinent had been brought under the umbrella of one state—the Mughal Empire. The Great or Grand Mughals, as the dynasty's first six emperors are known, left behind some of the most exquisite architecture in all of Asia, epitomized in the marble magnificence of the Taj Mahal in Agra and the ruins of Akbar's short-lived capital, Fatehpur Sikri. To some scholars, they remain the quintessential Oriental autocrats—their rule marked by ruthless struggles of succession and aggressive military conquests. Others stress the richness of the encounters between the Mughal court and the Sanskrit culture of India. In the popular imagination they were synonymous with incredible wealth, opulent palaces, and treasuries brimming with precious stones. In the early 1900s, the German traveler and philosopher Count Hermann Keyserling declared the Great Mughals to be "the grandest rulers brought forth by mankind": "They were men of action, refined diplomats, experienced judges of the human psyche, and at the same time aesthetes and dreamers." Such a "superior human synthesis" went beyond the attributes of any European king.

Adding substance to the dynasty's aura is the abundance of written material at the historian's disposal. The personalized memoirs of emperors were complemented by the writings of court chroniclers who recorded the minutest details of the day-to-day administration of their realms. The rise of the Mughals coincided with the age of European exploration and expansionism. English envoys bearing gifts in exchange for trading rights, Jesuit missionaries seeking converts, French jewelers bargaining for precious stones, Italian doctors offering quack cures for gout and impotency, as well as a miscellany of improbable adventurers left behind candid accounts of individual rulers, their attributes and eccentricities—as well as the splendor of their courts.

Mughal vs. Mongol

Outsiders would call the dynasty that Babur founded "the Mughals," using the Persian word for Mongol. Babur preferred to play up his father's Turkic roots. In the fifteenth century the term "Mongol" carried connotations of barbarism. As Babur would say: "Were the Mongols a race of angels, it would still be a vile nation."

The story of the Mughals begins in 1483, with the birth of Zahir al-Din Babur (d. 1530) in modern-day Uzbekistan. His father, a great-great-great grandson of Tamerlane, was the ruler of Ferghana, a small but exceptionally fertile province to the west of Samarkand, Tamerlane's old capital and the site of his magnificent tomb. His mother was directly descended from Genghis Khan, the founder of the Mongol Empire. A freak accident that killed his father brought Babur to the throne at the age of just eleven in 1494. A pigeon fancier, Babur's father had been tending his birds in a dovecote on the outer wall of his palace when the cliff below gave way. As Babur puts it so poetically in his memoirs: "Umar Shaikh Mirza flew, with his pigeons and their house, and became a falcon."

Two years into his reign, he made the first of three attempts to capture Samarkand. His initial bid failed, but he was able to take the city the following year—for a few months. In his absence, Ferghana was conquered by his half brother, leaving Babur without a kingdom. Destitute, Babur, his mother, and a small band of supporters spent the next few years wandering among the mountains and valleys of Central Asia. "It passed through my mind that to wander from mountain to mountain, homeless and helpless, has little to recommend it," he would later write.

Babur's memoir, the *Baburnama*, is a revealing account of these "throneless times," as he called them. Unlike the largely hagiographic ghostwritten memoirs of other Mughal rulers, Babur's is alarmingly frank—"both a Caesar and a Cervantes," as the contemporary Indian novelist Amitav Ghosh describes him. His aim, Babur informs his readers, is "that the truth should be reached in every matter, and that every act should be recorded precisely as it occurred." The *Baburnama* has been described as "among the most enthralling and romantic works of literature of all time," thanks largely to its candor. It recounts the future Mughal emperor's sexual shyness with his first wife; his love affair, unconsummated, with a bazaar boy in Andizhan; his pining for the melons of Kabul; and even the color of his excrement after an attempted poisoning—"an extremely black substance like parched bile."

In 1504, aged twenty-one, Babur gave up his dream of conquering Samarkand and instead set his sights on Kabul. The city's despotic ruler had just died, leaving his infant son as heir. Kabul was an easy conquest, and his success left Babur in control of several strategic crossroads linking India and Central Asia. A year later, he led his first of five expeditions into India. Initially these were pillaging raids. In 1514, after making one last unsuccessful attempt to conquer Samarkand, he began to look to northern India as territory where Timurid power could be rebuilt. Although he received some support from disaffected Lodi nobles, he found them to be untrustworthy, and on three occasions between 1519 and 1524 ordered his invading forces to turn back. It would not be until 1525 that he prepared to take on Ibrahim Lodi. Commanding a force of just eight thousand soldiers, Babur met little resistance as he advanced across the plains of Punjab, where Lodi's authority had largely collapsed. In April 1526, he reached Panipat, in present-day Haryana. What they lacked in manpower, Babur's forces made up with the latest military technology—matchlock guns and cannons. He also arranged his forces in a formation not dissimilar to that used by American pioneers taking on Native American tribes in the Wild West. Bullock-drawn wagons were roped together in a circle, creating a formidable barricade behind which his artillery took cover. When Lodi's forces finally attacked, they were mown down by shotgun pellets. Columns of cavalrymen held in reserve did the rest. It was all over in just a few hours.

Among the dead was Lodi, the only Muslim ruler of Delhi to fall in battle. As was customary, soldiers severed his head and presented it to Babur. Lifting it solemnly, he exclaimed, "Honour to your bravery." His two most senior emirs shrouded the body in a bolt of brocade, then bathed and buried it where it had fallen. As well as building a mosque to commemorate his victory, Babur laid out a symmetrical garden with interlocking canals and raised walkways reminiscent of a Central Asian oasis—a practice he would replicate in other parts of India.

After his victory, Babur rode to Delhi, staying just long enough for the *khutba*, or Friday prayer, to be read in his name, an act that signified the populace's tacit acceptance of their new ruler. Next, he marched to the Lodi capital, Agra, where his son Humayun (1508–1556) had captured the family of the raja of the important North Indian state Gwalior. As a token of his acceptance of the new ruling dispensation, the raja presented Humayun with a gift of jewels, including a diamond so large that its worth would provide "two and a half days' food for the whole world." Babur refused to accept it from his son. Years later Humayun would gift the stone, known as Babur's diamond, to the ruler of Persia. Anecdotal evidence, based on the stone's size, suggests that the fabled diamond was the Koh-i-Noor.

Babur took a bleak view of his newly conquered territories, as did his war-weary soldiers, who were pining for the cool mountain passes of Afghanistan. To dissuade them from returning, he asked, "Shall we go back to Kabul and remain poverty-stricken? Let no one who supports me say such things henceforth. Let no one who cannot endure and is bound to leave be dissuaded from leaving." India, he reminded them, was large and rich—even if it had little else to recommend it.

Babur's aim of bringing Timurid rule to North India was not without its hurdles, starting with what he described as the "remarkable dislike and hostility between [India's] people and mine." Moreover, the Mughals were far from being the dominant power in the land. With the eclipse of the Delhi Sultanate, much of northern India was controlled by semiautonomous Afghan principalities. The successive dynasties of the Delhi Sultanate had all relied on soldiers from Afghanistan and horses from Central Asia, imported by Afghan traders to keep their armies battle-ready. Many of these soldiers had become petty chieftains.

Babur on India from the Baburnama

"There is no beauty in its people, no graceful social intercourse, no poetic talent or understanding, no etiquette, nobility or manliness. The arts and crafts have no harmony or symmetry. There are no good horses, no good dogs, no grapes, musk-melons or first-rate fruits, no ice or cold water, no good bread or cooked food in the bazaars, no hot-baths, no colleges, no candles, torches or candlesticks."

Babur also had to contend with numerous Rajput clans, the strongest of which were the Sisodiyas. In 1527, determined to restore the Rajput empire of Prithviraj Chauhan, the Sisodiya ruler Rana Sanga (1482–1528) assembled a large army, left his stronghold of Mewar, and swiftly advanced northward to see off the invader who brought that dream a step closer by obligingly disposing of the Lodis. The morale of Babur's vastly outnumbered army plunged when an astrologer pointed out that Mars was in an inauspicious position, a sure omen for Timurid defeat. Babur tried to counter the omen by repealing some un-Islamic taxes and vowing to give up drinking wine. Three hundred of his commanders joined him in his pledge, and dozens of jars of the latest vintage brought from Kabul were poured into a specially dug stepwell. Gold and silver wine goblets were broken down and the pieces distributed to the poor. To further boost his soldiers' morale, he declared a jihad or holy war against the infidel Rajput ruler, and gave himself the title of a *ghazi*, or holy warrior.

The two armies came together at Khanwa, approximately forty miles west of Agra. True to their reputation, the Rajputs fought courageously. Babur repeated the tactics used at Panipat, creating a barricade of wagons behind which troops armed with matchlocks and cannons could pick off the Rajput warriors before his cavalry encircled the enemy forces. The tactic worked. To commemorate his victory, Babur ordered the erection of a pillar of severed heads as a warning to others who might contemplate taking on his forces.

By his mid-forties, Babur's health had begun to decline. The hardships he had endured in his early life were taking their toll. Hearing that his father was ill and fearing that nobles in the court were intriguing to install one of his uncles on the throne, Humayun returned to Delhi from Badakhshan, only to fall severely ill himself. One legend describes Babur walking around his son three times, praying for his recovery. By this rite he transferred Humayun's illness to himself and died soon after. The historical record, however, shows that several months passed between this event and Babur's death. Babur died on December 26, 1530, a mere four years after becoming the first Mughal emperor. His body was laid to rest in one of the parterre gardens he had created in Agra. It was later moved and placed in a grave on a terrace overlooking Kabul, where he used to sit and admire the view. No other structure was allowed so the grave would have full exposure to the snow and the sun.

Defeat and Exile

Humayun's succession would follow a pattern laid down by Genghis Khan and Timur. Although he was his father's chosen heir, his brothers Kamran, Askari, and Hindal were entitled to a share of his territories. Each harbored bitterness about not becoming the new Mughal emperor. Kamran, believing he had been shortchanged by receiving only Kabul and Kandahar to rule over, was the first to move against his brother by annexing the Punjab. Humayun had no choice but to acquiesce to the new status quo.

A more significant threat to Humayun's rule came from Bahadur Shah (1505–1537), the ruler of the prosperous maritime state of Gujarat. In 1535, Humayun marched south to confront Bahadur Shah's army, which was equipped with the latest cannons and employed Portuguese gunners. In a daring night action, Humayun's forces captured the fort of Champaner and looted Bahadur Shah's treasury. He then took the capital, Ahmedabad, and the hill fort of Mandu in Malwa, in India's central west. But instead of consolidating his conquests militarily and administratively, Humayun celebrated by holding magnificent banquets and enjoying royal entertainments. As the English writer Bamber Gascoigne blithely notes: "He invariably found the first fruits of victory more appealing than any possible long-term gains and would happily settle down to enjoy for months on end his favourite pastimes of wine, opium (which he took in pellet form with rosewater) and poetry."

Humayun returned to Agra to confront a new threat. Sher Shah Suri (1486–1545), an insignificant Lodi retainer ruling over a small fiefdom near Varanasi, had emerged as the leader of the Afghan resistance to Mughal rule in eastern India. In

1537, Sher Shah invaded Bengal and besieged the capital, Gaur. Humayun responded by sailing down the Yamuna River and the Ganges in a flotilla accompanied by his brothers Kamran and Hindal, with whom he had temporarily reconciled. But instead of proceeding to Gaur, he spent six futile months attempting to take Sher Shah's fortress of Chunar. The delay enabled Sher Shah to finally conquer Gaur and loot its treasury, using the proceeds to create one of the largest armies ever seen in northern India. Confident enough to crown himself the sultan, he adopted the title of Sher Shah, or king.

When Humayun learned of Gaur's fall, he tried to negotiate a power-sharing arrangement with Sher Shah, but they failed to agree on who would rule Bengal. On reaching Gaur, he found it largely abandoned. Once again, the Mughal emperor was diverted from pressing his advantage, this time by Gaur's "fairy faced girls and handsome maids, along with exhilarating gardens and soothing tanks."

While Humayun was indulging in "every kind of luxury" in his Gaur harem, his half-brother Hindal stormed the Mughal capital, Agra, where he proclaimed himself the emperor. Kamran, meanwhile, returned to the Punjab, but instead of helping Humayun subdue his opponents in northern India, he plotted with Hindal on how to divide up the spoils. Things went from bad to worse when Sher Shah took advantage of the turmoil in the Mughal court to take on Humayun's forces at Chausa in the monsoon of 1539. Considering him a lost cause, Kamran and Hindal ignored their brother's appeals for help. Three months of shoring up their respective defenses and engaging in faux diplomacy ended in June 1539, when Afghan forces launched a surprise attack that routed Humayun's army. While retreating across the swollen

Ganges, Humayun fell off his horse. He was saved from drowning by of one of his water bearers, who tossed him an inflated goat skin to use as a buoy. The servant would later be rewarded by being made king for a day.

The next encounter between two armies took place near Kanauj on the Gangetic Plains. Demoralized and depleted by desertions, the Mughals panicked and fled. "It was not a fight, but a rout, for not a man, friend or foe, was even wounded ... Not a cannon was fired—not a gun," one of Humayun's generals later complained. Once again, the Mughal emperor was forced to flee, this time crossing the Ganges on an elephant and retreating to Lahore. As far as Sher Shah was concerned, the losses at Panipat had been reversed. After just eleven years on the subcontinent, the Mughals were on their knees.

Humayun's exile in Lahore was short-lived. After Sher Shah threatened to take the city, he made plans to go to Kabul. But with Kamran in control of the Afghan capital, he had no option but to travel south to Sindh, hoping to regroup his forces and retake his kingdom. While Kamran and Askari remained in Afghanistan, implacably opposed to Humayun, Hindal joined forces with the exiled emperor. In 1541, Humayun married Hamida (1527–1604), the daughter of Hindal's tutor. A year later, after crossing the Thar Desert at the height of summer and reaching Umarkot in Sindh, she gave birth to a boy named Akbar, who would become the Mughal dynasty's greatest emperor. Leaving his infant in Kandahar, Humayun pressed on westward through Afghanistan, finally reaching the city of Herat, held by Shah Tahmasp, the Safavid ruler of Persia. In July 1544, he reached the Tahmasp's court in Qazvin, in modern-day Iran, where the Shah offered him protection on condition that he and his followers convert to the Shia sect of Islam. The price of protection included the Koh-i-Noor diamond.

In September 1545, using troops and funds supplied by the Shah Tahmasp, Humayun led a combined Mughal-Persian force that seized Kandahar from Askari. Three months later, Kamran was defeated in Kabul. Over the next eight years, Kamran tried unsuccessfully to retake the city four times. On his final attempt, he was captured and brought to Humayun, who had him blinded. Kamran is said to have begged with his jailers to be killed. When they refused, he bore the lancing of his eyes stoically. He then requested to make a pilgrimage to Mecca, where he died in 1557.

In Humayun's absence, Sher Shah proved to be a capable leader governing a realm that was stable, prosperous, and well-administered. He reorganized his army, rationalized the system of revenue collection with fixed tax rates on agricultural output, and tackled corruption. He upgraded and extended the Grand Trunk Road, entrusting local chiefs with its security. Shade trees were planted, and *caravanserais*, or rest houses, serving Hindus and Muslims, were spaced a day's travel apart. He also introduced a standardized silver coin known as the *rupiya*, which anticipated the currency of modern India and Pakistan. But his plans to set up Afghan colonies in Rajasthan, Malwa, and Bundelkhand never eventuated. While he was attempting to take the Rajput fortress of Kalinjar in 1545, an ammunition dump exploded, killing him instantly. Before his death, he had ordered the construction of a mausoleum in Sasaram that was larger than the tomb of any other Muslim ruler in India to date.

The leadership crisis that followed Sher Shah's death, which saw five rulers come and go in quick succession, emboldened

Sher Khan's 150-foot-tall, three-tiered mausoleum stands in the middle of a lake. Subsequent Mughal emperors would build ever larger and more elaborate tombs to outdo their Afghan adversaries, culminating in the Taj Mahal in Agra.

Humayun to retake his dominions. In 1555, his troops defeated the forces of Sher Shah's son at Sirhind, in the Punjab. By the middle of that year, Delhi had been captured. After a gap of fourteen years, Babur's monarchy was restored.

Humayun hardly had time to savor the fruits of his victory. In January 1556, just six months after recapturing Delhi, he was on the roof of his library in the Purana Qila in Delhi, consulting with his astrologers about the hour they expected Venus to rise. Hearing the call to prayer, he stood up, caught his foot in his robe, and fell down a steep set of stairs, injuring his head. He died a few days later, his last words being "I accept the divine summons."

The Greatest Mughal

Humayun's son Akbar (1542–1605), only thirteen at the time of his father's death, was put under the care and mentorship of Bairam Khan (1501–1561), the general who had masterminded Humayun's reconquest of India. An exact contemporary of Elizabeth I of England, Akbar would go down in history as the grandest of the Mughal emperors, with some historians elevating him to the status of the greatest of all Indian sovereigns. In *The Discovery of India*, Nehru credited Akbar's reign "with the cultural amalgamation of Hindu and Muslim in north India." Under Akbar, "the Mughal dynasty became firmly established as India's own."

This posthumous portrait of Akbar by the Hindu artist Govardhan (active c. 1596–1645) incorporates the Elizabethan-derived motif of a lion and calf living in peace under the emperor's benign rule.

Although he is touted as the poster boy of tolerance and moderation, the first years of Akbar's rule were particularly bloody, even by South Asian standards. Within months of his enthronement, Delhi was attacked by Hemu, a Hindu saltpeter dealer who had risen through the ranks to lead the Suri army. Akbar's vastly outnumbered forces challenged Hemu's military machine at Panipat. The late-sixteenth-century poet Padmasagara describes the young ruler as "flying at the Sur's army like the star Canopus headed towards the ocean. Amazingly, he caused those warriors to wither from merely hearing a syllable of his name, and he established immortality for his troops that was like an ocean filled with the taste of victory."

While fear was a factor, so was luck. The Mughal forces were saved when an arrow struck Hemu in the eye, causing his panic-stricken army to flee. Hemu was captured and brought before Akbar. Bairam allowed the youthful ruler to behead him. He was now a *ghazi*, a holy warrior.

As Akbar asserted his independence, his relationship with Bairam deteriorated. In 1560, he suggested that his guardian proceed to Mecca on a pilgrimage, and the general had no choice but to comply. He never made it. In January 1561, he was assassinated at Patan, in Gujarat, by an Afghan who bore him a grudge. Two years later, Akbar eliminated another rival to the throne, his foster brother Adham Khan, by throwing him over a palace balcony. When he did not die, his mutilated body was brought up and thrown over again, this time killing him.

At the age of nineteen, Akbar ruled over an empire that extended from Lahore in the east to Jaunpur in the west, but troublesome pockets of resistance remained. The need to neutralize challengers to the Mughal ascendancy would be a feature of his more than five-decade-long rule. Akbar's methods of empire-building differed markedly from his predecessors, especially with the Rajput kingdoms. Rather than engage them in battle, he integrated the Rajput lineages into the Mughal service, treating them as partners in the sovereign power and the wealth of his dominions, while leaving them free to manage their own affairs and administer their ancestral lands. Nor were they required to convert to Islam.

The change in policy came about almost accidentally. In 1561, Bharamal (1548–1574), the ruler of the Kachhwaha clan at Amber, approached Akbar for support to head off a challenge to his princedom. In exchange, Bharamal offered his daughter in marriage. An otherwise insignificant clan suddenly became one of the most important of the Rajput ruling dynasties. Amber's princesses would become Mughal queens and the mothers of future emperors. Its rulers would enter the Mughal service as generals. Bharamal's grandson Raja Man Singh led the Mughal army in campaigns against the Afghans and was made the governor of Bengal. Other Rajput lineages followed the Kachhwaha's example, including the rulers of Jodhpur and Bikaner.

Although Akbar's support enhanced the status of the Kachhwahas, the pre-eminent Rajput lineage remained the Sisodiyas of Mewar. The clan's ruler, Udai Singh (1540–1572), was descended from Rana Sanga, and openly despised those Rajput states who gave up their daughters to the Mughal harem. Determined to put the Sisodiyas in their place, Akbar led a massive army to attack Rana Sanga's stronghold of Chittor in 1567. Bolstered by the forces of two prominent Rajput chiefs, the Mughal emperor's camp extended some ten miles. The stage was set for a long, drawn-out siege.

Chittor's fort was stocked with enough food to last several years and had an ample supply of water. But it was not impregnable. The walls were breached after four months, and Akbar was credited with firing the shot that fatally wounded the fort's commander. Fires were then spotted at several points inside the fort. Believing death preferable to losing their honor, thousands of women committed *jauhar*, or self-immolation. Akbar then ordered the slaughter of the thirty thousand remaining inhabitants. Though they had been beaten for now, the Sisodiyas would continue their resistance throughout the Mughal period.

The defeat of the Sisodiyas left the core areas of the Mughal heartland more or less secure, allowing Akbar to turn his attention to administrative matters. A master policymaker, he implemented a systematic and centralized form of rule that enabled uniformity in the administration of his vast empire. One of Akbar's most important achievements was the reorganization of the Mughal army, which had grown sixfold since he had come to power and included soldiers and officers from a range of different ethnic and religious backgrounds. Instead of inheriting their titles or ranks, officers were assigned a performance-related numerical rank, or *mansab*, that ranged from ten to ten thousand, corresponding to the number of soldiers under their command. The system ensured that military forces could be mobilized at short notice.

Akbar's commitment to religious pluralism was one of the defining features of his reign—all the more remarkable given that religious intolerance was growing in other parts of the world, including Europe, where the Inquisition was underway. At the age of twenty-one, he abolished pilgrimage taxes and the jizya tax. All subjects of the Mughal Empire, regardless of religion, were now treated equally, at least in theory. Sharia law was set aside. Religious mendicants were granted land to set up monasteries. Hindu temples were rebuilt and repaired. Apostasy was no longer punished by death. Akbar and his courtiers celebrated important Hindu festivals such as Diwali. He also adopted the Hindu custom of having himself weighed against gold, silver, grains, and other commodities, and then distributing the result to the destitute and needy.

Like the rulers of the Delhi Sultanate and his Mughal predecessors, Akbar was a follower of Sufi mysticism. Presenting himself as an enlightened Sufi master, he undertook annual pilgrimages, sometimes on foot in the searing summer heat, to the shrine of the founder of the Chishti Sufi tradition in

The Buland Darwaza, or the "Door of Victory," was built in 1575 to commemorate Akbar's victory over Gujarat. It is the main entrance to the Jama Masjid at Fatehpur Sikri.

India, Mu'in al-Din Chishti, at Ajmer, in the northwest. He became a disciple of the Sufi saint Salim Chishti, who predicted the birth of his first son, Salim, the future Emperor Jahangir. So grateful was Akbar that he transformed the saint's village, Sikri, into his new capital, naming it Fatehpur Sikri, and erected one of the most magnificent tombs in India in Salim Chishti's honor. Fatehpur Sikri was modeled on one of his moveable imperial encampments and became an arena for playing out his vision of imperial rule. Today it stands like a perfectly preserved ghost town.

Inspired by Sufism's tolerance of other faiths and their pathways to reaching a union with god, Akbar used his residence in Fatehpur Sikri to engage in a systematic study of comparative theology and religion. He built a "House of Worship," where religious debates were held on Thursday evenings.

Representatives from all religious communities and sects were encouraged to enroll. Akbar was convinced that all religions, not just Islam, contained some element of truth. When a group of Jesuits visited his court, he went out of his way to please them, dressing in Portuguese clothes, kissing a Bible, and placing it on his head. The Jesuits found him so accepting of Christianity that they believed they had a convert, before realizing that he shared the same fascination with Hinduism, Jainism, Judaism, and Zoroastrianism while still observing Muslim prayer times. One of the Jesuits, Father Antonio Monserrate, accompanied Akbar and his army into Afghanistan. While advancing through the Khyber Pass, the emperor restrained an angry mob from stoning the priest to death after he denounced the Prophet.

Monserrate on Akbar's Leadership

"It is hard to exaggerate how accessible [Akbar] makes himself to all who wish audience of him. For he creates an opportunity almost every day for any of the common people or of the nobles to see him and converse with him; and he endeavours to show himself pleasant spoken and affable rather than severe toward all who come to speak with him."

Although he couldn't read (there is evidence to suggest that he was dyslexic), Akbar amassed a library of twenty-four volumes. He set up a department that translated Hindu epics such as the *Mahābhārata* and the *Rāmāyaṇa*, as well as Christian gospels written in Latin, into Persian and had copies made and distributed to libraries throughout his dominions. Sanskrit-speaking astronomers were appointed to his court.

Not everyone approved of Akbar's religious experimentations. His concept of a Divine Faith (*Din-i Ilahi*), an eclectic mix of religions with the emperor as its sacred sovereign, led his enemies to accuse him of abjuring Islam. Among those who detested Akbar's multi-faith enthusiasm was the court chronicler Badauni (1540–1615), who became his fiercest critic. Akbar seems to have taken a morbid enjoyment in assigning him the four-year task of translating the *Mahābhārata*, which Badauni later described as containing nothing but "puerile absurdities." Badauni criticized Akbar for memorizing the 1,001 Sanskrit names for the sun, worshipping the heavenly object four times a day, and interviewing "famed holy men of all sects." Akbar in turn complained that Badauni was a fanatic: "No sword can slice through the jugular vein of his bigotry."

In 1589, Akbar commissioned his head vizier and court poet, Abu'l-Fazl (1551–1602), to "write with the pen of sincerity the account of the glorious events of our dominion-increasing victories." A liberal-minded scholar and gifted historian, Fazl produced two monumental works, the *A'in-i Akbari*, or *Constitution of Akbar*, and the *Akbar-nama*, or *History of Akbar*. A combination of gazetteer, almanac, rule book, and statistical digest, the *A'in-i Akbari*, which in English editions runs to 1,500 pages, contains information on everything from "regulations for oiling camels and injecting oil into their nostrils" to mathematical methods for calculating the Earth's size. At 2,500 pages, the *Akbar-nama* is a eulogistic history of his reign that portrays Akbar as a divine mystic with supernatural powers. As Fazl writes: "He sought for truth amongst the dust-stained denizens of the field of irreflection and consorted with every sort of wearers of patched garments such as [yogis, renouncers, and Sufi mystics], and other solitary sitters in the dust and insouciant recluses."

During the latter part of his reign, Akbar could be found mingling with Hindu holy men who "employ themselves in various follies and extravagances, in contemplations, gestures, addresses, abstractions and reveries, and in alchemy, fascination and magic." His obsession with understanding human nature prompted him to order a Kaspar Hauserian experiment where dozens of infants were moved to a special house; no one was allowed to talk to them in the belief that as they grew older the natural language of humankind would be revealed. The infants were also watched to see "what religion and sect [they] would incline to and above all what creed they would repeat." When Akbar visited the house in 1582, four years after the children were placed there, he heard "no cry . . . no talisman of speech, and nothing came out except the noise of the dumb."

The final years of Akbar's life were marred by tragedy. All three of his legitimate sons were alcoholics, and he would outlive two of them. In his thirties and impatient to inherit the throne, his eldest son, Salim (1569–1627), launched an abortive uprising against his father in 1600. Two years later, he had coins forged in his name as emperor and ordered the killing of Fazl. Father and son reconciled, but only after the intervention of Akbar's wife. Salim was designated the heir apparent, but instead of preparing himself for the duties, he indulged in the excessive consumption of opium and wine. "[Akbar] had achieved more than he could possibly have hoped, only to find his successes undermined by the irony that none of the sons seemed able or worthy to inherit what he had established," writes Bamber Gascoigne.

The World's Richest Empire

On ascending the throne after his father's death in 1605, Salim took the name Jahangir, or "Seizer of the World." While global domination was a pipe dream, the empire he inherited was the richest and most extensive in the world at the time. It stretched over most of northern India and what is now Pakistan, Bangladesh, and Afghanistan. Its population of a hundred million was five times that of the Ottoman Empire at its height, and it produced about a quarter of the world's manufactures, including textiles, spices, sugar, and weaponry.

Jahangir is often portrayed as lazy and languorous. Although his opium and alcohol addictions would incapacitate him in his later years, he was in fact an enlightened and tolerant ruler who followed and tried to improve on many of his father's policies. The Indian art historian Ashok Kumar Das describes Jahangir as an "aesthete": "He was an aristocrat with the eye of a naturalist, the vision of a poet, the taste of a connoisseur and the philosophy of an epicurean." Like Babur, he left a detailed memoir, the *Jahangirnama*, that reflects his fascination with the natural world (he could name every bird in northern India) and his patronage of the arts. Henry Beveridge, the nineteenth-century translator of Jahangir's memoirs declared that the emperor would have been a "better and happier man" as the "head of a Natural History Museum."

Among the thousands of paintings he commissioned is an image of the now extinct Mauritian dodo. The painting by the court artist Ustad Mansur is the world's only accurate depiction of the bird drawn from a living specimen. His memoir also

A painting depicting the dodo ascribed to Ustad Mansur dated to the period 1628–1633. The flightless bird was probably brought to Jahangir's court via Portuguese-controlled Goa.

contains detailed observations of the breeding habits of the sarus crane and the outcome of an experiment in which a lion was dissected to find the physical origin of what made it so brave.

When his favorite courtier, Inayat Khan, was dying from opium addiction, he ordered that he be drawn and painted. A Jaina monk who lived in Jahangir's court, Upadhyaya Bhanucandra Gani, poignantly captured the decadence of the time:

> Jahangir enjoyed and amused himself as Indra does in heaven—sometimes residing in wonderful rest-houses, sometimes on the banks of the Indus, sometimes on pleasure-mounts, sometimes in mansions of variegated colours, sometimes revelling in the exquisite performance of the best female dancers, sometimes listening to the soft music of beautiful damsels, and sometimes attending to dramatic performances.

Among the numerous European visitors to Jahangir's court was Sir Thomas Roe (1581–1644), who arrived in 1615 with letters and gifts from James I to secure a trading agreement for the East India Company. Of all the gifts that Roe bestowed, those Jahangir prized most were English paintings and miniatures, which he ordered his artists to copy. Roe spent three years in India, leaving behind a detailed account of, among other things, the emperor's court as it moved from camp to camp during Jahangir's periodic tours of his empire. More than a thousand elephants, camels, and bullocks were required to transport the royal tents alone. Roe calculated that when the camp halted for the night, it covered an area twenty miles in circumference and equal in greatness to any town in Europe.

Roe was not the first trader to go to the Mughal court. A multitude of trading communities—ranging from the Jewish and al-Karimi networks in Mamluk, Egypt, to the Rasulids of Yemen, as well as the Portuguese—had by the sixteenth century established deep commercial networks with India, trading mainly in spices such as pepper and cardamon from Kerala. Pepper bought in the markets of Cochin could get eight times the price in Lisbon. Demand from the Persian and Ottoman empires and Ming China led to significant increases in pepper output from the early 1500s onward. Payment in gold, silver, ivory, copper, and slaves flowed into the coffers of Indian merchants. Under Akbar and Jahangir, foreign craftsmen, including Europeans, were encouraged to settle in India and teach weavers improved techniques of cloth-making, at times introducing Iranian, European, and Chinese patterns into Indian ones.

Like his father, Jahangir sought out intellectuals and teachers from a range of religions at his court and read texts translated from Sanskrit. Pictures and statues of the Madonna decorated his palaces. Though he remained a devout Muslim, he had a secular outlook. "All sorts of religions are welcome and free, for the king is of none," noted Roe. The exception was Hindu yogis: though they, too, were tolerated, he described them as lacking "all religious knowledge" and perceived in their ideas "only darkness of spirit."

In 1611, Jahangir married Mihru n-Nisa (1577–1645), the widow of one of his lieutenants. Though only thirty-four, she quickly rose to dominate her husband's court, taking on the title Nur Mahal (Light of the Palace) and then Nur Jahan (Light of the World). Coins were struck in her name—the first time a woman had been honored in this way in Islamic India. No public business was carried out unless it was referred to her.

"She governs him and winds him up at her pleasure," noted Roe of her relations with her husband. She was also an excellent shot, killing four tigers by firing just six bullets from a curtained-off *howdah* (seat) atop an elephant in a single day. She dictated orders, issued proclamations, and appointed members of her family to senior court positions. Her insistence that visitors bring her gifts fostered a level of corruption never seen before in the Mughal Empire.

One of those who earned Nur Jahan's favor was Khurram (1592–1666), Jahangir's son by an earlier marriage. Khurram's ascendancy was partly due to his success in subduing the Sisodiyas. Following Akbar's assault on Chittor, the Sisodiya leader Rana Pratap (1540–1597) had led a protracted guerrilla campaign against the Mughals. During his first military assignment in 1614, Khurram took on Pratap's successor, Amar Singh (1559–1620). Facing defeat against a much stronger Mughal army, Singh sued for peace. A year later, the two sides concluded an agreement that exempted the Sisodiyas from entering into marital relations with the Mughals or sending representatives to their court. It also allowed them to administer their own territory and returned to their possession Chittor's fort.

A triumphant Khurram became Jahangir's chosen successor, but his increasingly rebellious behavior drove his father to rename him *bidalwat* (wretched). Nur Jahan, who had taken advantage of her husband's drug-addled behavior and deteriorating health to become the de facto ruler of the empire, also turned against Khurram and began favoring one of Jahangir's younger sons, Shahryar. To get Khurram out of the way, she persuaded Jahangir to send him to Burhanpur to secure the southern flank of the Mughal Empire from the remnants of the Delhi Sultanate, no doubt in the hope that he would not survive the campaign.

Jahangir's death on October 28, 1627, set off an all-too-familiar succession scenario as Nur Jahan tried to seize the chance of putting a sickly Shahryar (he was suffering from a form of leprosy) on the throne, but her plans were thwarted by Asaf Khan, a general in Jahangir's army loyal to Khurram who put her under house arrest. Khurram was still in South India, a three-month march from Agra, when news of his father's death reached him. Twelve days after entering the city on January 24, 1628, on a date chosen by astrologers as auspicious, he was crowned the new emperor as Shah Jahan or "King of the World." One of his first acts was to order the execution of Shahryar and his supporters. Nur Jahan was exiled to Lahore, where she died in 1645.

Born of a Rajput mother, Shah Jahan had more Indian than Mughal blood, but never forgot his Islamic roots. He took a more orthodox approach to matters of religion and state than his father. The practice of prostration before the sovereign, considered un-Islamic, was banned. Patronage of the annual Hajj pilgrimage was reinstated, and the policy of allowing the building and repair of non-Muslim places of worship was stopped. The presence of Jesuit missionaries at his court, however, was tolerated and, like Akbar, he employed Hindus to command his armies.

Pursuing an aggressive military strategy, Shah Jahan added parts of eastern India, Sindh, and the northwestern frontier with Afghanistan to the empire. Treaties were also signed with two major kingdoms in the Deccan, the Adil Shahs of Bijapur and the Qutb Shahs of Golconda. His attempts to retake Timurid territories in northern Afghanistan and Central Asia were less successful. The real significance of these wars was the outcome they had on the fortunes of the two sons who would later vie to replace him—Dara Shukoh and Aurangzeb.

Always accompanying Shah Jahan on his military campaigns was his favorite wife, Mumtaz Mahal (1593–1631). The other wives in his harem did not command "one-thousandth part of the affection" that he did for her, noted the contemporary writer Inayat Khan. Mumtaz Mahal was consulted on all matters of state and her royal seal was affixed to official documents. When in 1631 she died in a thirty-hour labor, giving birth to her fourteenth child, Shah Jahan was so distraught that he did not appear in public for a week. "From constant weeping he was forced to use spectacles; and his august beard and moustache, which had only a few white hairs in them before, became in a few days from intense sorrow more than one-third white," Inayat Khan recorded.

Mumtaz was buried in a garden by the banks of the Tapti River in the city of Burhanpur, where she'd died. Six months later, her body was taken to Agra and reburied on the banks of the Yamuna. On the site of her tomb would rise the greatest of all the Mughal monuments in India: the Taj Mahal. Clad

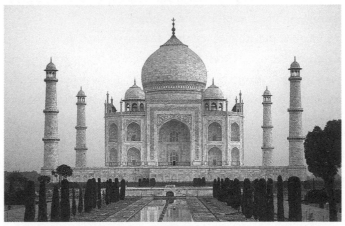

Seeing the Taj Mahal just after its completion in 1648, the French physician François Bernier was adamant that it was much more deserving to be counted as one of the wonders of the world "than those unshapen masses," the pyramids of Egypt.

in white marble, much of it inlaid with semiprecious stones, the building would become, in the words of Shah Jahan's court historian Qazwini, "a masterpiece for ages to come" and "provide for the amazement of all humanity."

Of all the succession struggles that beset the Great Mughals, that of Shah Jahan's four sons was the grisliest. In April 1657, the emperor fell ill when he returned to Delhi from his summer holiday. The Venetian traveler and quack doctor Niccolao Manucci attributed his illness to the overuse of aphrodisiacs, "for being an old man . . . he wanted still to enjoy himself like a youth." Shah Jahan recovered, but not before rumors of his imminent demise swept through his empire. Prior to returning to Delhi, he had designated Dara Shukoh (1615–1659), his eldest and favorite son, as his successor. Like Akbar, Dara Shukoh was a Renaissance man, who once commented that "the essential nature of Hinduism was identical with that of Islam." The fatal flaw in Shah Jahan's succession plan was his failure to disarm the other princes coveting the throne: Shuja, Aurangzeb, and Murad.

During the nine years that followed Shah Jahan's near-death experience, it was Aurangzeb (1618–1707) who would vie for power most vigorously. Austere in his personal behavior and religiously orthodox, he despised his older brother and everything he stood for. Dara Shukoh, he complained, had won his father's favor by "flattery, smoothness of tongue and much laughing." While Shukoh was in Afghanistan making an unsuccessful attempt to seize Kandahar, Aurangzeb took Agra in 1658 and imprisoned Shah Jahan in the Red Fort. On his return to India, Shukoh was betrayed by one of his generals, captured, and brought back to Delhi, where he was paraded through the city on a grubby elephant and in chains.

"Everywhere," said the French doctor François Bernier, "I observed the people weeping and lamenting the fate of Dara in the most touching language: men, women, and children wailing as if some mighty calamity had happened to themselves." After being charged with apostasy, he was sentenced to death and beheaded.

On being proclaimed emperor in May 1659, Aurangzeb took as his title Alamgir, or "World Compeller," the Persian word engraved on the sword his captive father had given him. Aurangzeb's reputation as a religious conservative is well entrenched in India today. His almost-fifty-year reign would mark the end of Mughal ties to the Sanskrit cultural world. As Bamber Gascoigne writes, "Akbar [had] disrupted the Muslim community by recognising that India was not an Islamic country: Aurangzeb disrupted India by behaving as if it were." He spent months memorizing the Koran and would lay down his carpet and recite his evening prayers even in the midst of battle. "Aurangzeb was, first and last, a stern Puritan," one of his earliest biographers, Stanley Lane-Poole, noted. "Nothing in life—neither throne, nor love, nor ease—weighed for an instant in his mind against his fealty to the principles of Islam."

Scholars such as Audrey Truschke and Katherine Schofield have since challenged this view of his religious zealotry. The long-held notion that he banned music because

A painting attributed to the Mughal court artist Bichitr depicting Emperor Aurangzeb seated on a golden throne in his durbar, c. 1660.

it was un-Islamic was just one of the many myths that have now been discounted on closer historical scrutiny. Despite his adherence to orthodox Islam, he moved cautiously against Hindus in the first decade of his reign. His sons and nobles continued to celebrate Hindu religious holidays, patronize poets, and enjoy music and wine. That changed in 1669, when he ordered the governors of all provinces under Mughal rule to destroy Hindu temples, following up the decree a few years later with another that banned Hindus from higher office. However, these orders were never carried out systematically, and temple demolitions were confined to a few areas around northern India.

In 1679, he reinstated the jizya tax on non-Muslims that Akbar had abolished 115 years earlier. Soon after the decree was issued, an earthquake struck Delhi. Believing it to be an omen, the city's mullahs entreated the emperor to reconsider his actions. Aurangzeb refused, saying that the trembling of the earth was "the result of the joy it felt at the course I was adopting." So entrenched was Hinduism that wiping it out completely was far beyond the capacity of any ruler. As Manucci observed, even destroyed temples were "venerated by the Hindus and visited for the offering of alms." Those that remained were thronged with worshippers.

During his reign, Aurangzeb would expand the Mughal Empire to its greatest extent. But his campaign of conquest came at considerable expense. The military and administrative resources of the empire were spread thin and discipline was breaking down. When Sir William Norris, trade representative of King William III, visited Aurangzeb a few years before his death, he reported that his soldiers had not been paid and his courtiers could be bribed for a bottle of wine. "All administration has disappeared," wrote one eyewitness. "The realm is desolated, nobody gets justice, they have been utterly ruined."

Adding to this parlous state was the fact that Aurangzeb's most formidable foes, the Marathas in the Deccan and the Sikhs in the Punjab, were unvanquished. Under Śivaji, the various Maratha tribes were united into an effective military force that used a network of impregnable forts along the Western Ghats to launch punishing guerrilla raids on Aurangzeb's forces; these are still glorified today. The emperor had alienated the Sikhs by condemning the ninth guru, Tegh Bahadur, for blasphemy and executing him. Since its founding in the late fifteenth century, Sikhism had become a movement for religious and social reform, as well as a formidable military force. Aurangzeb was particularly infuriated by the large number of Muslims converting to the faith. The assassination of Gobind Singh, the tenth and last guru, by Aurangzeb's successor, Bahadur Shah, in 1708 unleashed a series of wars that would undermine the remnants of the Mughal Empire for a century to come.

Determined not to repeat the chaos that surrounded his own ascension to the throne, Aurangzeb had tried in vain to lay the groundwork for an orderly transfer of power. Fearing that they would rebel against him, he imprisoned three of his five sons for petty crimes such as embezzlement. Another was dispatched to a post at a far-flung corner of the empire. But in the end, it all came to naught. The death of the last great Mughal on March 3, 1707, touched off a debilitating fratricidal struggle that saw son conspire against son, puppet against pretender, often with murderous consequences. In the course of a dozen years, no fewer than seventeen aspirants would jockey

After drawn-out sieges, Aurangzeb conquered the key Shia Muslim states of Bijapur and Golconda, bringing most of the Indian subcontinent under his control.

for the throne. Aurangzeb's death also opened the way for new players to enter this eighteenth-century great game for the control of the Indian subcontinent and its vast wealth. No longer would wars be fought solely between Hindu and Muslim armies. Britain and France, once content to send emissaries such as Roe and Norris bearing gifts to win favors from local rulers, were about to become full-blown rivals for trade and territory.

CHAPTER 6

Merchants and Mercenaries

In 1772, London theatergoers flocked to the Haymarket Theatre to see Samuel Foote's new play, *The Nabob*. It told the story of Sir Matthew Mite, a dissolute employee of the East India Company (EIC) who returns to England intending to use his ill-begotten fortune to marry into an aristocratic family and buy a seat in the House of Commons. Sir John Oldham, a respectable aristocrat who has fallen on hard times, is in debt to Mite, who wants to marry his beautiful daughter Sophy. Mite is a gambler "profusely scattering the spoils of ruined provinces" and "voluptuously riot- ing in pleasures that derive their source from the ruin of others." He confesses to wanting to set up a seraglio guarded by "three blacks from Bengal" and threatens to send Oldham to a debt- ors' prison if he can't make Sophy his wife. In the end, Oldham's cousin Thomas Oldham stumps up the ten thousand pounds that Mite is owed, saving the family seat—and Sophy's honor.

Nabob is a corruption of the Persian word *nawab*, meaning governor. As the English public's indignation toward the Company's barbaric business practices grew in the 1770s, the word was applied to rapacious employees like the fictional Mite. The inspiration for Foote's play was the most rapacious of them all, Robert Clive, who rose through the EIC's ranks, amassing a fortune so large it astonished his contemporaries.

Clive was nineteen when he disembarked at Madras in 1744 to take up the position of junior tally clerk. He was the eldest of thirteen children from a family of minor gentry. As a boy, he was known for being "out of measure addicted" to fighting, a trait that would serve him well on the subcontinent. His starting pay was a mere five pounds a year, but if he survived the climate and life-threatening tropical

Knighted for his victories in southern India and Bengal, Clive arguably did more to lay the foundations for the British Empire in eighteenth-century India that any other individual.

diseases, he stood a good chance of progressing to a junior merchant, councillor, or even governor. In one of his first letters home, the young Clive said his aim was nothing more than "to provide for myself & . . . being of service to my Relations." The culture of the EIC would not allow for such modesty.

By the time of Clive's arrival, the "Honourable Company," as it was later known, had grown from a small trading entity to a highly profitable publicly listed corporation with more than a dozen "factories" (the word derived from the Portuguese *feitoria*, meaning fortified trading post) scattered around the coast of India and along its major waterways. Senior merchants were known as factors and junior employees such as Clive as writers. Just a few dozen permanent employees operating out of a cramped office on Leadenhall Street in London would ultimately run a corporation that controlled half the world's trade and whose customs receipts provided the British exchequer a tenth of its total revenue. Between 1600, the year in which the company was granted its charter by Queen Elizabeth I, and 1833, ships sailing under the Company's colors made about 4,600 voyages from London to Asia. By the end of the eighteenth century, the size of the EIC's armed forces was double that of Britain's.

The rise and fall of the EIC has been well covered by historians, including most recently by William Dalrymple, who describes its gradual takeover of India as "a corporate coup unparalleled in history": "the military conquest, subjugation and plunder of vast tracts of southern Asia . . . almost certainly remains the supreme act of corporate violence in world history."

When eighty hardheaded businessmen met in London in 1599 to establish the EIC, they set their sights not on India but on the spice trade with the Indonesian archipelago. Their main competitor was the Dutch Vereenigde Oost Indische Compagnie or VOC, which had ten times the capital base and was hauling in huge profits from the Spice Islands. After being soundly beaten in several skirmishes with Dutch traders keen to protect their monopolies, the Company decided it was better to cut its losses than persevere. As a fallback, India was a tempting prize. It was closer to home and manufactured the world's finest textiles.

In 1608, Captain William Hawkins landed in Surat, on India's western coast, becoming the first commander of an EIC vessel to set foot in India. He immediately departed for a yearlong journey to Agra, the imperial capital of the Mughal Empire. But his gifts, which consisted of meager bundles of cloth (the rest had been stolen by an agent working for the Portuguese), failed to inspire Jahangir. Instead of being granted a *farman*, or imperial directive, giving the Company trading rights throughout the Mughal Empire, he returned with only the emperor's present of an Armenian Christian wife.

Hawkins was followed seven years later by Sir Thomas Roe, who arrived at the Mughal court carrying camel-loads of presents, including English mastiffs and hunting dogs, crates of red wine, and a state coach. England's main competitors were the Portuguese. Although they had been in India as traders for almost a century, their standing with the Mughals was shaky. Muslim pilgrims wanting to travel to Mecca for the Haj relied on Portuguese shipping: before boarding a vessel, they needed a passport issued by Portugal that was stamped with idolatrous images of Jesus and Mary. Roe's arrival coincided with English victories in two skirmishes with Portuguese vessels. With British help, Roe promised, Jahangir would become "lord of the seas."

Once again there was no *farman*, but the emperor obliged Roe by granting permission for a trading post in Surat. On his return to England, Roe offered the Company's directors the following advice: "Let this be received as a rule that, if you will profit, seek it at sea and in quiet trade; for without controversy it is an error to affect garrisons and land wars in India."

Over the next several decades, the EIC's presence in India grew steadily. Madras was acquired from a local ruler in 1639, and in 1661 Bombay, with its magnificent harbor, was "gifted" to Charles II as part of the marriage dowry he received from Catherine of Braganza.

Trade boomed. By 1680, the EIC's two thousand stock-holders were receiving an annual dividend of 50 percent, a level repeated in 1682, 1689, and 1691. Although its fortunes varied over the subsequent decades, the Company would remain crucial to the English economy. In 1700, it shipped over half a million pounds of goods from India and accounted for 13 percent of England's imports. Textiles had overtaken spices as the main trading commodity, with fine Indian cottons from Bengal, Gujarat, and the Coromandel and Konkan finding ready markets in Southeast Asia, East Africa, and Safavid Persia. "Indian cloth started functioning as currency in Africa, a wage good in Southeast Asia, and a fashion article in Europe," writes the scholar Giorgio Riello.

In what has become a depressingly familiar scenario, the greater the turnover, the larger the scope for corporate malfeasance. In 1693, the EIC's governor and the lord president of its council were impeached for insider trading and using funds to buy off parliamentarians who had threatened to clip the Company's wings.

ASIA-BOUND SHIPPING TONNAGE AMONG EUROPEAN COMPANIES

Period	English	Dutch	Portuguese	French	Danish	Swedish	England % of Total
1581–90	0	0	55, 419	0	0	0	0
1631–40	31,179	63,970	20,020	3,000	4,000	0	25.5
1681–90	47,879	130,849	11,650	17,500	4,000	0	22.6
1731–40	67,880	280,035	13,200	53,891	12,267	7,368	15.6
1781–90	228,315	243,424	8,250	130,490	63,461	0	33.9
1820–29	859,090	178,000		168,180	22,779	6,730	60.0

It was not the first time the Company had overstepped the mark. In 1688, its bellicose governor in London, Sir Josiah Child, disregarded Roe's advice about "quiet trade" and foolishly decided to take on the hundred-thousand-strong Mughal war machine. Responding to complaints that Mughal officials were extorting money from English traders at its factories in Bengal, Child sent two ships carrying a total of 308 soldiers up the Hooghly River to teach them a lesson. When the ships made landfall, their soldiers were picked off by Mughal sentries as easily as if they were "swatting flies." On India's western coast, a company official, who was also called Child, decided to pick a similarly disastrous fight against Mughal shipping. What became dubbed the "Children's War" led to the loss of the Company's factories in Bengal, Bombay, and Surat. Officials had to go begging to Aurangzeb to restore their trading rights. They were reinstated only after the payment of a massive indemnity and the promise of better behavior in the future.

In 1690, Job Charnock, the chief of the Company's operations in Bengal, returned to the Hooghly to select a new site for a settlement. Charnock's choice—on the river's east bank near a cluster of villages—had few fans. "For the sake of a large shady tree . . . he could not have found a more unhealthful place on all the River," ship captain Alexander Hamilton wrote shortly after the settlement's establishment. Although the population had grown to around one thousand by 1692, Hamilton noted that there were already 460 deaths registered, among them Charnock's. What his soldiers christened Golgotha would become the site of Calcutta, the imperial capital of the British Raj.

Described by Aurangzeb as "the Paradise of Nations," Bengal was by far the richest province in India and the single

Calcutta in the early seventeenth century. Known today as Kolkata, it is one of the world's largest urban conglomerations, with a population of 15 million.

most important supplier of goods from Asia to Europe. After traveling through eastern India in 1657, Bernier declared Bengal's "fertility, wealth and beauty" far greater than Egypt's, which was considered at the time "the finest and most fruitful country in the world." Portuguese, Dutch, and French companies had also set up trading posts on the Hooghly.

Like the EIC's other factories, Charnock's trading post depended on the goodwill of local rulers for its survival. By the early eighteenth century, it had become apparent that goodwill was no substitute for security. To ensure the post's protection, British officers commanded small armies primarily of locally trained soldiers, or sepoys. These armies were expensive to maintain, requiring revenue, which meant setting up an administrative structure to collect taxes, which in turn necessitated courts and a justice system. A trading empire gradually acquired the attributes of a state.

On New Year's Eve 1716, an enfeebled Mughal emperor, Farrukh Siyar, was finally bullied into issuing a *farman* granting the EIC full trading rights. Dubbed the "Magna Carta of the Company in India," it was celebrated among its directors as granting "such favour as had never before been granted to any European nation." The Company was now inducted into the political hierarchy of Mughal India through a direct relationship with the emperor. Half a century later, Clive would use the decree to justify the overthrow of Bengal's nawab.

With its main settlements at Pondicherry, a day's sailing south of Madras, and at Chandernagore, about fifteen miles north of Calcutta, the EIC's chief challenger was the French Compagnie des Indes, founded in 1664. For much of the eighteenth century, Anglo-French rivalry in continental Europe would be played out by their respective trading companies in India. The outbreak of the War of the Austrian Succession (1740–1748) and the Seven Years' War (1756–1763) coincided with power struggles in South Indian states that had become independent of Mughal rule. This gave both companies the opportunity to intervene politically and militarily in what were purely domestic affairs.

The architect of this policy was Joseph-François Dupleix (1697–1763). Described by the English scholar Lawrence James as "a man of dynamic energy who combined ambition, cupidity, Anglophobia and belligerence in roughly equal parts," Dupleix would become Clive's chief rival. In 1742, he was transferred from Chandernagore to assume the governorship of French possessions on the Coromandel Coast. When Britain's fleet threatened Pondicherry in 1745, he appealed for protection to the nawab of the Carnatic, an independent state to the north of Madras with its capital at Arcot. The attack on Pondicherry never materialized, but the appeal was a game changer. As Thomas Macaulay, one of Dupleix's earliest biographers, wrote, the Frenchman had recognized "it was possible to found a European empire on the ruins of the Mogul monarchy."

Favorable trading rights were just one of the factors that determined the EIC's fortunes in India. Promising to hand over territories, local rulers increasingly looked to the British and French for support in their battles with competing kingdoms. The revenue raised by the Europeans from these territories would be ploughed into bolstering their respective militaries. Even when not officially at war, the British and French supported competing Indian princes to wage proxy conflicts on their behalf.

Local rulers quickly learned the advantages of such support. Using small corps of highly disciplined troops trained in European methods of attack and defense, English- and French-led forces could accomplish what had once taken enormous Indian armies months or even years to achieve. Handsomely remunerated soldiers of fortune from America, Ireland, Britain, France, Switzerland, Poland, and even Armenia came to play a pivotal role in changing the face of warfare in South Asia.

Clive and the Making of a Colonial Legend

The first Indian ruler to engage a military force under the command of a European commander in exchange for a grant of territory was Muzaffar Jung (?–1751), the grandson of the nizam of Hyderabad. Nizam ul-Mulk's death in 1748 had set off a four-year succession crisis that saw six sons and one grandson compete for the throne of South India's richest and most powerful state. Muzaffar Jung was proclaimed the new nizam in an elaborate ceremony at Pondicherry in 1750 after French-led troops defeated his rival, Nasir Jung (1712–1750).

Dupleix's choice of Pondicherry over Hyderabad was significant. He wanted to remind the Muslim world that power had passed from the Viceroy of the Deccan to the French. In return for his support, Muzaffar Jung declared Dupleix the viceroy of the whole of southern India from the Krishna River to Cape Comorin. The Frenchman now ruled thirty million people with almost absolute power.

Jung's rule was never recognized by the Mughal emperor in Delhi, and he lasted a mere six weeks on the throne before being killed in an ambush. But by engaging the French, he had set a precedent that would change India's political map forever. From now on, those Indian rulers wanting to maintain power with the help of English-led troops had to pawn off swathes of territory and pay for subsidiary forces stationed in their states, ostensibly for protection against internal and external aggression. They were also expected to host a British "Resident" at their capital who would have the final say in matters such as royal marriages and successions. Prevented from pursuing independent foreign or military policies, these Indian rulers found themselves mere surrogates of empire-builders in London.

Dupleix's adventurism proved his undoing. In 1754 he was relieved of his post by the French naval commander Charles Robert Godeheu de Zaimont, who had been dispatched to India to patch up relations with the English. That left the arena clear for Clive, who had quickly risen up through the Company's ranks and had developed a reputation as a military strategist and brilliant leader.

The legend that became "Clive of India" was first formed during the siege of Arcot in 1751. A city of one hundred thousand, Arcot was the capital of the Carnatic, the coastal region to the north of Madras, which had been ruled by Nizam ul-Mulk's deputy, Anwar-ud-Din. When he was killed in battle in 1749, the French supported their stooge, Chanda Sahib (?–1752), to become the new nawab. To prevent the succession and avoid a scenario where the French and their puppet ruler in the Carnatic would encircle Madras, Clive proposed attacking Arcot. With a force of only two hundred European soldiers and three hundred Indian sepoys, Clive managed to take Arcot's fort. Forces under the command of Chanda Sahib's son and bolstered by 150 French soldiers surrounded the fort and used heavy artillery to bombard the English positions. Despite losing almost half his men, Clive held off the combined French and Indian troops for fifty-three days until reinforcements arrived from Madras.

Like the later defenders of Jalalabad, Lucknow, and Chitral, Clive's men epitomized "the doggedness and steady courage of the British race," James enthuses. "Those who manned the ramparts were presented as defenders of order and civilization and their strongholds were breakwaters around which surged the waters of chaos and barbarism." As the governor of Madras, Thomas Saunders, announced to the directors in London, Arcot had shown the weakness of the Indians: "'Tis certain any European nation resolved to war on them with a tolerable force may overrun the whole country."

In 1753, Clive left for England, returning two years later as deputy governor of Fort St. David at Cuddalore, south of Madras. For once, the French and English were at peace, but the deceptive calm was about to be shattered. On August 16, 1756, news reached Madras that Calcutta had fallen to the nawab of Bengal's army, and upward of one hundred English prisoners had died in a prison cell dubbed the Black Hole.

Calcutta had by then grown into a thriving port with a population of some four hundred thousand, only a small fraction of whom were British. The city far outshone nearby trading posts belonging to the French, the Dutch, and the Danes. Relations between the European traders and Nawab Alivardi Khan (1671–1756) had been cordial and mutually beneficial. The nawab's death in 1756 coincided with the outbreak of the Seven Years' War. English and French company directors responded to the news from Europe by ordering the reinforcement of their respective garrisons.

The enhanced fortifications unnerved Alivardi Khan's successor, Siraj ud-Daula (1733–1757), who saw them as a threat to his power and ordered them to be stopped. The French obliged but the British ignored his demand. When Siraj ud-Daula's envoy went to negotiate an end to the standoff, he was slapped by a British officer and expelled. On returning to his capital, Murshidabad, he reportedly told Siraj: "What honor is left to us, when a few traders, who have not yet learnt to wash their bottoms reply to the ruler's orders by expelling his envoy." When a last-ditch appeal from Siraj ud-Daula urging the English to "behave themselves like merchants" failed, he assembled a large army and marched southward to Calcutta.

Although there was plenty of warning of his advance, hubris got the better of Calcutta's defenders and they did little to prepare for its defense. Military officers wanted houses close to Fort William demolished to allow a better field of fire, but the owners refused, believing they would never get compensated. By June 16, 1756, Siraj ud-Daula's forces had reached Dum Dum, the site of today's international airport, prompting scenes of chaos and panic in the fort, where 2,500 mainly British residents of the city had sought shelter. As the enemy soldiers closed in, there was a rush to escape on one of the twenty-odd vessels moored in the river. Among those who fled was the city's governor, Roger Drake.

Within hours the nawab's men had taken control of Fort William, but instead of killing the remaining defenders, they rounded them up. Siraj ud-Daula promised the prisoners that "not a hair of their heads" would be hurt. But when a blind drunk English sailor shot dead a Mughal solider who was plundering their valuables, the mood changed. All of the survivors were herded into the fort's tiny punishment cell, measuring fourteen by eighteen feet, with only one small window and hardly any water.

"Deplorable Deaths"

The mythology of the Black Hole owes much to an account of the incident by the garrison's British commander, Josiah Holwell (1711–1798). According to Holwell, when the door of the cell was unlocked ten hours later at 6 AM, corpses were piled up inside and only twenty-three of the prisoners were still alive. He referred to the experience as "a night of horrors I will not attempt to describe, as they bar all description." After returning to England the following year, he published *A Genuine Narrative of the Deplorable Deaths of the English Gentlemen and Others, Who Were Suffocated in the Black Hole*. More recent estimates put the number of people imprisoned as low as forty-three. Siraj ud-Daula did not order the prisoners to be shut in the Black Hole and knew nothing about it until afterward.

A Most Successful Business Deal

The Black Hole would come to symbolize barbarity of the Indians in the minds of English policymakers and be used to strengthen the case for British rule. In the short term, the atrocity would become a rallying cry for the recapture of Calcutta and then the rest of Bengal. In January 1757, a British naval force took the city with little difficulty. But instead of returning to Madras, Clive pushed on to capture the French trading post at Chandernagore, leaving the British in control of the region. The stage was now set for the decisive Battle of Plassey.

Most historians dismiss Plassey as a mere skirmish. A morning cannonade was followed by a severe monsoonal storm that put most of the nawab's ammunition out of commission, while the British protected theirs with tarpaulins. A spontaneous attack caused by the overenthusiasm of a British officer ended in victory for Clive's forces. On paper, eight hundred Europeans and two thousand local troops had routed an enemy force of fifty thousand men, but in reality Siraj ud-Daula never stood a chance. Traders and nobles wanting to get rid of the nawab had enlisted the support of his commander-in-chief, Mir Jafar (c. 1691–1765), who held back his forces just when they were needed. Bankrolling the conspirators were the Jagat Seths, the biggest financiers in Bengal, who had lost faith in Siraj's ability to provide the security needed for trade to flourish. Their involvement prompted the English historian Nick Robins to refer to Plassey as "more of a commercial transaction than a real battle." Rather than being considered as the first step in the creation of the British Empire in India, Plassey "is perhaps better understood as the East India Company's most successful business deal."

Clive rewarded Jafar with the governorship of Bengal, though he was essentially a puppet ruler. Siraj ud-Daula was hunted down and murdered near his capital, Murshidabad. Aged just thirty-two, Clive found himself the conqueror of Bengal—and a very rich one at that. Despite strict instructions from London to repulse French attacks and not pick fights with local rulers, Clive had taken things into his own hands, seeing the opportunity for personal enrichment and political and economic gain for the Company. In a single stroke, he had netted 2.5 million pounds for the Company and 234,000 pounds for himself, making him one of the wealthiest men in England.

Clive returned to England in 1760 a hero, leaving as his successor Black Hole survivor Josiah Holwell. Eager to exploit the potential succession crisis that followed the death of Jafar's son, Holwell wanted to take over the administration of Bengal. But this was opposed by the Company's directors, who decided to make Jafar's son-in-law Mir Qasim (?–1777) the new ruler. When Jafar tried to resist the move, he was deposed.

The British soon came to regret their support for Qasim. The newly installed nawab dismissed local officials suspected of collaborating with the Company, increased revenue demands, harassed English shipping, and began reorganizing his forces along European lines with the help of two Christian mercenaries: Walter Reinhardt, an Alsatian soldier of fortune, and the Isfahani Armenian Khoja Gregory. After receiving reports that Qasim had killed Company prisoners and their Indian allies at Patna, the EIC's council in Calcutta formally declared war on the nawab on July 4, 1763, and vowed to put Jafar back on the throne.

To reverse the losses of Plassey and restore Bengal's independence, Mir Qasim created an alliance between the Mughal emperor Shah Alam II (1728–1806) and the nawab of Awadh, Shuja-ud-Daula. Shah Alam had been reinstated to the throne in Delhi after Afghan forces led by Ahmad Shah Durrani defeated the Marathas at the decisive battle of Panipat, north of Delhi, in 1761. When the emperor's overtures to the British to support him in return for granting the Company the *diwani*, or fiscal administration, of Bengal were rejected, he entered into an alliance with Mir Qasim.

As the tripartite army began its march on Calcutta, British sepoys under the command of Major Hector Munro rode out to meet them. To make doubly sure there would be no desertions on the British side, those Company sepoys who refused orders "were strapped to cannons by their arms, their bellies against the mouths of the guns, which were then fired in front of their quaking colleagues." For only the second time in the Company's history, its soldiers were engaged in fighting Mughal troops. The Battle of Buxar, which saw the defeat of the three great armies of the Mughals, left the EIC the dominant force in northeast India: "At Buxar all that still remained of Mogul power in northern India was shattered." It was "perhaps the most important battle the British ever fought in South Asia," writes British historian John Keay.

At a humiliating ceremony in Clive's tent at Allahabad, Shah Alam handed over the diwani of Bengal. The collection of taxes, once the domain of Mughal revenue officials in Bengal, Bihar, and Orissa, was now subcontracted to the Company. What had been a company of "foreign merchants" was transforming itself into a capitalist colonial state—creating laws, administering justice, assessing taxes, making peace, and waging wars. It became the first trading company to mint coins, monetizing its reserves of gold bullion and making it easier to conduct trade.

A massive 1818 canvas by the artist Benjamin West captures the moment when Shah Alam handed a scroll to Robert Clive that transferred tax-collecting rights in Bengal, Bihar, and Orissa to the East India Company.

News that the Company had been granted the diwani sent its shares skyrocketing between 1767 and 1769. But these bountiful times were fleeting. Answerable only to its shareholders, the Company had no stake in the just governance of the regions it now ruled over. The failure of the monsoon in 1769 severely affected rice crops in Bengal and Bihar, forcing the commodity's price five times higher in some places. Millions were on the verge of starvation. By June 1770, there were reports of villagers feeding on corpses. No effort had been made to stockpile surpluses. Instead, Company officials were accused of making massive profits by hoarding grain and controlling distribution. As the British writer Michael Edwardes succinctly described it: "A lust for gold inflamed the British, and Bengal was to have little peace until they bled it white."

As the famine worsened, the company's land revenues fell precipitously, forcing its directors to ask the British government for a bailout of £1.4 million to avoid bankruptcy. So important was EIC to Britain's economy that the bailout request sent the share market crashing. With 40 percent of members of parliament holding Company stock, a rescue package was never in doubt, but the price was steep. The *Regulating Act* placed the EIC under government supervision. A governing council appointed by parliament and based in Calcutta was charged with the day-to-day running of the Company. The interests of the EIC and the state were now intertwined. The Act marked the beginning of British colonial rule in India.

As the company had continued to acquire territory, its administration was divided between three "presidencies"— Calcutta, Bombay, and Madras. One of the key provisions of the *Regulating Act* was the establishment of the post of governor-general, based in Calcutta, who was given authority over the presidencies of Bombay and Madras. The first governor-general was Warren Hastings, a controversial figure whose greatest sin, according to one historian, was that "he loved India too much." To hold the Company to account, Hastings wanted British sovereignty to be exercised through Indian officers and systems of government. Justice would be dispensed by Indian judges, and Indian officials would negotiate matters relating to landholdings. His vision was too radical for its time, and if implemented would have been reversed by his successors. His most lasting legacy was encouraging the study of Indian history and languages, such as Sanskrit. It was under Hastings that Orientalists, such as William Jones and Charles Wilkins, did their pioneering work, translating Hindu epics and linking Sanskrit to the Indo-Āryan group of languages. But for all his philanthropy and idealism, Hastings was still a nabob who saw his primary role as generating wealth for the Company, its shareholders, and himself. Under Hastings,

Bengal's salt and opium production was monopolized for the Company's benefit, and the first shipment of opium was smuggled to China in defiance of a long-standing import ban.

When Hastings returned to England in 1785, he expected to be welcomed by his peers for putting the EIC's affairs in order. Instead, he found himself under attack by members of parliament, notably the corporation's most vocal critic, Edmund Burke. To the Anglo-Irish Whig politician, the Company was the "kingdom of magistrates": "separated both from the Country that sent them out and from the Country in which they are." Within two years of his return from India, Burke managed to get Hastings impeached. He was charged with twenty-two articles, including extortion, bribery, corruption, and waging an unprovoked war against the Rohillas. After a marathon impeachment trial lasting seven years, Hastings was acquitted of all charges.

His replacement as governor-general was Lord Cornwallis (1738–1835), who, in 1781, had overseen the surrender of Yorktown in the American War of Independence. Cornwallis was the exact opposite of his predecessor. An army man with a deep distaste for trade, he described the Company's presence in India as "a system of the dirtiest jobbing." Setting out to reform the administration, and stamp out corruption and nepotism, he divided the Company into commercial and political wings. Based on his belief that "every native of Hindustan I verily believe is corrupt," he Europeanized the services. "No person, the son of a Native Indian, shall henceforward be appointed by this court to Employment in the Civil, Military, or Marine Service of the Company," he declared.

Cornwallis also sought to bind the fate of India's landed elites closer to the Company by fixing the amount of revenue paid by large landlords, or *zamindars*, at a permanent rate. The move was also meant to boost agricultural production because every extra rupee earned would be retained by the landlord. Zamindars also bore responsibility for collecting revenue from those peasants who worked on their lands, previously the burdensome task of British officials. The dominance of trade in the Company's affairs was now usurped by its administrative arm.

The Road to Supremacy

While the Battle of Buxar had secured the Company's hold over eastern India, its interests in west and south of the subcontinent faced a series of threats from the 1760s onward. The most formidable challenges came from the kingdom of Mysore and from the Maratha Confederacy. Both used French arms and officers in their respective armies, making them dangerous proxies for French power in India. It would take four wars to defeat Mysore and three to defeat the Marathas, culminating in Britain's supremacy in India in 1818.

This crucial chapter in India's history begins with the capture of Mysore in 1761 by Hyder Ali (c. 1720–1782). Destined to become a thorn in the Company's side, Ali was a brilliant tactician. His artillery included camel-mounted rockets with a range of up to a mile. He even had a small navy, commanded at different times by English and Dutch mercenaries, comprising several warships and smaller transport vessels. A visionary ruler, he established a state trading company and encouraged investors to buy shares in it. He also explored setting up "factories" in the Ottoman Empire and in Pegu in Burma.

Fearful that Ali would turn his sights on Madras, British soldiers marched on Mysore in 1767 but were beaten back for the first time since Josiah Child's disastrous campaign against the Mughals a century earlier. In 1780, Ali joined forces with the nizam of Hyderabad and launched a lightning strike on the suburbs of Madras, "surrounding many of the English gentlemen in their country houses, who narrowly escaped being taken." Meanwhile, his son Tipu Sultan (1751–1799) engaged the British at Polilur, near modern-day Kanchipuram. Almost half of the eighty-six English officers leading a contingent of British and Indian sepoys were killed, together with 280 rank-and-file soldiers and 1,700 sepoys. It was Britain's worst defeat in India to date.

The loss at Polilur coincided with the trouncing the British received at Yorktown, prompting widespread dismay in England. "India and America are alike escaping," predicted the anti-imperial Whig Horace Walpole. A senior Company army officer warned parliamentarians that Britain's foothold in India was "more imaginary than real." If there were to be more defeats like Polilur, the Indians "will soon find out that we are but men like themselves, or very little better." The fears were not unfounded. After their reverses in the Second Anglo-Mysore War, one in every five British soldiers stationed in India was a prisoner of the Indians. Stories of forced circumcisions, slavery, and torture incensed the British public.

Ali's death in December 1782 left Tipu the undisputed ruler of Mysore. In Britain, Tipu would be vilified in plays, cartoons, and other media, cast as an "intolerant bigot" and fanatical Muslim tyrant bent on persecuting Christians and driving Europeans from the Indian subcontinent, long after his death. A more subtle reading of his rule shows that he was a social reformer who recognized the importance of trade and sound administration. Under his watch, liquor, prostitution, and female slavery were banned, as was polyandry. All this mattered little to the British. After two humiliating defeats, the crushing of Mysore became an obsession.

Cornwallis would wait three years after arriving in India to seek Britain's revenge, but once he set his sights on the Tiger of Mysore, there was no going back. In 1789, supported by Maratha and Hyderabadi forces, he encircled Tipu's capital, Seringapatam, in the southeast. After holding out for almost a year, Tipu was forced to accept a humiliating set of terms, including an eight-figure indemnity and the surrender of almost half his territories, which were shared among the British and their allies.

One of the items brought back to London after Tipu's defeat and installed in the EIC's headquarters was a wooden automaton showing a near-life-size tiger eating a British soldier. Built by Indian artisans, French toy  manufacturers, and Dutch organ makers, it was Tipu's favorite toy. A crankshaft on the body of the tiger would cause the automaton to emit a deep roar, while the man would wave his arms and wail. Stories of Tipu's atrocities involving tigers and Englishmen only increased the automaton's notoriety, and it became the centerpiece of the newly created East India House Museum.

Tipu's defeat did little to halt the growing influence of the French in India. The nizam of Hyderabad and the Maratha Peshwa of Pune had switched sides and were now engaging French mercenaries to train their soldiers. Back in Europe, Britain and France were at war yet again.

The fourth and final Mysore War was executed by Richard Wellesley (1760–1842), an uncompromising empire-builder who arguably did more than Clive to establish the British hegemony in India. The decision to declare war followed the discovery that Tipu was in communication with the French at Île de Bourbon in the Indian Ocean. In 1797, more than fifty French soldiers stationed in Seringapatam were reported to have formed a Jacobian Club and proclaimed the rights of man—though recent research has dismissed this as British propaganda. News of Napoleon Bonaparte's intended invasion of Egypt prompted fears that the French ruler might use Egypt as a springboard for an invasion of India with the connivance of local rulers, such as "Citoyen Tipu." Although Nelson's smashing of the French fleet at Abukir Bay in August 1798 neutralized the threat, it did not stop Wellesley marching on Seringapatam.

After a month-long siege, twenty-four British troops, supported by a similar number of soldiers belonging to the nizam of Hyderabad, successfully stormed the city. When Tipu's still-warm body was found, his jeweled sword-belt had been looted. As Wellesley would later recall, there was so much booty that "every soldier had to relieve himself of the burden by throwing away a portion of it." Inside Tipu's palace, soldiers found three live tigers and a mechanical one.

Following Tipu's death, the Marathas were the last remaining barrier to Wellesley's empire-building plans. Once capable of forming a powerful united front, the Marathas had never recovered from their defeat by Afghan forces at Panipat. Although they were split into sometimes competing kingdoms—the most powerful of which were the Holkars of Indore, the Scindias of Gwalior, the Gaekwads of Baroda, and the Bhonsles of Nagpur—they were still capable of intervening militarily in much of the subcontinent. The presence of French soldiers of fortune employed as military advisers added weight to Wellesley's determination to defeat them once and for all.

In 1803, Wellesley and his political agent, John Malcolm (1769–1833), marched from Srirangapatnam to Pune. Along the way, they sought allies from among local chiefs and eventually arrived at the city with a combined force of forty thousand soldiers. After taking Pune without a fight, they chased down Scindia, Holkar, and Bhonsle forces in a cat-and-mouse campaign across northern India, capturing Delhi in the process. Seated on the diamond-and-jewel-studded Peacock Throne commissioned by Shah Jahan was the blind and aging Shah Alam, a king in title only. So enfeebled was Shah Alam that Wellesley decided it was more prudent to allow him to live out his days than depose him. When he died in 1806, the British allowed his son Akbar Shah to succeed him, but real power in the old Mughal capital for the next five decades would remain firmly in the hands of a British intermediary or Resident, who oversaw all aspects of the administration.

The capture of Delhi and subsequent signing of peace treaties with the Scindias, the Bhonsles, and the Holkars left the East India Company the strongest power in India. But the Marathas would prove to be stubborn foes. Soldiers loyal to Gwalior's ruler continued to harass British forces, promoting Wellesley to demand more funds to bolster his war machine. Viewing Wellesley's territorial aspirations as unbecoming of the head of a trading company, the EIC's directors turned him down. When Prime Minister William Pitt accused him of acting "imprudently and illegally," he quit.

The third and final Anglo-Maratha war was unlike any military encounter the British had faced in India before. Their chief foes were bandit armies made up of Pindari warriors recruited by the Maratha ruling houses. On horseback and armed with spears, the Pindaris ravaged the countryside of central India, plundering villages for sustenance, and launched raids on Company outposts. Alongside them were Afghan marauders. To suppress these twin scourges, in 1817 the Company began assembling the largest army ever seen in India—110,000 troops, including 20,000 irregular soldiers lent by Indian allies. Operating in scattered groups over thousands of square miles of often inaccessible terrain, the Pindaris were an elusive foe. As Malcolm complained, "Nowhere did [the Pindaris] present any point of attack . . . Their chief strength lay in their being intangible." After a sustained British onslaught, most of the Pindaris and Afghans simply disappeared, only to reemerge in later years as highway robbers. But as a fighting force, they were no longer the threat they once were. One by one, the ruling houses of the Marathas submitted to British hegemony.

The year 1818 marked the beginning of British supremacy in India, but as the British Indologist Jon Wilson writes, it was "a comma, not a full stop, a moment of hiatus rather than a termination of a process." Peace in British India would always be a violent enterprise. "The submission of Indian leaders to the expansion of British money and violence was reluctant, edgy and conditional," Wilson continues. "The defeat of the Marathas did not mean conquest."

CHAPTER 7

The Lighting of the Fuse

Few events in Indian history have been analyzed and debated, romanticized and demonized as the mutiny of 1857. The apocalypse that started with an insurrection by sepoys in Meerut on May 10 has variously been described as India's First War of Independence, the Great Uprising, the Sepoy Rebellion, or simply as the Indian Revolt. None of these terms, however, reflect the true nature of a sequence of events that culminated in the dethronement and deportation from Delhi of the last Mughal emperor, Bahadur Shah Zafar (1775–1862), the end

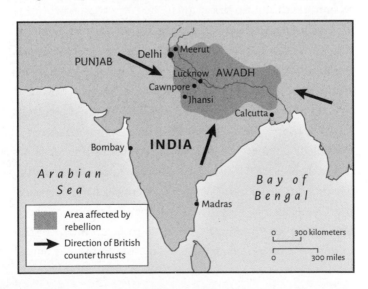

of East India Company rule, and the proclamation of Queen Victoria (1819–1901) as Empress of India. The first large-scale uprising against British rule was also a colossal failure that saw horrendous atrocities committed by both sides. It would reset the relationship between Britain and its "jewel in the crown." It would also bolster the arguments of those wanting to take greater military and administrative control of India while providing an inspiration for Indian nationalists fighting for independence.

The upheavals of 1857–1858 raise many questions. What were the true causes of the rebellion? Why was it confined mainly to the north—Delhi, the United Provinces, parts of Central India, and Bihar—and not pan-Indian? Plenty of groups had a legitimate grievance against the British—Sikhs, Marathas, Rajputs, and Gurkhas—but remained aloof. If it was "anti-colonial," why did it not affect those cities where colonization was felt most strongly, such as Calcutta? The bulk of India's princes stayed neutral or even lent their forces to suppress the mutineers.

Part military rebellion, part peasant revolt, part holy war, the rebellion raged for more than a year, but from the very beginning there was a lack of unity and purpose. Although the sepoys secured the blessings of Bahadur Shah, who became a figurehead for both Hindus and Muslims, he could give only moral support. The fact that the rebels put their faith in a symbol of defunct Mughal legitimacy made the rebellion distinctly backward-looking. Had it succeeded, it is doubtful whether any regime or system of government that replaced the Company Raj would have improved the lives of those who had taken up arms. Princes who took advantage of the unrest were interested only in reestablishing the old feudal order. The rebellion's scattered and divided leadership offered no coherent program for change. But the changes that came in its wake were profound, and would influence the course of India's history well into the twentieth century.

Stoking the Flames

The underlying causes of the 1857 revolt have their roots in the evolution of British attitudes toward India since the late 1700s. The prevailing wisdom—that India should be governed by its laws and that the ruling class be treated with respect—was eroded by Lord Cornwallis's reforms, which effectively banished Indians from all administrative and legal posts. The impact was felt acutely in the army, where it was impossible for an Indian soldier to reach the rank of an officer, let alone a junior subaltern. Close contact between English officers and those under their charge became the exception rather than the norm. Writing after the rebellion, the sepoy Sita Ram Pande (c. 1795–c. 1873) recalled that when he joined the army in the early part of century, "the sahibs" mixed with their Indian servants and subordinates: "When I was a sepoy the captain of my company would have some of the men at his house all day long and he talked with them . . . I know that many officers nowadays only speak to their men when obliged to do so." The alienation between ruler and ruled extended to the private sphere. At the close of the eighteenth century, one in three Company employees left part of their estates to their Indian *bibis*, or consorts. By the middle of the nineteenth, almost none did so.

The consolidation of British rule after the defeat of the Marathas boosted British confidence. As the predominant power on the subcontinent, the British embarked on a mission to "civilize" their subjects. One of the conditions

Images such as this, taken from an 1833 edition of Penny Magazine, *helped reinforce attitudes among many in Britain that India was a land inhabited by superstitious heathens.*

of the renewal of the Company's charter in 1813 was to allow Christian missionaries to operate in India. It won the support of the anti-slavery activist William Wilberforce, who equated emancipating Hindus from the "wickedness and cruelty of idolatry" with abolishing the slave trade. Drowned out in the shrill rhetoric of the times was the advice of Warren Hastings. Coming out of retirement, he testified for three hours before a parliamentary committee examining the EIC charter. His warning was clear: "A Surmise had gone abroad that there was an intention of forcing our Religion on the Natives. Such an opinion propagated among the Native Infantry might be attended by dangerous consequences." Indeed, he added, it "might create a religious war."

The pace of reform would pick up considerably under Lord William Bentinck (1774–1839), the governor-general from

1828 to 1835. Serving twice as prime minister, the great-great-grandfather to Elizabeth II was convinced that the British had "a great moral duty to perform in India." At the top of his to-do list was abolishing the practice of *sati*, in which a Hindu widow would immolate herself on the funeral pyre of her dead husband, sometimes against her will. The practice, which first appeared during the Gupta era, was particularly widespread among Rajputs and in Bengal, where more than three hundred instances were recorded in 1803–1804 within a thirty-mile radius of Calcutta. While the prevailing wisdom had been that the "rites and superstitions of the Hindu religion should be allowed with the most unqualified tolerance," sati crossed a line. During the tenure of Lord Minto (1751–1814), who became governor-general in 1807, colonial officials sought to regulate the practice by making it mandatory for a police officer to be in attendance to ensure there was no coercion, and that the widow was not under sixteen years of age or pregnant. Minto's successor, Lord Hastings (no relation to Warren), declared sati an "outrage against humanity" but believed that to abolish the practice would be "perilous" and had the potential to incite unrest in the army. Bentinck found himself torn between sending "hundreds of innocent victims to a cruel and untimely death" and jeopardizing "the safety of the British Empire." Making the case for its abolition, he argued that Britain was strong enough to resist any challenge to its rule and that the landowning zamindars would support such a move. Laws making sati illegal were passed in Bengal in 1829 and in Bombay and Madras shortly afterward.

The laws had the support of Hindu reformers such as Rammohun Roy (1772–1833), who cited cases where women were forced on the funeral pyre by relatives who would inherit their properties, or who unsuccessfully tried to flee before being "carried back by their relations and burnt to death." Fluent in English, Arabic, Persian, Hebrew, Greek, Latin, and Sanskrit, in addition to his native Bengali, he championed women's rights and petitioned the government to limit the amount that the peasants could be asked to

Rammohun Roy, dubbed the father of modern India, was the first educated Indian to advocate for his country's freedom through constitutional means.

pay landowners. Although he was a Brahmin, he was critical of the caste system, which he said "has been the source of want of unity among us." Roy spent three years in England, impressing all those he met, including the philosopher Jeremy Bentham, who wanted him to sit in the House of Commons.

Elites such as Roy were a tiny minority. Indian society in the early 1800s was still overwhelmingly peasant-based, with more than 70 percent of the population engaged in agriculture. Average life expectancy was around twenty-six years. But historiography is also changing our view of India in the period following the disintegration of the Mughal Empire. The traditional characterization of eighteenth-century India as "an epoch of decay, chaos, greed and violence" has been overtaken by new research showing economic growth, urbanization, and commercialization, particularly in the more dynamic northern regions. Indian families were smaller than those of Europeans, largely due to female infanticide, high child mortality, and child marriage, which often led to early widowhood. An

1822 survey of cities such as Calcutta, Dacca, and Allahabad found that the average size of households was between 3.5 and 4.1 persons; by comparison, the average in England at the time was 4.75. Yet the pitiful condition of women in early-nineteenth-century India was never in doubt. As the Bengali social reformer Ishwarchandra Vidyasagar lamented: "In a society in which the menfolk have no mercy, no religion, no sense of justice, no sense of good or bad, in which mere conventionality is considered the chief activity and the supreme religion, let no more women be born."

Bentinck's civilizing zeal extended to education, where a debate ensued between the Orientalists, who argued for traditional learning in classical languages such as Sanskrit and Persian, and the Anglicists, who wanted to promote Western learning in English. If Indians wanted to study the *Bhagavad Gītā*, the latter view contended, they could get as much from an English translation as from the original Sanskrit. The divide did not run along racial lines. Among those supporting the Anglicists was Roy, who argued that modern education was the "key to the treasures of scientific and democratic thought of the modern West."

The matter was finally settled by Thomas Babington Macaulay (1800–1859), the son of an evangelist, who became the first law member on Bentinck's administration. Reflecting his utilitarian belief in the superiority of European culture and science, Macaulay declared that the old languages of India contained "neither literary nor scientific information, and are moreover so poor and rude that, until they are enriched from some other quarter it will not be easy to translate any valuable work into them." His objective was to create "a class of persons Indian in colour and blood, but English in tastes, in opinions, in moral and in intellect." Macaulay famously pronounced that he could not find one Orientalist "who could deny that a single shelf of a good European library was worth the whole native literature of India and Arabia."

The criticism Macaulay endures today is at least partly negated by the zeal with which he embarked on creating a uniform penal code for India and designing the Indian Civil Service. Often contradictory systems of Hindu and Muslim law operating side by side in conjunction with Company regulations had created a legal quagmire, made worse by Cornwallis's insistence that no Indian should preside over courts of law. Macaulay's new criminal code restricted the death penalty to crimes of murder and treason. In an effort to bring uniformity to existing laws, the code enshrined a woman's right to property almost half a century before similar laws came into force in England. Today's frustratingly slow but surprisingly resilient Indian bureaucracy owes its longevity to Macaulay's framework. Without it, India may not have survived as a nation following the traumas of Partition.

The influx of missionaries boosted the numbers of Europeans in India not connected with the EIC or its various armies, though the numbers were still small—rising from around 2,150 "non-officials" in 1830 to 10,000 in 1850. European professionals ranged from undertakers, taxidermists (to stuff tigers bagged on hunting expeditions), distillers, and billiard-table makers. Men vastly outnumbered women, giving rise to the so-called "fishing fleets"—the thousands of young British women who sailed to India desperate to find a "£300-a-year man—dead or alive"—a reference to the average annual salary of a junior officer in the Indian Civil Service.

Bentinck ended his tenure in India disappointed. His proposal to admit Indians into the senior ranks of the Company was never implemented by its directors in London. He also sought to raise the salaries of Indian judges tenfold; the Company merely quadrupled them. Nor did his reforms suppress the increasingly hawkish voices in the Company's ranks. Writing in 1820, Sir Charles Metcalfe (1785–1846), a former Resident in Delhi, declared: "I abhor making wars, and meddling with other states for the sake of our aggrandisement—but war thrust upon us, or unavoidably entered into, should, if practicable, be turned to profit by the acquisition of new resources, to pay additional forces to defend what we have, and extend our possessions in future unavoidable wars."

This attitude backfired when Britain became entrapped in the First Afghan War, described by the author James Morris as "the worst disaster to overtake the British in the East prior to Japan's World War II invasion of Malaya and capture of Singapore exactly a century later." The cause of the war was Lord Palmerston's anxieties about Russia's intentions toward India. The British prime minister feared that the Afghan ruler, Dost Mohammad (1793–1863), was too sympathetic toward Russia and would look the other way as Czarist troops marched down the Khyber Pass and invaded India. The first major conflict of the Great Game, as the scramble for spheres of influence in Central Asia between Russia and India was dubbed, ended with a widescale uprising against the British occupation and the wholesale slaughter of its retreating army and hundreds of civilians by Afghan tribals. Despite being promised safe passage, thousands of British soldiers and Indian sepoys, as well as women and children, were massacred as they made their way from Kabul. The only survivor of the retreat was William Brydon (1811–1873), a surgeon with the Army Medical Corp, who stumbled into the British garrison at Jalalabad on his half-dead horse. For days afterward, fires were lit and bugles sounded to attract survivors, but none arrived.

More successful, but no less brutal, was the British annexation of Sindh in 1843. Following two short wars fought between 1845 and 1849 with the Sikhs, Britain added the Punjab and Kashmir to its empire. Under the terms of the Last Treaty of Lahore, signed in 1849, the infant Sikh Maharaja Duleep Singh

Lady Elizabeth Butler's painting Remnants of an Army, *depicting Dr. William Brydon reaching the safety of Jalalabad fort, was first exhibited at the Royal Academy in London in 1879.*

(1838–1893) was forced to surrender the Koh-i-Noor diamond to the Queen of England. After being temporarily misplaced by John Lawrence, a member of the triumvirate of British officials who took over the administration of the Punjab, the brilliant was found by his valet and entrusted to the new governor-general, Lord Dalhousie (1812–1860), who transported it from Lahore to Bombay. When Queen Victoria received the stone at Buckingham Palace in July 1850, she was unimpressed, noting in her diary that "it is not set 'à jour' & badly cut, which spoils the effect." The diamond's reputation for bringing bad luck—several of its owners had either died or lost their thrones shortly after taking possession of the stone—may have dulled Victoria's enthusiasm. Furious at her reaction, Dalhousie would later write, "If H. M. thinks it brings bad luck, let her give it back to me. I will take it and its ill-luck on speculation."

Opinion on Dalhousie's legacy as governor-general is divided. Remembered for bringing the railway to India, initiating a series of needed irrigation projects and stringing thousands of miles of telegraph lines across the country, his nine-year tenure is held by some as one of the most successful of any administrator. Under his watch, new laws were introduced, allowing widows to remarry, Hindu converts to Christianity to retain their inheritance rights, and different castes to mingle in railway carriages. But however noble in intention these reforms were, they constituted a flagrant breach of Hindu customs on religion and caste.

His most controversial legacy, however, was to invoke the "doctrine of lapse," a policy that had existed on paper since 1841 but never been implemented. The doctrine held that Britain, as the paramount power, could take control of a princely state whose ruler was either manifestly incompetent or whose death triggered a succession crisis. Believing that the states were a bulwark against modernization, the doctrine became an opportunity, in Dalhousie's words, for "getting rid of those petty intervening principalities which may be a means of annoyance, but which can never, I venture to think, be a source of strength."

Nearly a dozen states would come under this interventionist policy, the most important of which was Awadh, a rich province that lay between the Ganges and Yamuna rivers. Once considered one of Britain's strongest allies, Awadh was a major source of soldiers for the British Army and bought large quantities of British goods. The capital, Lucknow, combined "the monumental magnificence of Shah Jahan's Delhi with the scented allure of Scheherazade's Baghdad." The British had long concluded that the conduct of the nawabs of Awadh left a lot to be desired. William Sleeman, who was appointed Resident in Lucknow in 1848, described the province as "a scene of intrigue, corruption, depravity, neglect of duty and abuse of authority." Its ruler, Wajid Ali Shah (1822–1887), was said to spend his time in "delights of dancing and drumming, and drawing, and manufacturing small rhymes"—a reference to his love of Urdu couplets.

In January 1856, Shah was asked to sign over his state to the East India Company. He refused, but instead of calling for a rebellion, he sent an envoy to Britain to plead his case before the queen, the parliament, and the press. When that failed and the province was annexed, he moved into a sprawling mansion on the banks of the Hooghly in Calcutta, where he created the city's first private zoo with a menagerie of monkeys, bears, tigers, a rhinoceros, a snake pit, and eighteen thousand pigeons. He spent much of his leisure time flying kites—a sport he excelled at.

Dilli Chalo!

The decision to annex Awadh angered sepoys in the Bengal army, most of whom came from the province. Adding to their grievances was an 1834 ruling that widened the army's recruitment base, threatening what had been the near monopoly of high-caste Brahmins. Another order in 1856 made all recruits liable for overseas service, causing affront to orthodox Hindus, who believed that crossing the *kala pani*, or black waters, would break the rules of caste.

Dalhousie was not around to see the anger he had sown flare into open rebellion. He left India in February 1856, handing over the governorship to Lord Canning, just as the annexation of Awadh was being formalized. While the doctrine of lapse is often cited as one of the main causes of the rebellion of 1857–1858, other important factors were at play. The first Indian account of the rebellion, written by the Muslim leader Sayyid Ahmad Khan in 1873, argued that the "mutineers were for the most part men who had nothing to lose," and the uprising was not an attempt by the Muslim elite "to throw off the yoke of foreigners." William Dalrymple puts the cause down to imperial arrogance and self-confidence. "So removed had the British now become from their Indian subjects, and so dismissive were they of Indian opinion that they had lost all ability to read the omens around them or to analyse their own position with any degree of accuracy."

Most historians agree that the final indignation was the introduction of the new Enfield rifle. Though it was easier to load and much more accurate, rumors soon spread among sepoys that its cartridges were greased with tallow made from cows, which was degrading to Hindus, and pig fat, offensive to Muslims. To make matters worse, the end of the cartridge containing the powder had to be bitten off so that the charge would ignite. Unease over the use of the cartridges sparked a protest at Barrackpore in Bengal in March 1857. Order was quickly restored, but not before a rebel sepoy named Mangal Pandey (1827–1857, today celebrated as the mutiny's first martyr and glorified in a Bollywood blockbuster) was executed. A month later, fires were lit at Ambala cantonment, leading to the regiment being disbanded.

By May, the unrest had spread to Meerut. Believing they would be defiled en masse if they used the cartridges, eighty-five sepoys staged a mutiny. As they were captured and led off to start ten years' imprisonment, the remaining sepoys revolted, setting fire to their barracks and shooting every European in sight, accompanied by shouts of *Dilli chalo!* ("On to Delhi!")

The sepoys marched on the old Mughal capital, reaching it on the morning of May 11. By nightfall, the city was in their hands. They were received by Bahadur Shah Zafar, who still resided in the Red Fort, the traditional seat of Mughal power, but whose status had been reduced to "King of Delhi." More of a philosopher and poet than a military leader, Zafar provided a moral sanction for the rebellion but little else.

Peasant leaders now joined in the revolt, attacking British garrisons in the vicinity of Delhi and Meerut. By the beginning of June, the unrest had spread to the area around Kanpur (then Cawnpore), where the worst of the massacres of Europeans took place. Nana Saheb (1824–1859), the son of the last Maratha Peshwa, declared his support for the mutineers. After two weeks of bombardment, he offered the four-hundred-strong British community safe passage out of the cantonment. But as the residents boarded boats to take them down the Ganges, they were attacked by sepoys. Saheb rescued about two hundred women and children and locked them up in the Bibighar, or Ladies' House, to use as a bargaining tool in case of a British attack. When a British relief force converged on Cawnpore, sepoys attacked the Bibighar, executing those inside. Their bodies were cut up and thrown down a well. As John Keay describes it, "Their slaughterhouse methods, clumsy rather than sadistic, constituted an atrocity which would haunt the British till the end of their Indian days."

Canning's attempts to suppress the rebellion were stymied by a lack of British troops. Thousands had left India to fight the Crimean War and had yet to be replaced. There were just forty-five British soldiers in India in 1857, half of them in the Punjab. Communications between different army divisions was crude and, with rebellions breaking out across a wide swathe of northern India simultaneously, forces were overstretched. The first breakthrough came when Brigadier General Henry Havelock defeated Nana Saheb at Cawnpore just days after the massacre.

Using recruits from areas not affected by the mutiny, the British were able to turn the tide of the rebellion. After the recapture of Delhi in September 1857, the focus of military operations shifted to Lucknow, where the British commissioner, Henry Lawrence, had fortified the Residency with trenches and booby traps. Among the 855 British troops and officers barricaded inside the grounds was Dr. Brydon, the only survivor of the retreat from Kabul. Just over a thousand civilians, most of them Europeans, were also crowded into the thirty-three acres of the compound. Brydon would survive the siege, but not Lawrence, who was killed by a shell that landed in his room. It would take two relief columns to break the siege and bring the survivors to safety.

Still revered for her bravery by many Indians today is the Rani of Jhansi, Lakshmi Bai (1828–1858). Born in Varanasi, she excelled at horse riding and swordsmanship from an early age. Marrying into the royal family of Jhansi, she found herself regent when her husband died before she had produced an heir. Despite the local British representative expressing confidence in the young widow's ability to lead her state, Jhansi was annexed under the doctrine of lapse. When the rebellion broke out, she declared that she hoped the rebels would go "straight to hell." But in early 1858, as British reinforcements from Bombay were advancing toward Jhansi, she decided to throw in her lot with Nana Saheb's protégé, Tatya Tope (1814–1859). After the British laid siege to Jhansi, Bai led the resistance herself, before donning a disguise and, according to legend, escaping the fort by leaping over the ramparts on her horse. In June 1858, she and Tope managed to seize Gwalior despite its impregnable fortress and determined to make a last stand. But after holding the fort for only three weeks, Lakshmi Bai died in a hail of British bullets. The fall of Gwalior signaled the end of the main phase of the rebellion.

Had the rebels been able to combine their forces and take both the Punjab and the Deccan, they might have succeeded in driving the British from Indian soil. Instead, the rebellion became a patchwork of isolated insurrections. It was

Lakshmi Bai, the Rani of Jhansi, defiantly rode her horse through enemy lines, her sword raised in the air, to become an icon of the freedom movement.

not until July 8, 1859, that Canning was finally able to declare that peace had been restored.

British reprisals were severe. Revenge was the order of the day. Summary executions became the norm, with mutineers sometimes being tied to the mouths of cannons and blown to pieces. Others were made to lick the blood from floors where Europeans had been killed. Depending on their religion, some had beef or pork stuffed down their throats before being hanged. Bahadur Shah Zafar was put on trial for supporting the mutineers. He was then transported to Rangoon. Denied paper or pens, he used charcoal to scrawl couplets on the walls of the house where he was incarcerated. He died in 1862 after developing paralysis of the throat and was buried in an unmarked grave in a compound near the Shwedagon Pagoda.

An Anomaly Becomes an Anachronism

Even before the revolt was over, Britain's parliament set up a royal commission of inquiry to investigate its causes. Known as the Peel Commission, it recommended a significant increase in the number of European troops and a decrease in the proportion of native soldiers. A ratio of one British soldier to every two Indian sepoys was maintained in the Bengal presidency, where the revolt had started, and one to three in the presidencies of Bombay and Madras. Recruitment would favor those regions that remained neutral or sided with the British. To avoid the possibility of the sepoys forming a united front in the future, the Commission recommended that native regiments be composed of different nationalities and castes. The governor of Bombay, Mountstuart Elphinstone, was one of those pressing for such reforms, declaring, "*Divide et impera* was the old Roman motto and it should be ours." Subsequent

British policies would see the principle applied more widely, setting Hindu against Muslim and leading to the partition of the subcontinent in 1947.

In many ways, the events of 1857 came as a long overdue opportunity to take action against the East India Company. As British historian Percival Spear points out, the Company "was held to have failed to gauge Indian opinion, to be inert and backward looking. The occasion of the Revolt was thus a convenient way to end an administrative anomaly which had become an anachronism." In Britain, public unease about the Company's role in stoking the grievances that led to the mutiny was also growing. The outcome was a complete overhaul of the way in which India had been ruled. Passed by parliament in 1858, the Government of India Act transferred power from the East India Company to the Crown. The Company closed for trade in 1874, "unhonoured and unsung, but maybe not altogether unwept." In 2010, it was relaunched as a luxury foodstuff brand in London.

Pax Brittanica

On November 1, 1858, Queen Victoria issued a proclamation that was partly a mission statement setting out how India would be administered and partly a set of preventative measures to ensure that British rule in India would never be threatened again. Read out in multiple languages in all main Indian cities and towns, the proclamation stated, "In their prosperity will be our strength; in their contentment our security." British officials were ordered to abstain from interfering with Indian beliefs and rituals, however "abhorrent" and "primitive" they might be. Victoria also disavowed any "desire to impose Our convictions on any of Our subjects." The Anglicist cause, championed so enthusiastically by Macaulay and others half a century earlier, had effectively been reversed.

The doctrine of lapse was also scrapped. The British "desire no extension of Our present territorial possessions," the queen's proclamation insisted. Instead of liquidating the princely states, the directive became to transform their rulers into allies. Some 560 princely states would remain nominally independent, with the day-to-day running of their administration in the hands of local rulers but with British residents and political agents to keep a watchful eye over them. Foreign and defense policy would be in the hands of the Crown.

Landowners—such as those in Awadh, who had their lands confiscated before 1857—were now allowed to retain their holdings in perpetuity. By making them local magistrates, they became incorporated into the new ruling structure as rajas and rais (overlords). Indian affairs were now overseen through a ministerial portfolio, with a secretary of state for India based in London. Governors-general became viceroys. Enjoying absolute power and ruling over one sixth of the world's population, they were handsomely rewarded, receiving up to twenty-five thousand pounds per annum, the highest salary of any public official in Britain.

Finally, Victoria proclaimed that Indians had a right to take part in the management of their country by holding positions in the Indian Civil Service, whatever an individual's "education, ability and integrity" qualified him for. This last concession was more in spirit than in practice. Competitive examinations were held in English at a level of mastery that few Indians had. Even fewer could afford a fare to London to sit the examinations. By 1870, there was only one Indian member of the civil service.

A lasting legacy of 1857 was an elevated level of racial arrogance among the British toward India. Mutiny memorials to the British dead sprung up in Delhi, Cawnpore, and Lucknow, but as Nehru would later complain, there were no memorials to the Indians who had died.

By 1901, there were almost 170,000 Europeans in India, around 90 percent of whom were British. Of these, around half were soldiers and their families. The remainder worked on the railways, as tea and coffee planters, as business owners, or as middle management in textiles and other industries. The "club" became the focus of social life, a bulwark against "native" society. Dances and theatrical productions, bridge and lawn parties, tennis and polo tournaments were the orders of the day. Homes away from home, the clubs had gardens filled with roses and petunias that barely survived in the tropical heat. Kitchens served Anglo-Indian fare: "bottled peas, pseudo-cottage bread, fish . . . pretending to be plaice, more bottled peas . . . trifle, sardines on toast," to quote E. M. Forster's *A Passage to India*. Indians were prohibited from the clubs—with the notable exception of freemason lodges.

Cut off from social intercourse with Indians due to caste and racial barriers—except perhaps for those household servants doing all the domestic chores—many European women found India a lonely and frustrating country. Others, such as travel writer Fanny Parkes, enjoyed "the pleasure of vagabondising over India" and left behind vivid descriptions of the land and its people. But Parkes was the exception rather than the rule. Queen Victoria's son, the Duke of Windsor and the future Edward VIII (1841–1910), was shocked by "the rude and rough manners" of many Britons he met during his tour of India in 1875–1876. He was particularly offended by certain racial slurs used to describe Indians. The proportion of Indians in the civil service would never exceed 6 percent. Given the insipid racism that prevailed, it was not hard to see why.

In 1876, the queen announced to the British parliament that her Indian subjects were "happy under My rule and loyal to My throne." On the advice of Indian prime minister Benjamin Disraeli, she adopted the title of "Empress of India" and, for the benefit of her Indian subjects, "Kaiser-i-Hind." The title was suggested by the Hungarian Orientalist G. W. Leitner because it conveniently combined the imperial titles of the Roman "Caesar," the German "Kaiser," and the Russian "Czar"—and there was less chance of it being mispronounced. To confirm the new title, Viceroy Lord Lytton (1831–1891) spared no expense, organizing an Imperial Assemblage in Delhi in January 1877. Among the eighty-four thousand who attended were sixty-three ruling princes and hundreds of chiefs and nobles, as well as former members of Bahadur Shah Zafar's household. The empress was represented by a bejeweled crown resting on a gilded cushion. "The union of India with England has been asserted to be indissoluble," officials proclaimed.

The "indissoluble" union had grown closer with the opening of the Suez Canal in 1869, which shortened the travel time between India and England by two weeks. A year later, the two countries were connected via an undersea telegraph cable that revolutionized communications. Public works assumed greater importance. The railway network grew from about 8,400 miles in 1860 to 15,900 miles by 1890. Land under irrigation expanded rapidly with the building of the Ganges Canal and other massive projects. By 1891, more than ten million acres, supporting one-eighth of India's population of 285 million, was under irrigation.

If all this infrastructure was meant to bolster the legitimacy of British rule over India, it failed. As the scholar Jon Wilson points out, neither the railways nor the canals had much effect on ordinary Indians. New settlements or canal colonies were created in the Punjab, but the initial boom was usually followed by a long decline in agricultural productivity. Similarly, railways could not compete with bullock carts for transporting heavy goods, and human-powered river transport was cheaper than steam-powered vessels. "Without the kind of political leadership able to coordinate the productive activity of Indians for the benefit of society as a whole, the dreams of 'improvement' projected by the prophets of modernity in the 1840s and 1850s ended up as illusory fantasies," Wilson writes.

Nor did the canals prevent a series of devastating famines in the 1870s and 1890s, due to a protracted drought that caused crop failures. The famine of 1877, which claimed up to 5.5 million lives in the Deccan, coincided with Lytton's ostentatious Assemblage. A die-hard Tory, Lytton believed that free-market forces were the best way to resolve the problem. Grain continued to be exported during the famine. He also insisted that taxes be collected from peasants in the Deccan, prompting the editor of the *Indian Herald* to complain that "millions had died for the axiom of the political economy." Perhaps distracted by his disastrous decision to embroil Britain in the Second Afghan War, Lytton was unmoved by the images of skeletal villagers being published in newspapers in India and abroad, declaring, "Mere distress is not sufficient reason for opening relief work." A royal commission into the famine produced a report that was widely criticized as a whitewash. It exonerated the government for its failure to prevent the famine and its mishandling of the crisis. Most importantly, it contained no practical measures to avoid a repeat of the disaster.

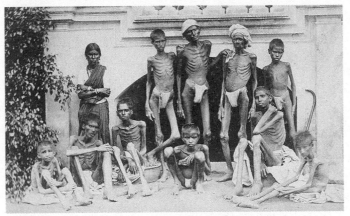

The horror of the 1877 famine came to the attention of the British public thanks to reporting by journalists, and to photographs, sometimes taken by missionaries, published in newspapers and magazines.

The contrast between Queen Victoria's insistence that her subjects were happy and loyal and the realities on the ground did not go unnoticed. Stirrings of anti-imperial protest were just around the corner. The moniker of "India's first revolutionary" is generally applied to Vasudev Balwant Phadke (1845–1883), who led an uprising in the countryside around Pune composed of low-caste tribals demanding independence for India. Phadke was arrested in 1879 and sentenced to transportation to Aden. He escaped jail in 1883, but was captured soon after. He died after going on a hunger strike, an ominous precursor to what would become a potent weapon against British rule in the decades to come.

By the late 1890s, revolutionary societies were being set up in Maharashtra and in Bengal. Even Britain's supposedly loyal civil servants were getting anxious about the inevitability of future famines and the need for a safety valve to keep discontent spilling over once again into a full-scale revolt.

CHAPTER 8

The Long Road to Freedom

India's freedom movement is synonymous with the towering figures of Mahatma Gandhi, Jawaharlal Nehru, and Mohammad Ali Jinnah. Yet the Indian National Congress (INC), which guided 340 million Indians to their "tryst with destiny" in 1947, was founded by an English ornithologist.

Allan Octavian Hume (1829–1912), the son of the fearless Scottish reformer James Hume, was twenty when he arrived in India in 1849. He rose quickly through the ranks of the Bengal civil service. While stationed as a district magistrate at Etawah, near Cawnpore, he was reluctant to impose the death penalty on sepoys who had taken part in the 1857 revolt, earning him a reputation for fairness and moderation. He was also, in his own words, "an unsafe, impulsive, insubordinate officer," qualities that led to his eventual demotion from the civil service. Freed from the strictures of officialdom, he devoted himself to becoming an expert on the game birds of India. In the hill station of Simla, he built Rothney Castle to house his collection of eighty thousand bird skins and nests, which he later donated to what would become the Natural History Museum in London.

The catalyst for the formation of the INC was the Ilbert Bill of 1883, which allowed Indian judges to preside over the trials of British subjects. The bill threatened to unleash a "white mutiny" of irate Europeans, mainly indigo planters and merchants, who believed their position as the "ruling race" was being forever undermined. Hume was among those outraged by the European backlash to the bill. In March 1883, with Viceroy Lord Dufferin's (1862–1902) blessing, Hume addressed an open letter to the graduates of Calcutta University, encouraging them to form an association for national regeneration. Such an association of educated Indians would also act as a safety valve "for the escape of great and growing forces" of discontent in India.

The INC's inaugural meeting took place in Bombay on December 28, 1885, with the seventy-two invited delegates affirming their loyalty to the British Crown. Their key demand "was that the basis of the government should be widened and that the people should have their proper and legitimate share in it." Forty-four years later, the INC would be fighting for total independence from Britain.

For the first decade of its existence, the INC met once a year, over Christmas, so as not to interfere with the work of its members, who were mainly lawyers, journalists, and civil servants. Proceedings were conducted in English. Ominously, there were few Muslims in its ranks. This rankled Muslim leaders such as Sir Sayyid Ahmed Khan, who in 1875 had founded the Muhammadan Anglo-Oriental College at Aligarh. Khan insisted that representative government might work in societies "united by ties of race, religion, manners, customs, culture, and historical traditions" but "in their absence would only injure the well-being and tranquility of the land." His arguments would later be used to justify the partition of India and the creation of the Muslim-majority state of Pakistan.

The INC's endorsement of British rule (its members explicitly complimented an "empire on which the sun never sets") drew the ire of right-wing Hindus. Prominent among them was Bal Gangadhar Tilak (1856–1920), whose politicization resulted from his opposition to the 1891 Age of Consent Act, which raised the age for the consummation of marriage to twelve. In his writings, Tilak quoted the *Bhagavad Gītā* to justify the killing of oppressors. After two British officers were killed in June 1897, he was charged with incitement to murder and sentenced to eighteen months' imprisonment. On his release, he was revered as a martyr for the nationalist cause.

Acts of such violence were rare, with luminaries such as the social reformer Aurobindo Ghose (1872–1950) and the poet, philosopher, and educationalist Rabindranath Tagore stressing passive resistance and economic self-reliance in preference to confronting the Raj directly. The British maintained their aura of benevolent rule. Once Indians gained sufficient experience to manage their own affairs, it was suggested, Britain could gradually withdraw and Indians could at some future undefined time rule themselves as a self-governing dominion. Little did they realize, this process was about to be sped up.

"The Greatest Power in the World"—for Now

The trigger for the first sustained mass movement against British rule in almost half a century came as a surprise. In 1903, the viceroy, Lord Curzon (1859–1925), announced that Bengal, India's most populous province, was to be partitioned.

George Nathaniel Curzon, Baron of Kedleston, an Oxford graduate, seasoned traveler and explorer—and the holder of a gold medal from the Royal Geographical Society for discovering the source of the Oxus River—had long coveted the position of viceroy. No stranger to controversy, Curzon took a dim view of Indians' ability to govern themselves and opposed facilitating their entry into the civil service. When it was suggested that an Indian be elected to the executive council, he retorted, "In the whole continent there is not one Indian fit for the post." One of his ambitions as viceroy, he wrote to his superiors, was to assist the "unrepresentative" and "tottering" INC to a "peaceful demise." He won few fans from educated Indians when he told an audience at Calcutta University that "truth was a Western concept." India's princes were dismissed as "a set of unruly and ignorant and rather undisciplined schoolboys."

Curzon was not all bad. He did stand up for ordinary Indians, traveling widely in rural areas and ordering the expulsion of a whole regiment to Aden because of a conspiracy to protect soldiers who raped a Burmese woman. Among his least contentious achievements was setting up the Archaeological Survey of India, which was charged with restoring what he termed "the greatest galaxy of monuments in the world."

When Curzon became viceroy, Bengal had a population twice that of Great Britain and encompassed Bihar, Orissa, Assam, and present-day Bangladesh. Predominantly Hindu in the west and Muslim in the east, Bengal's partition was justified in the interest of stimulating growth in the underdeveloped eastern region of the province. The real reason was more sinister—"to split up and thereby weaken a solid body of opponents" to the Raj, namely the well-educated, high-caste Bengalis of Calcutta.

Curzon, the Imperialist

"For as long as we rule India, we are the greatest power in the world."

Despite London warning that "the severance of old and historic ties and the breaking up of racial unity would backfire," partition went ahead on October 16, 1905. Angry demonstrations erupted almost immediately in many cities and towns in eastern India, spreading quickly to the rest of the country. Congress leaders urged people to boycott British goods, which were burned on massive bonfires across the country, and purchase *swadeshi* ("of one's own

Even while at Oxford, Curzon exhibited the self-importance and sense of entitlement that inspired the famous Balliol rhyme: My name is George Nathaniel Curzon, / I am a most superior person / My cheek is pink, my hair is sleek, / I dine at Blenheim once a week.

country") instead. What became known as the Swadeshi Movement saw coarse Indian-grown cotton woven on local hand-looms replace sophisticated Manchester textiles. Locally made sugar, salt, and other goods took precedence over imported manufactures.

The partition of Bengal led to a schism in Congress between moderates and radicals. The moderates espoused dialogue and believed British promises that power would gradually devolve to Indians until they became self-governing states within the British Empire, such as Australia and Canada. Warnings from moderates such as Gopal Krishna Gokhale that "only madmen outside lunatic asylums could think or talk of independence" cut little ice with radicals who wanted direct action. They took their inspiration from Irish nationalists and saw the boycott of British goods as "part of a great turning of the national consciousness away from foreign ideas and institutions." Self-government was the only way forward, Tilak declared. "*Swaraj* is my birthright and I will have it."

The rupture between the two sides came to a head at the Surat Session of the INC in 1907. The British took advantage of the split by arresting prominent radicals, including Tilak, who was jailed for six years. Editors of pro-independence newspapers were charged with sedition and their publications suspended. A penal colony set up on the remote Andaman Islands was soon overflowing with prisoners. Cases of persons being sent to jail without being charged or tried inspired even more young Indians to join the nationalist cause.

Curzon departed just after the partition of Bengal came into effect. His replacement was Lord Minto (1845–1914), who, together with John Morley (1838–1923), the new secretary of state for India, began drawing up a program of political reform. The Morley-Minto Reforms, also known as The Indian Councils Act, came into effect in 1909, increasing the size of existing central and provincial legislative councils and enabling more Indians to be represented. For the first time, an Indian was allowed to be admitted to the viceroy's executive council. Controversially, the Act also provided separate electorates for Muslims, who argued they had been under-represented in official bodies. The concession, wrested from the British by the recently formed Muslim League, would entrench existing communal differences and for many nationalists served as proof, if any were needed, that the British were engaged in a policy of divide and rule.

The high-tide mark of the Raj came in 1911, with the staging of Delhi Durbar to commemorate King George V's visit. Unprecedented in scale and extravagance, it marked the first and only visit by a reigning British monarch to India. The king and his wife, Queen Mary, sat on golden thrones under the gilded dome of the royal pavilion before an audience of a hundred thousand. The first order of business was bestowing decorations on India's leading princes. In a procession of bejeweled splendor, each ruler halted before the king, bowed, and took three steps backward—except the nationalist Gaekwad of Baroda, Sayajirao, who merely cocked his head and abruptly turned his back on the king. The alleged snub (the Gaekwad blamed an attack of nerves, though it is doubtful) did not register as heavily as it might have, given what came next. George V made a surprise declaration: the capital of India would be transferred from Calcutta to Delhi. No one had expected this news. After a brief, stunned silence, the crowd erupted with cheers.

List of Viceroys: 1899–1947
Lord Curzon (1899–1905)
Lord Minto (1905–1910)
Lord Hardinge (1910–1916)
Lord Chelmsford (1916–1921)
Lord Reading (1921–1926)
Lord Irwin (1926–1931)
Lord Willingdon (1931–1936)
Lord Linlithgow (1936–1944)
Lord Wavell (1944–1947)
Lord Mountbatten (1947–1948)

Moving the capital to Delhi made sense geographically and symbolically—the city had been the seat of power for much of the Mughal period—but it had yet to recover from the ravages of the 1857 revolt. The decision was also meant to signal British single-mindedness in the face of Bengali intransigence. While the decision was welcomed by most Indian princes, who would now be closer to the seat of power, it received a lukewarm response in England. One of those critical of the move was Curzon, who believed Calcutta was a symbol of everything the British stood for, while Delhi was "a mass of deserted ruins and graves." Here Curzon was missing a vital point. By creating a new capital on the ruins of past empires, Britain would be able to write itself into India's past. As Viceroy Lord Hardinge proclaimed, "Every walled town in India has its 'Delhi Gate,' and among the masses of the people it is still revered as the seat of the former Empire." To soften the blow to Bengali pride, George V announced that the partition of Bengal had been revoked.

The Gandhi Factor

The outbreak of World War I, which came only three years after George V's visit, punctured the myth of British invincibility. But it also saw an outpouring of loyalty from both Congress and the Muslim League, as well as the princes. Ultimately, more than one million Indian combatants and support staff served in theaters as diverse as Gallipoli, Flanders, and Mesopotamia. For nationalists such as Tilak, the unstinting support for the war effort was proof that Indians could run their own affairs. After returning from exile in Burma in 1914, he teamed up with the rights activist Annie Besant (1847–1933). Her Irish parentage, trade-union background, Fabian principles, and indefatigable energy made her the perfect champion of Indian home rule. In 1916, she and Tilak founded the Home Rule League, which advocated self-government within the British Empire for all of India. Two years later, Besant was elected chair of the INC, which officially adopted the goal of home rule as part of its platform.

Mixed signals on the political front only strengthened the hand of those wanting Britain off their backs. In August 1917, Edwin Montagu (1879–1924), India's secretary of state, told the House of Commons that substantial steps were needed to realize responsible self-government in India "as an integral part of the British Empire." Montagu embarked on a five-month tour of the country with the new viceroy, Lord Chelmsford (1868–1933). At the end of 1919, they submitted a report to the British government for legislative changes that would become known as the Montford reforms. Enshrined in the Government of India Act 1919, these changes broadened the democratic base of India's administration. Legislative councils, elected by Indians in each of the provinces, would be responsible for areas such as education, public health, and public works, while law enforcement, taxation, and defense would be looked after by imperial bureaucrats responsible to the viceroy. The reforms were immediately dismissed by hard-line nationalists as being too limited. Only 5.5 million landholders, or one tenth of the adult male population, could vote in provincial elections.

But the reforms were largely stillborn, negated by the Rowlatt Report. Published in April 1918, it recommended that the near-totalitarian wartime powers of the Defence of India Act 1915 to control public unrest and terrorist activities be made permanent. For the millions of Indians who had been willing to sacrifice their lives for the empire, the passing of the Rowlatt Bill in March 1919 was an insult, and signaled Britain's readiness to use repression to silence its enemies.

Closely monitoring the reaction to the Rowlatt Bill was Mohandas Karamchand Gandhi (1869–1948). Forty-nine at the time, he had spent the majority of his formative years agitating for the rights of Indians in South Africa. Gandhi would become the most influential figure in the Indian independence movement, yet he was only ever briefly president of the Congress Party and spent far more time in jail or in one of his ashrams than in directly steering India to freedom. Nor did he make a concerted attempt to present his political doctrine in print. His changing and often contradictory ideas are contained in the ninety volumes of his *Collected Works*. Those looking for consistency in his views on everything from Western medicine, which he described as "black magic," to caste and untouchability (the former was necessary even though it was responsible for the latter) need look no further than a passage he wrote in his newspaper *Harijan* on September 30, 1939: "At the time of writing I never think of what I may have said before. My aim is not to be consistent with my previous statements on a given question, but to be consistent with truth as it may present itself to me at a given moment. The result is that I have grown from truth to truth."

Gandhi was born in 1869 in Porbandar, a small principality in Gujarat, where his father served as a *diwan*, or prime minister. He was thirteen when he married his wife, Kasturba, who was one year older than him, and at the age of nineteen he went to England to study law at the Inner Temple in London. After a short and unremarkable tenure at the Bar, he was invited to South Africa by a fellow Gujarati Muslim merchant seeking a legal adviser. His first encounter with South African racism came in 1894, while traveling by train to Pretoria. A white male passenger alerted railway officials that an Indian was seated in a first-class compartment in defiance of rules that restricted colored people to third class. After pointing out that he had a valid ticket and refusing to vacate his seat, Gandhi was forcibly ejected from the train and left on a platform in the middle of a cold winter's night.

Over the next twenty years he fought for the rights of 150,000 Indian migrants in Cape and Natal provinces, described in the statute books as "semi-barbarous Asiatics or persons belonging to the uncivilised races of Asia." In 1908, he composed his first political pamphlet, *Hind Swaraj* ("Indian Home Rule"), while traveling by ship from London to South Africa. Influenced by the pacifism and anti-materialism in the writings of Leo Tolstoy, and by John Ruskin's respect for labor and the rights of the poor, *Hind Swaraj* was a critique of modernity. In this seminal text, Gandhi articulated the use of nonviolence as a political weapon, extolled the interdependent life of a utopian village community, and argued for the equivalence of all religions and classes—though not for the abolition of untouchability. His advocacy for communal harmony attracted the support of many Muslims and lower-caste Hindus. His championing of nonviolent resistance based on moral strength earned him a legion of admirers in the West, among them the Nobel-winning French essayist and novelist Romain Rolland, who compared Gandhi to Jesus. The only thing lacking, Rolland wrote, was "the cross." His role in bringing Britain to its knees became an inspiration for millions of individuals and movements around the world, from the civil rights movement in America to the Prague Spring.

Having failed in his legal appeals to the South African government to grant Indians equality under the Constitution, Gandhi switched to direct protest, which he called *satyagraha*, or "holding firmly on to truth." Satyagraha drew on the nonviolent Jaina and Vaishnava traditions of his native Gujarat and elevated suffering and denial into a quasi-religious discipline, like yoga or meditation. For Gandhi, satyagraha was the quality of the soul that enabled individuals to endure suffering for what they believed was morally right. More than a weapon for resisting oppression, it was a vehicle for converting his opponents to his beliefs.

Gandhi on Satyagraha

"Satyagraha does not mean meek submission to the will of the evil-doer, but it means the pitting of one's whole soul against the will of the tyrant. Working under this law of our being, it is possible for a single individual to defy the whole might of an unjust empire, to save his honour, his religion, his soul, and lay the foundation for that empire's fall or its regeneration."

Gandhi returned to India from South Africa in 1915, and two years later started his political career. In India, the pool of potential recruits to his cause rose to three hundred million, few of whom ultimately would be untouched by his work. At first, he concentrated on campaigns against the exploitation of indigo workers in the district of Champaran and of mill workers in Ahmedabad, succeeding in improving conditions for both groups. The agitation against the Rowlatt Bill was to be his first real test on Indian soil, "the greatest battle of my life." And it would backfire spectacularly.

Gandhi was one of the most photographed and discussed individuals of his time, yet so varied are the interpretations of his life and influence that he remains an enigma. Indian schoolchildren are taught that the first person to refer to Gandhi as the Mahatma or "great soul" was Tagore in 1915.

Gandhi's call for a peaceful *hartal* (strike of workers and businesses) and for a day of fasting and prayer resulted in violence in Delhi, Bombay, and many other cities. The population was incensed, and there was little appetite for airing their dissent respectfully. Angry mobs attacked British civilians; police fired on demonstrators. When Gandhi discovered the unrest was spreading to small towns, he admitted he had made a "Himalayan miscalculation" in calling on people to undertake civil disobedience before they were ready to do so.

Gandhi's ability to influence events across a country as vast as India was limited. Ignoring his calls for an end to demonstrations, thousands of protesters in Amritsar ran amok, murdering five British men and beating up a female missionary, who they left for dead. (She survived thanks to a Hindu family who dragged her to their house and handed her over to the British.) The commander of troops at Amritsar was Brigadier General Reginald Dyer (1864–1927), a man known for his short temper and for overreacting when under pressure. On April 13, 1919, an estimated twenty thousand people congregated in Jallianwala Bagh, an area of open ground enclosed by high walls. Most were there for the Sikh harvest festival of Baisakhi and were unaware that Dyer had issued an order that morning prohibiting gatherings, religious or otherwise. At 4:30 PM, Dyer personally led a force of Gurkha, Sikh, Pathan, and Baluchi riflemen to Jallianwala Bagh and, without warning, ordered them to open fire. With troops blocking the narrow entrance to the Bagh and its walls too high to scale, there was no escape for those inside. Official figures put the death toll at 379. An enquiry by Congress put the figure at over a thousand.

Condemnation of Dyer's actions came swiftly. Winston Churchill (1874–1965) called the mass shooting "without precedent or parallel in the modern history of the British empire . . . an extraordinary event, a monstrous event, an event which stands in singular and sinister isolation." Rabindranath Tagore, who had been knighted for his services to literature, protested the massacre by returning his award. Gandhi declared that "cooperation in any shape or form with this satanic government is sinful."

Called before a committee of inquiry in Lahore several months later, Dyer justified the shooting, claiming it was calculated to sap "the morale of the rebels." Dyer was dismissed, but on his return to England became a cause célèbre for die-hard Tories and Unionists who believed that conquest, not partnership, was needed to maintain Britain's empire. His deification only served to increase Indian antagonism toward British rule.

Gandhi reacted to the Amritsar massacre by staging a fast. For the Mahatma, fasting was a weapon that could be employed by the weakest and the poorest against the mightiest of opponents. He also saw it as a means of atonement for his own sins, errors, and shortcomings. As Wendy Doniger writes, Gandhi's fasting "was intended first to control himself, then to control his own people, getting them to unite in protest but to pull back from violence; and then to control the British, getting them to let him out of jail on several occasions and, eventually, to quit India."

Tilak's death in 1920 left Gandhi the undisputed leader of the INC. Under his guidance, an organization once derided as an upper-middle-class debating society transformed into a national body with roots in small towns and villages, and an efficient hierarchical structure. A total of fourteen thousand delegates attended the INC's 1920 meeting in Nagpur, in central India. His emphasis on mass civil disobedience caught on, serving to politicize large sections of Indian society, especially in rural areas, which accounted for 90 percent of the population. Thousands of upper-caste lawyers and professionals were ordered to the villages to recruit new members. For most, it was their first encounter with India's impoverished masses. Gandhi also made inroads into the working class, which was small (less than 1 percent of the population in the 1920s) but significant because it was concentrated in the larger cities.

The growing split between Hindus and Muslims alarmed Gandhi. He believed that the INC's support for the Khilafat Movement, which had sprung up during the First World War to oppose Muslim troops being used against the Constantinople-based Caliph, offered an opportunity of uniting the two communities "as would not arrive in a hundred years." When the Treaty of Sèvres effectively erased Turkey from the map, and with it the Caliph's control over the holy places of Islam, the movement gathered strength. So eager were its leaders to attract Hindu support, they told Gandhi they were prepared to ban cow slaughter—an offer he brushed aside.

In December 1921, the INC authorized Gandhi to start a campaign of civil disobedience. Promising *swaraj* (self-rule) within a year, he urged his supporters to deliberately break British laws. Civil servants were told to leave their posts; no taxes were to be paid and courts were to be boycotted. By making India ungovernable, the British would be forced to leave.

But India was not ready for the Mahatma's vision. In February 1922, a crowd of Congress and Khilafat volunteers was fired on by police in the village of Chauri Chaura, in the United Provinces. The crowd retaliated by setting fire to a police station. Twenty policemen were either hacked to pieces as they tried to flee or burned to death to the cries of *Mahatma Gandhi ki jai* ("Victory to Mahatma Gandhi"). Horrified, he called off the campaign, telling his followers to educate the masses, extend grassroots organizations, and take up the spinning wheel. His entreaty for the latter was simultaneously a practical way of achieving swadeshi by spinning cotton, a potent symbol of unity against the oppressor and a spiritual exercise. The British responded by giving him a six-year prison sentence, though he was released on health grounds after serving less than two.

The Politics of Polarization

Gandhi responded to the failure of the civil disobedience movement by withdrawing to his ashram near Ahmedabad, where he could be found seated at his spinning wheel, holding daily prayer meetings and staging numerous fasts to protest acts of injustice. His retirement from active politics commenced in 1927 with Congress's rejection of the Simon Commission. Set up by Stanley

Baldwin's conservative government, the commission was tasked with reviewing the workings of the Montford reforms and to prepare a constitution for a self-governing India. Angered by the absence of a single Indian on the commission, Congress voted to boycott it "at every stage and in every form" and resolved for the first time to make complete independence from the British its goal. A year later, representatives from all major independence groups drafted their own constitutional reform scheme.

Approved by Congress in December 1928, the Nehru Report, produced under the presidency of Motilal Nehru (1861–1931), stated that the "next immediate step" for India must be dominion status, as enjoyed by Canada, Australia, and other independent former colonies of Britain. India would be a federation, having at the center a sovereign two-chamber parliament to which the ministry would be responsible. The report rejected the idea of separate electorates for minorities, instead providing for their protection through a system of reservations.

The report was opposed by Congress radicals, who saw the acceptance of dominion status as a step back from the goal of complete independence adopted the year before. Abandoning the principle of separate electorates also angered the Muslim League, headed by Mohammad Ali Jinnah (1876–1948). Like Gandhi, Jinnah had studied law at the Inner Temple, and in 1896 became the youngest Indian to be called to the Bar. In 1906, two years after returning to India to practice as the sole Muslim barrister in Bombay, he joined the overwhelmingly Hindu INC. In 1913, he became the leader of the Muslim League. His impact on pre-independence India was based on his brilliance as a politician, even though the verdict is still out on whether his demand for a separate state of Pakistan was a strategy to win more concessions for Muslims or an end in itself.

The Muslim League's rejection of the Nehru Report hastened the inevitable breakdown of a working relationship between it and Congress. For many Muslims, the powers proposed for a future central government reinforced their belief that the British Raj would be replaced by the Congress Raj, limiting their ability to share power and protect their interests in a future democratic and independent India.

Although Jinnah campaigned for a state founded solely on the basis of religion, his Islam was moderate and progressive. It was said he could not recite any passages from the Koran and rarely prayed at mosques.

The December 1929 conference of the Congress Party in Lahore was a watershed moment for the freedom movement. At midnight on New Year's Eve, the tricolor flag of an independent India was raised on the banks of the Ravi River amid shouts of *Inquilab zindabad* ("Long live the revolution"). Gandhi declared January 26, 1930, to be Independence Day, and presented the viceroy Lord Irwin (1881–1959) with an eleven-point program that, if accepted, would be tantamount to granting independence. To pressure the British, he devised his most spectacular satyagraha so far—the salt march.

Ever since the days of the Mughals, the production and sale of salt had been a state monopoly. The tax was minimal, less than three annas a year, but because salt was a necessity for rich and poor alike, it was regressive, impacting the

The police use of steel-tipped lathis against marchers when they reached Dandi was memorably captured in Richard Attenborough's film Gandhi.

poorest drastically. Followed by journalists and newsreel cameramen from around the world, Gandhi left his ashram at Sabarmati on March 12, 1930, for the 240-mile walk to Dandi, on Gujarat's western coast, telling those accompanying him not to return until India was free. His daily prayer meetings drew massive crowds. By the time he reached Dandi, tens of thousands had joined his march. On April 5, he bathed in the sea and picked up a handful of salt from the beach, a trivial but highly symbolic act. The government treated the whole episode with indifference, concentrating instead on the mass arrest of Congress leaders. Gandhi was jailed but, in the weeks and months that followed, hundreds of thousands followed his example, a response that Gandhi had never expected.

By the closing months of 1930, both sides recognized that an impasse had been reached. Fearing that Congress might turn to more violent methods, Irwin invited Gandhi for talks in Delhi. In Irwin, Gandhi at last had a viceroy who was sympathetic to the demands of moderate national-ists. He considered the Mahatma a leader with "a very good mind; logical, forceful, courageous, with an odd streak of subtlety." The respect was mutual: Gandhi would later say, "I succumbed not to Lord Irwin but to the honesty in him." Photographs of the leader of the freedom move-ment striding up the steps of the vice-regal palace wearing his trademark dhoti and carrying a walking stick prompted Churchill to deride Gandhi in the House of Commons as a Middle Temple lawyer turned half-naked "fakir of the type well known in the East." Nevertheless, the talks were a success, producing the Gandhi-Irwin Pact. Civil disobedi-ence would be suspended in return for the release of most of the sixty thousand jailed for participating in the salt marches. Gandhi also agreed to attend a second Round Table Conference in London (the first had been boycotted by Congress) to work out a constitution for India.

Gandhi sailed to England, arriving in London on Sep-tember 12, 1931. Three days later, still wearing a dhoti and shawl, he addressed more than a hundred delegates at the conference. His presence in London descended into a media circus. Weeks of talks were bogged down over the reserva-tion of seats for religious and other minorities. His demand for immediate and full responsible government was ignored. Disillusioned, he left London in December 1931.

By the time he returned to India, Irwin had been replaced by the arch conservative Lord Willingdon (1866–1941), who made clear his intention to preserve British power in India whatever the cost. Congress reacted by announcing a second national disobedience campaign. The government responded with even greater repression than before, outlawing Congress and arresting more than a hundred thousand people. As deadly clashes escalated, Gandhi was once again forced to suspend the agitation.

The ensuing stalemate was broken by the Government of India Act 1935, the longest piece of legislation ever passed by the British parliament. The Act, which became law in August, allowed for provinces with elected politicians to be given autonomy from the central government, increased franchise to about a sixth of the Indian population, and allowed women the right to vote for the first time. The complex franchise provisions were spread out over fifty-one pages with people being excluded from electoral rolls for reasons such as being a Sikh in a Muslim constituency. An assembly in Delhi comprising 250 seats, half occupied by members from the princely states, would form a power-sharing executive with the central government. Although it was a step forward, the Act was seen as just another bid to buy time.

One of those disappointed in the Act was Jawaharlal Nehru (1889–1964). Born in 1889, Nehru was a graduate of Harrow and Cambridge and, like Gandhi, had studied law at the Inner Temple. His father, Motilal, was a barrister at the Allahabad High Court and was elected president of Congress in 1919. In 1923, Nehru was elected Congress general secretary and quickly became its chief ideologue. His writings, composed mainly during his long stints in jail, countered the British narrative that India was a fragmented entity divided by caste, religion, and language, needing the benevolent guiding hand of colonialism to unite it. Nehru dismissed the Act as a "Charter of Slavery" designed to preserve British rule, referring to the safeguard-ridden document as "a machine with strong brakes but no engine."

Jawaharlal Nehru (left) and Rabindranath Tagore (right) shared a vision of a secularist India. Nehru in turn was influenced by the Bengali Nobel Laureate's writings and his theory of universality.

Nehru on Indian Unity

"Some kind of a dream of unity has occupied the mind of India since the dawn of civilisation. That unity was not conceived as something imposed from outside, a standardisation of externals or even of beliefs. It was something deeper and, within its fold, the widest tolerance of belief and custom was practised and every variety acknowledged and even encouraged."

Despite Nehru's misgivings, Congress members participated in the March 1937 Indian provincial elections. When the votes were counted, the party had won absolute majorities in five provinces and was the largest single party in four others. After demanding assurances that the government would not use its special powers, it formed ministries in all provinces except for Punjab, Sindh, and Bengal. In contrast, the Muslim League scraped together barely one quarter of the 482 seats reserved for Muslims. Jinnah's overtures to form coalitions in several provinces received the cold shoulder from Congress, which found itself riding a wave of popular support and now had control over most aspects of government, aside from security and defense.

The League's rebuff from Congress marked the end of any real chance that Hindus and Muslims would march toward independence hand in hand. The growing alienation and insecurity Muslims felt was fanned by Hindu chauvinist parties, the most prominent of which was the All-India Hindu Mahasabha. According to the Mahasabha's president, V. D. Savarkar (1883–1956), Hindus were united by "the tie we bear to our common fatherland, and the common blood that coursed through our veins and also by the tie of a common homage we owe to our great civilisation or Hindu culture." Only followers of religions that originated in India could be Hindu—a criterion that included Sikhs, Buddhists, and Jains but excluded Muslims. (The division is still at the core of Hindu nationalist or Hindutva ideology today.) In 1938, Nehru tried unsuccessfully to assuage Muslim fears by insisting that Hindu fundamentalists would be banned from Congress. It was too little too late. By the time the League met in Lahore in 1940, the idea of a separate nation for Muslims was not only a goal, but it had also taken on a name: Pakistan, or "the land of the pure."

Quit India and the Countdown to Independence

When Britain, and therefore India, declared war on Germany on September 3, 1939, Congress was not consulted. Instead, it was presented with a raft of new laws limiting the autonomy of provincial governments and restricting civil liberties. Despite his commitment to nonviolence, Gandhi declared his support for Britain at a meeting with Viceroy Lord Linlithgow (1887–1952). The Congress Working Committee followed suit, passing a resolution reaffirming its "entire disapproval of the ideology and practice of Fascism and Nazism and their glorification of war and violence and the suppression of the human spirit." But it also stressed that "the issue of war and peace for India must be decided by the Indian people." The British government was asked "to declare in unequivocal terms what their war aims are in regard to democracy and imperialism and the new order that is envisaged, in particular, how these aims are going to apply to India and to be given effect to in the present." For Britain to fight in the name of freedom while refusing to let Indians rule themselves was seen as hypocritical. When Linlithgow sidestepped the issue, Congress's nine provincial ministries resigned in protest. For the Muslim League, the resignations were cause for celebration: Congress rule, they believed, was finally over. In March 1940, the League adopted what was called the Pakistan resolution, demanding "independent states" in the northwestern and eastern parts of India. A plan on how to achieve that goal was conspicuous by its absence.

With the entry of Japan into the war in September 1940, the sudden fall of Singapore in February 1942, and the rapid Japanese advance through Burma, an invasion of India seemed just a matter of time. In Bengal, more than forty thousand boats were scuttled to prevent them from falling into Japanese hands. In Madras, government officials were dispersed into the interior, and tigers at the zoo were shot in case they were released from their cages and began roaming the streets.

Ready to back the advancing Japanese was the Indian National Army (INA). Made up of thousands of Indian prisoners of war who had been interned by the Japanese forces, the INA was led by Subhas Chandra Bose (1897–1945), who had briefly held the position of Congress president before being ousted by Nehru and Gandhi for his radical views. After being arrested in late 1940 for organizing anti-British protests, Bose staged a spectacular escape, traveling to Germany via Afghanistan and Moscow. The Indian population of Axis-held Europe hailed him as "Netaji." In 1943, he arrived in a submarine in Japanese-occupied Singapore before sailing to the Andaman Islands, the only Indian territory in Japanese hands. The Andamans became Azad Hind or Free India, with Bose as head of state. In the end, the INA never posed a threat to India. Of the six thousand soldiers who saw action, more died from disease than in battle, and many suffered abuse and neglect by their supposed allies, the Japanese. Bose would die in a plane crash on his way to Tokyo just weeks before Japan's surrender.

In March 1942, Stafford Cripps (1889–1952), a socialist member of Churchill's war cabinet, flew to India with the most far-reaching proposal for Indian independence yet. In return for supporting the war effort, the government promised "the earliest possible realization of self-Government." A "new Indian Union" would be created—a "Dominion, associated with the United Kingdom and the other Dominions by a common allegiance to the Crown, but equal to them in every respect, in no way subordinate" to them. Congress was invited to join the Viceroy's Council and act as the Cabinet of the Indian government. Once the war was over, India would gain complete freedom within or outside the British Empire—the choice would be up to its new leaders.

While some Congress leaders, including Nehru, were prepared to accept the proposals, hardliners and representatives of other parties doubted the truth of Britain's declared intention to share executive power, especially in critical areas such as defense. A provision allowing provinces and states to eventually secede was seen as an attempt to appease the Muslim League and the princely states. In the end, Cripps left India without making an agreement. Gandhi described the Cripps offer as a "post-dated cheque on a failing bank."

Bankruptcy of another kind was also on Gandhi's mind. Noncooperation had not succeeded in dislodging the British from India, his fasts had had little effect, and negotiations with viceroys and at the Round Table Conference in London had produced few results. Convinced that Britain could not resist an Axis advance, Gandhi decided it was time for the Raj to "leave India to her fate." On August 8, 1942, the All-India Congress Committee endorsed his riskiest and audacious move yet, the "Quit India Resolution" authorizing "the starting of a mass struggle on nonviolent lines on the widest possible scale." As Gandhi declared the following day: "I am not going to be satisfied with anything short of complete freedom. We shall do or die. We shall either free India or die in the attempt."

It would be his last declaration until the war was over. No sooner had he made his statement than he was arrested, together with nearly all of the Congress leadership. With no one to direct them, volunteers took things into their own hands. Largely peaceful protests were staged in many cities and towns, but these soon turned violent after police responded with *lathi* (metal-tipped wooden staves) charges, firings, and more arrests. Factories making war provisions were sabotaged and telegraph lines cut. Europeans were dragged out of derailed trains and killed. In some areas "national governments" were established. Writing to Churchill, Linlithgow described the unrest as the "most serious rebellion since that of 1857."

Gandhi's Quit India Movement has been described as his "final throw of the dice." Jinnah would call it "the Mahatma's Himalayan blunder." Most historians agree. The jailing of Congress leaders allowed the Muslim League to gain strength and press for partition. In the midst of a world war, the British had few worries about public opinion at home if they went hard after Congress—and they did. With Japan now occupying the bulk of Southeast Asia, India was needed more than ever as a source of money, materials, and manpower. Giving into Congress demands, British officials argued, risked igniting communal strife—something the country could ill afford. There was also pride at stake. Britain had never given up territory except through war, and India was the jewel in its imperial crown. As long as the arch-imperialist Churchill was prime minister, Indian independence was a low priority, if not a lost cause.

Alongside the threat of war on India's doorstep came another nightmare: famine in Bengal. Several years of poor rice harvests, a lack of boats for distributing food supplies, the cutting off of rice supplies from Burma due to the war, and hoarding by Indian traders all combined to produce one of the worst famines of the twentieth century. Churchill's intransigence about diverting ships from Europe's defense to deliver food to the starving contributed to the disaster. Famine or no famine, it didn't matter, Churchill crowed, because "the Indians will breed like rabbits." Anywhere between 1.5 and 3 million people would die before the incoming viceroy Lord Wavell (1883–1950) overruled Churchill and ordered the Indian Army to start distributing food supplies.

A Tryst with Destiny

The end of the war in Europe on May 7, 1945, saw the curtain finally start to fall on Britain's Indian empire. On July 26, Churchill's Tory-led government was defeated by Labour, which had long been a supporter of Indian independence. The new prime minister, Clement Attlee, ordered the release of Congress leaders from jail. Early the following year, Britain sent a Cabinet Mission to India. The issues on the table were no longer whether Britain would pull out of India or under what circumstances, but how soon a handover could be achieved and, most importantly, to whom.

As far as Nehru was concerned, the Muslim League was a creation of the British, part of its divide-and-rule strategy. He believed that once the British left, Muslims would flock to Congress. But his dream of a united India did not reflect the reality. Elections for provincial assemblies held in December 1945 and January 1946 only deepened communal divisions, with Congress dominating in Hindu-majority areas and the League triumphant in areas with a high concentration of Muslims. As the undisputed leader of India's Muslims, Jinnah now had the mandate to press for their own state.

After two months of deliberations, the Cabinet Mission came up with a complicated three-tier governing structure. The Muslim League accepted the plan, even though it contained no provision for an independent homeland. After some reservations, Congress also agreed to an arrangement where it would share cabinet posts with the League. It was Gandhi who sabotaged this last hope that India could remain united by refusing to endorse any deal that gave the League and Congress equal constitutional representation, calling such parity "worse than Pakistan." Relations between the two sides deteriorated drastically. After meeting Nehru in Bombay, Jinnah declared he would have nothing more to do with his adversary and announced a Direct Action Day on August 16, 1946, "to oppose Congress tyranny" and support the creation of Pakistan. Black flags hung over the houses of Muslims. His declaration sparked what became known as the Great Calcutta Killings, which left thousands dead in a week-long orgy of communal bloodletting.

Fearing that India was rapidly descending into civil war, Wavell announced a Breakdown Plan that would see Britain withdraw province by province, south to north, by March 31, 1948. The plan was rejected in London as a surrender of power rather than an orderly transfer. Wavell was recalled and the date for Britain's departure was amended to June 1948. In the same announcement, Attlee confirmed that the last viceroy of India would be Louis Mountbatten (1900–1979). The former supreme allied commander in Southeast Asia and a cousin of King George V, Mountbatten would have free rein to obtain a settlement without having to refer to his superiors in London. For once, both Congress and the League applauded the move.

Within days of his arrival in India on March 22, 1947, Mountbatten started a charm offensive, using his inauguration speech to stress that his was "not a normal" viceroyalty, and that he sought "the greatest goodwill of the greatest possible number" of Indians. His engaging frankness quickly won over Gandhi and Nehru and other senior Congress leaders. Nehru formed a particularly close relationship with Mountbatten's wife, Edwina (1901–1960), which "raised many eyebrows," according to Shahid Hamid, military secretary to the commander of Indian forces, Claude Auchinleck. Mountbatten, however, failed to win over Jinnah, whom he privately referred to as an "evil genius," a "lunatic," and a "psychopathic case."

It soon became clear to the new viceroy that partition was inevitable. Congress finally accepted the principle on April 28, with Nehru believing that Pakistan would not survive more than a few years and would eventually return to the Indian fold. It was a view shared by Mountbatten, who likened Pakistan to a Nissen hut—a temporary structure easy to dismantle. Under pressure from the viceroy, Jinnah had to drop his dream of a contiguous state, settling instead for what he called a "mutilated and moth-eaten" Pakistan consisting of the Muslim-majority districts of West Punjab and East Bengal separated by more than twelve hundred miles of Indian territory. Among those who questioned its viability was R. G. Casey (1890–1976), the governor-general of Bengal, who predicted that the more populous and linguistically and ethnically distinct East Pakistan would eventually break away. His prophecy proved correct. From the ashes of a bloody civil war, the state of Bangladesh would be created in 1971.

On June 4, 1947, the day after the plan for partition was agreed by both parties, Mountbatten told a press conference that the transfer of power "could be about the 15 August," shortening the previous timetable by almost a year. The date, which he later admitted had been plucked out of thin air, left the government with just seventy-three days to make the necessary constitutional military and economic arrangements for independence. By now, Congress had accepted that partition was inevitable. But two major hurdles remained. The first was to convince the hundreds of princes whose states made up a third of the subcontinent to relinquish their power and join either India or Pakistan. The second was to draw up the boundaries of the soon-to-be-independent states. The man given this almost impossible task was London lawyer Cyril

Radcliffe (1899–1977), who had never been to India before, something Jinnah and Nehru both welcomed—his lack of experience was preferable to bias. The majority of princes accepted their fate, but the Hindu, Muslim, and Sikh communities on either side of the soon-to-be demarcated boundaries were bracing for the worst.

Just before midnight on August 15, 1947, a time chosen by astrologers as being auspicious, Jawaharlal Nehru addressed the legislative assembly in New Delhi, declaring: "Long years ago we made a tryst with destiny, and now the time comes when we shall redeem our pledge . . . At the stroke of the midnight hour, when the world sleeps, India will wake to life and freedom." Two days earlier, the Mountbattens had flown to Karachi, where ceremonies marking Pakistan's independence were to take place on August 14. After speeches at the assembly hall, the viceroy sat next to Jinnah, now the first governor-general of Pakistan, in an open-topped borrowed Rolls Royce for a procession through the city. Mountbatten had been told of a plot to assassinate Jinnah and believed his presence would prevent any such attempt by Hindus or Sikhs.

There was no such protection for those caught up in the ethnic bloodletting that was already spinning out of control in newly partitioned districts. Historians are divided on whether hastening the transfer of power avoided a civil war or helped precipitate violence. Killings had begun as early as July, when gangs of Sikhs and Hindus attacked Muslims who had begun migrating westward, fearful that they would be trapped in a nation hostile to their faith. The violence intensified when the final draft of Radcliffe's boundary map was leaked to the League and Congress a week before its official August 16 release date.

Partition, when it came, triggered the largest and, by some estimates, bloodiest forced migration in history. Up to fifteen million Hindus, Muslims, and Sikhs crossed the newly demarcated borders to their promised homes. The brutality that accompanied the settling of scores was medieval, with axes, scythes, swords, spears, and clubs used. Thousands of women were raped, abducted, or mutilated. Recent research puts the death toll at between five hundred thousand and six hundred thousand, divided more or less equally between Muslims and non-Muslims. With the British Army already beginning its withdrawal and Mountbatten ordering intervention only when English nationals were in danger, there was little that local police and military personnel could do. A fifty-thousand-strong boundary force was largely ineffectual, as it was made up of Hindu and Muslim troops not inclined to intervene against their own communities. Despite the massacres, Nehru remarked, "I would rather have every village in India go up in flames than keep a single British soldier in India a moment longer than is necessary."

Absent from the ceremonies marking independence in Delhi was Mahatma Gandhi. He was nine hundred miles away in Calcutta, fasting, spinning, and praying. When government officials asked him for a statement in honor of August 15, he responded that "he had run dry. There is no message at all. If it is bad let it be so." Gandhi's disillusionment related to the partition of the subcontinent, which he had fought so hard to oppose. His presence in Calcutta secured a temporary reprieve to the savagery that had beset the city for more than a year, with Hindus and Muslims marching together to celebrate independence. But what was regarded as the "Calcutta Miracle" lasted for only nine days. When Hindu and

Muslim mobs renewed their attacks, Gandhi resorted, yet again, to fasting. This time, gang leaders came to his bedside and promised to mend their ways, some weeping as they confessed their guilt.

After peace was restored, the Mahatma made his way to Delhi, where rioting was continuing unabated. He set about touring Muslim refugee camps, reassuring their occupants that they had a future in India, and plunged himself into relief work to help traumatized Hindus and Sikhs. In January 1948, Gandhi, who was seventy-eight and suffering the effects of kidney failure, declared he would fast for as long as it took to end the violence. The effect was immediate, with both Hindu and Muslim organizations pledging to work for peace. Groups were formed to repair damaged temples and mosques. The only party to repudiate the peace pledge was the far-right Hindu Mahasabha.

On January 30, 1948, twelve days after Gandhi ended his fast, a Hindu Mahasabha worker arrived at his daily prayer meeting at Birla House in Delhi. As the Mahatma was being helped to the prayer ground by two of his young female assistants, Nathuram Godse pushed his way through the crowd. When he was directly in front of Gandhi, he pulled out a Beretta pistol and fired three shots, killing him almost instantly. The Mahatma's last words were *Hey Ram*. Just a few months before, Gandhi had written: "Even if I am killed, I will not give up repeating the names of Rama and Rahim, which mean to me the same god. With these names on my lips, I will die cheerfully." He had got his wish.

Although he is still revered around the globe for his belief in nonviolent change, Gandhi's legacy continues to divide Indian historians. Sunil Khilnani writes:

> In a society with no history of large-scale collective action, where politics was for most a domain of distant and spectacular power, Gandhi made people believe they could make a difference. He built a movement, shaped a nationalist imagination, and expanded the world's repertoire of dissent, protest and peaceful disagreement.

Professor of Indian history R. C. Majumdar lowers Gandhi's pedestal, insisting he was "lacking in both political wisdom and political strategy." Far from being infallible, he "committed serious blunders, one after another, in pursuit of some utopian ideals and methods which had no basis in reality." The truth, as always, falls somewhere in between.

For all the hagiography surrounding Gandhi, it can be argued that India would have achieved independence without him. As British scholar Judith Brown surmises:

> Far deeper economic and political forces than the leadership of one man were at work loosening the links between Britain and India—forces that had their origins in India, in Britain, and in the wider world economy and the balance of power. Yet his skills and his particular genius marked the nationalist movement and gave it a character unlike that of any other anti-imperial nationalism of the century.

It was now up to Nehru and other political leaders to turn Gandhi's struggle for a free India into reality.

CHAPTER 9

Creating the Nation-State

Mahatma Gandhi's assassination cast a long shadow over the early years of India's independence. The forces of communalism had struck the country at its most vulnerable moment. But Gandhi's vision for a new India proved more resilient than the message of hatred his killers had used to justify their actions. Jawaharlal Nehru was a strong and charismatic leader. Backed by Congress, Asia's largest and effective political organization, he set about erecting the four pillars of the new Indian state: secularism, democracy, socialism, and nonalignment.

The challenges faced by the new nation were extreme. Around eight million refugees had to be fed, housed, and integrated into society. When India conducted the first post-independence census in 1951, the literacy rate was just 16 percent. In rural areas, just 4.9 percent of women could read and write. Life expectancy was thirty-two years, and 47 percent of the rural population lived below the poverty line (the proportion would peak at 64 percent in the mid-1950s). The British may have left India with an enviable network of railways and irrigation canals, but industry accounted for a mere 6.5 percent of national income and employed less than 3 percent of the labor force—a figure that had hardly changed since the beginning of the century. Out of 640,000 villages, just 1,500 had access to electricity. For a population of 360 million in 1951, there were only 735 primary health clinics. India's new leaders also faced the challenge of unifying a heterogenous society divided by language, religion, geography, ethnicity, and, above all, caste: a hierarchical order that was opposed to the idea of political equality. In the northeast, Naga tribals had launched an armed insurrection demanding a separate homeland, and a communist insurgency had taken hold in the Deccan.

The immediate threats to India's survival as a nation came from an unexpected quarter. Just prior to India's independence, the rulers of 562 princely states were given the choice of joining India, throwing their lot in with Pakistan, or remaining independent. Aside from those that found themselves within the borders of the new country of Pakistan, all but three acceded to the Indian Union. Of those that held out, the smallest was Junagadh, on the Kathiawar peninsula in western India. Its canine-obsessed Muslim prince, Nawab Muhammad Mahabat Khan (1900–1959), who spent more than 10 percent of the state's income on the upkeep of the royal kennels, presided over an overwhelmingly Hindu population. On August 15, 1947, the nawab acceded to Pakistan. Threats of Indian military intervention and a popular insurrection by his Hindu subjects caused him to cut his losses. After handing over the administration of his state to India, he fled with four of his favorite hounds to Karachi. India's annulment of Junagadh's accession has never been recognized by Pakistan, which still shows the tiny state as part of its territory on official maps.

A much more serious crisis was brewing in Hyderabad, whose ruler, Nizam Osman Ali Khan (1886–1967), was considered the richest man in the world on account of his vast holdings of land and jewelry. As in Junagadh, the nizam was a Muslim ruling over a majority-Hindu population. Encouraged by Islamic zealots known as Razakars, he declared Hyderabad's independence, something the new Indian government was not prepared to countenance given the state's strategic position, its size (roughly the same as France), and the precedent this would set. Despite the best efforts of Lord Mountbatten, who had remained in India as its first governor-general, Khan refused to back down. His patience exhausted, Nehru decided to settle the matter by force. An Indian army invasion made short work of Hyderabad's poorly equipped forces, which surrendered on September 18, 1948. Jinnah, who died just a few days earlier, had predicted that a hundred million Muslims would rise up if Hyderabad was invaded. There was no uprising but "Operation Polo," the code name for the Indian annexation, left thousands of civilians dead and unleashed a wave of reprisal attacks by Hindus against Muslims.

The state of Jammu and Kashmir presented the most complex conundrum. Its Hindu maharaja, Hari Singh (1895–1961), ruled over a heterogeneous state that shared a border with the new dominions of India and Pakistan. The district of Jammu was predominantly Hindu, while Ladakh in the far east of the state was mainly Buddhist. Only the stunningly beautiful Kashmir valley had a Muslim-majority population. The Maharaja had toyed with the idea of independence as early as July 1946, harboring dreams of making his state "the Switzerland of the East"—independent and neutral. Unlike Junagadh and Hyderabad, the state had a well-organized opposition led by the charismatic Muslim politician Sheikh Abdullah (1905–1982). A close ally of Nehru, he wanted Kashmir to remain part of India.

Singh's choices were stark. He detested Congress as much as it detested him. Joining India would see the end of his feudal autocracy. A similar fate awaited if he joined Pakistan. The question was settled when tribal militias, mainly Pathans from the North-West Frontier Province of Pakistan, started crossing into Kashmir on October 22, 1947. There is still no definitive answer, three quarters of a century later, as to why they invaded and who was helping them. What is certain is that India was caught completely off guard. When the invaders were just fifty miles from Srinagar, the Maharaja sent out an urgent plea for military assistance. Nehru agreed, but the price was Kashmir's accession to India. Hari Singh had no choice but to comply. Within hours of signing the accession agreement, thousands of Indian troops were being airlifted to Srinagar. Having secured the capital, the troops proceeded to retake towns captured by the Pakistani irregulars. Although Kashmir had been saved, its future was still to be negotiated. And hostilities were not at an end. Fighting resumed in 1948 after the winter snows had melted, and better equipped Pakistan-supported forces made significant inroads in the north of the state.

By the time of a hastily brokered United Nations cease-fire in 1948, Pakistan was in possession of the mountains and valleys to the north of the Kashmir valley and to the west. The Line of Control became a de-facto frontier. Nehru agreed to a plebiscite that would allow the Kashmiri people to choose their own future, but this never took place. His failure to honor his promise turned Sheikh Abdullah against the prime minister. For the rest of his life, he would spend more time in jail for advocating separatist views than as a free man. Today, the disputed status of Kashmir remains the subcontinent's most intractable and dangerous political problem.

The Birth of the Indian Republic

Nehru's commitment to secularism was unwavering. Writing in *The Discovery of India*, he insisted it was "entirely misleading to refer to Indian culture as Hindu culture." Guaranteeing the rights of minorities was a central tenet of India's Constitution. Four years in the making, the Constitution came into effect on January 26, 1950, transforming India from a dominion with the British monarch as head of state into a full-fledged republic. The Constitution had 395 articles and eight schedules, making it the longest in the world. The chairman of the drafting committee was B. R. Ambedkar, the country's first law minister and leader of the Untouchables. Supporters of Mahatma Gandhi had advocated a constitution based on locally elected village republics. At the other extreme were those arguing for an American-style presidential system. Both models were rejected in favor of a Westminster model, with a lower chamber, or Lok Sabha, elected on the basis of universal franchise, and an upper chamber, or Rajya Sabha, that acted as a house of review. Its members would be either appointed by the president or indirectly elected by members of the state legislature. A complex system of fiscal federalism governed the collection of taxes.

Disillusioned with the state's failure to abolish untouchability, Ambedkar and thousands of Untouchables converted to Buddhism in a mass ceremony in 1956.

Democracy in Action

India's first national election was held in 1951. All citizens aged over twenty-one, at the time numbering over 170 million, had to be registered despite the lack of identity documents and the fact that 85 percent could not read or write. Elections were to be held simultaneously for 489 seats in the Lok Sabha and another 4,000 in provincial assemblies. The exercise required 56,000 presiding officers and 224,000 police to maintain security at 132,560 polling stations. Political parties were identified by myriad symbols. In Calcutta, stray cows were inscribed with slogans imploring people to vote for Congress—its symbol was two bullocks and a plough. Turnout was just under 46 percent. Congress won by comfortably picking up 364 seats in the Lok Sabha and 45 percent of the vote. The Communist Party of India, the main opposition, could only muster sixteen seats in parliament. By the 2019 general election, the total number of eligible voters (aged eighteen and over) had risen to 911 million. Voter turnout was 67 percent, the highest ever, and the percentage of women voters was a record 68 percent. There were just over one million polling stations, many with electronic voting machines. More than 2.25 million police and paramilitary officers provided security. The BJP won 303 of the 543 seats in the Lok Sabha, while Congress was reduced to fifty-two seats. The total number of women candidates rose from 2.9 percent in the 1957 elections to just under 8 percent in 2019. With just sixty-six women in the Lok Sabha, India ranks 149th out of 193 countries by percentage of women representatives in parliament.

The Constitution enshrined the principles of the separation of powers, equality before the law, freedom of religion, and freedom of expression. Discrimination on the grounds of religion, race, caste, or sex was prohibited. Article 17 abolished Untouchability. While it made no provision for reservations for Muslims or women, the Constitution recommended job quotas for government positions and university places, as well as reserved seats in state legislatures. Its most contentious aspect was the power it gave to the president to impose a state of emergency, suspend the Constitution, and detain anyone perceived to be a threat to the security of the country. A quarter of a century later, Indira Gandhi (1917–1984) took advantage of these powers to trigger a state of national emergency that lasted for nearly two years. The president also has the power to suspend state legislature and impose direct rule from Delhi, a practice that would be used with increasing regularity from the 1980s onward. Although equality was guaranteed by the Constitution, women fared poorly. Child marriage was common, divorce was difficult, and inheritance and property rights were severely limited, as was access to education.

"The Hindu Rate of Growth"

Nehru's economic mantra of self-reliance was socialist in its outlook and implementation. After visiting the Soviet Union in 1927, he was euphoric, declaring, "If the future is full of hope, it is largely because of Soviet Russia and what it has done." The philosophy of Marxism, he wrote in his autobiography, "lightened up many a dark corner of my mind." But he was under no illusion that socialism would not have to be adapted to Indian conditions. While the state would control the commanding heights of the economy, the private sector was allowed to invest in high-priority industries approved by the government. To create a society based on social justice, ceilings were placed on land ownership, and wealthy individuals and corporations were slugged with steep tax rates. The importation of foreign goods was heavily restricted.

Five-year plans set production targets and monitored the country's economic progress. The goal was self-reliance in industry led by a state-controlled public sector that grew to be the world's largest outside the communist bloc. Nehru's "new temples of modern India" consisted of massive steelworks, oil refineries, power stations, cement works, and fertilizer plants. Huge dams were constructed with little regard for their environmental impact or the thousands of poor farmers they inevitably displaced. Highly protectionist tariff barriers that typically saw duties of 350 percent ensured that obsolete, inefficient, and shoddy products proliferated, the most recognizable of which was the Ambassador car.

Based on the Morris Oxford Series III, the Ambassador rolled off the production line from 1956 to 2014 with minimal modifications. According to one reviewer, it "had a steering mechanism with the subtlety of an oxcart, guzzled gas like a sheikh, shook like a guzzler, and yet enjoyed waiting lists of several years at all dealers."

The Ambassador was manufactured by the Birla corporation, one of several high-profile, family-run companies that had risen to prominence under British rule, but now found themselves stymied by regulations. Even if Hindustan Motors, the Birla company that produced the Ambassador, wanted to improve its performance by adding something as basic as power steering, its managers would come up against a wall of bureaucratic hurdles that stifled innovation. All aspects of the manufacturing process, from hiring and firing to building new plants, were regulated by what became known as the "Licence Raj." Foreign-exchange regulations made it nearly impossible to import new technology and equipment. Yet the Birlas could hardly complain. Protected from cheaper and better-made cars in East Asia by high tariff barriers, there was no competition. That left little incentive to improve their products or increase efficiency.

The same applied to the state sector. In the mid-1980s, the Steel Authority of India employed 247,000 people to produce 6.6 million tons of steel, whereas it took only 10,000 South Korean workers to manufacture 15.4 million tons. Adding to the economy's poor performance was lack of investment in ports, roads, railways, power generation, and communications. In the first four decades following independence, India's economy barely moved out of the much-maligned "Hindu rate of growth" of around 3.5 percent, or slightly ahead of an annual population growth rate of 2.5 percent. During the same period, Pakistan managed a 4 percent economic growth rate, while South Korea hit 9 percent. From a per capita income twice the size of India's in 1947, South Korea's grew to be twenty times larger in 1990.

The fourth main pillar of Nehru's vision for the new India was nonalignment. Articulating the policy in 1947, he said that India would not choose the United States over the Soviet

Union "in the hope that some crumbs might fall from their table." With European decolonization, Nehru saw India's independence as part of an Asian resurgence. A nonaligned bloc could act as a stabilizing influence in an increasingly bipolar world. In 1955, Nehru played a leading role in the Bandung Conference in Indonesia, which was attended by representatives from twenty-nine countries and is considered the beginnings of the Non-Aligned Movement. The following year, India concluded a friendship treaty with China based on the principle of noninterference in internal affairs, peaceful coexistence, and territorial integrity.

But Sino-Indian friendship, or "Hindi-Chini Bhai Bhai," came to a crushing end in 1962 when China inflicted a humiliating blow on its southern neighbor by seizing large chunks of territory of what is now the northeastern state of Arunachal Pradesh, and laying claim to the disputed Aksai Chin region to the north of Ladakh. The earlier failure to demarcate the border between the two countries, and India's embrace of exiled Tibetan spiritual leader the Dalai Lama when he fled Chinese oppression in 1959 with thousands of followers, had raised tensions between the two Asian giants. An ill-prepared Indian military was no match for the People's Liberation Army. China's unilateral withdrawal saved India further humiliation, but Nehru would never recover politically. Opposition parties stepped up their attacks on his leadership and his failure to read the early warning signs of Chinese aggression. Congress lost a string of by-elections and regional parties grew in strength.

Nehru's death on May 27, 1964, triggered a brief power struggle within Congress that led to the selection of Lal Bahadur Shastri (1904–1966) as the new prime minister. Believing Shastri was a weak and ineffectual leader, Pakistan's military dictator, Field Marshal Ayub Khan (1907–1974), decided India was vulnerable. Troops disguised as "civilian volunteers" poured across the Line of Control into Indian-administered Kashmir in April 1965, hoping to capture Srinagar and foment a pro-Pakistan uprising in the valley. Srinagar did not fall, and there was no uprising. Shastri responded by ordering the army to take Lahore. A humiliated Khan was forced to sue for peace. His standing forever tarnished, he was overthrown in a popular uprising two years later. For India, the defeat of Pakistan was a sublime moment, coming just three years after its own humiliation at the hands of China. But Shastri had little time to savor it. On January 11, 1966, he died of a heart attack in Tashkent a day after signing the peace accord with Pakistan that formally ended the 1965 war.

This time the party's president, K. Kamaraj (1903–1975), decided to back Nehru's daughter, Indira, who had served as information and broadcasting minister in Shastri's government. Kamaraj and his clique believed that this "dumb doll," as they called her behind her back, could be easily influenced. They were wrong. From her father, Indira had learned the art of political manipulation. She also became a master of political survival. Her first hurdle was addressing the country's dire economic situation, exacerbated by the fallout of the wars with China and Pakistan and a series of monsoon failures (i.e., the monsoon fell far short of its normal rainfall). India's dependence on US food aid and an emergency IMF bailout to keep the economy afloat led her enemies to accuse her of selling India out to foreign interests. Despite clocking roughly 15,000 miles on the campaign trail and speaking at over 160 rallies, Indira failed to stem the rot that was eating away at her party. The 1967 polls saw Congress's majority reduced to 283 out of 520 seats. The main beneficiaries of this decline were communist parties, with forty-two seats, and the far-right Jan Sangh, which picked up thirty-five, as well as regional groupings such as the Akali Dal in Punjab and the DMK in South India. The Nehru magic was fading.

The election result also strengthened the hand of Indira's main rival for prime minister, Morarji Desai (1896–1995), who had the backing of the party's power-

Indira Gandhi became one of the world's most powerful women, but her legacy was tarnished when she declared a state of emergency in 1975.

ful provincial leaders, known as the Syndicate. Indira met the challenge by moving the party's ideology sharply to the left, announcing a program of bank nationalization and scrapping privy purses and other perks enjoyed by India's erstwhile royals, a number of whom had gone into politics and won seats in the Lok Sabha on anti-Congress platforms.

All in the Family

Political dynasties have thrived in South Asia. In Sri Lanka, Sirimavo Bandaranaike (1916–2000) took over from her husband to become the first woman head of state in a democracy. Indira Gandhi in India would be the second. In Pakistan, Benazir Bhutto (1953–2007) stepped into the shoes of her father, Zulfikar Ali Bhutto

(1928–1979), after he was executed by the country's military dictator. In Bangladesh, Sheikh Hasina still dominates politics in the country her father founded. The roots of dynasticism in India go back to 1929, when Motilal Nehru made his son, Jawaharlal, Congress president. Jawaharlal repeated the exercise with his daughter Indira in 1959 (her surname came from her brief marriage to Feroze Gandhi, no relation to the Mahatma). Following her assassination in 1984, the baton passed to her son Rajiv (1944–1991). After his death in 1991, the party reached out to his Italian-born Roman Catholic wife, Sonia (b. 1946). She turned down the offer but went on to become Congress president. Her son Rahul (b. 1970) led the party to its humiliating defeats in the 2014 and 2019 elections.

Indira's populist policies caused a split in Congress. In 1969, she turned on Desai and the Syndicate by forming a breakaway faction known as Congress (Requisitionists), taking the bulk of the party's old guard with her. Internal party elections were abolished and loyalty became the sole qualification for electoral tickets for senior party positions in the center and the states. The party's transition from being a functioning political party to a Nehru family patrimony was complete.

Indira's popularity was about to get a further boost. In 1970, elections were held in West and East Pakistan, ending decades of military rule. The vote highlighted the deep divisions between the country's two wings. In East Pakistan, Sheikh Mujibur Rahman's (1920–1975) Awami League rode to victory on a wave of discontent over the lack of resources being invested by the central government, and in March 1971 he made good his party's election pledge by proclaiming Bangladeshi independence. Pakistan responded by sending tanks into the streets of Dhaka, triggering a civil war. Millions of refugees streamed into West Bengal. In December 1971, the Pakistani air force started shelling Indian airfields, providing India with an excuse to send its troops into East Pakistan. Pakistan responded by invading India's western border. News that the US Seventh Fleet was heading to the Bay of Bengal raised hopes that America would intervene on the side of its ally, Pakistan. But it was too late. On December 16, after a two-week war, India accepted the surrender of ninety-three thousand Pakistani troops in East Pakistan. A ceasefire was ordered on the western front, where India had pushed back Pakistani forces and occupied some five thousand square miles of territory. By unilaterally ending the war, Indira had restored India's pride. The press likened her to Durgā, the tiger-riding Hindu goddess of war. After a millennium of humiliating defeats by Muslim invaders from the West, European colonizers and most recently the Chinese army, Indians could savor victory. Indira was at the height of her power and, according to a Gallup poll, the world's most admired woman. Promising to end poverty, she called an election in March 1971. Her Congress (R) bounded back with 352 seats. The party's other faction, Congress (O), could muster only sixteen. But the halcyon days were not meant to last.

Just two years after winning office, Arab members of the Organization of the Petroleum Exporting Countries cut production and quadrupled the price of oil in retaliation for the Yom Kippur War. Heavily dependent on imported oil, India's economy shuddered to a halt and inflation hit 33 percent per annum. With her unrealistic campaign promise of abolishing

poverty sounding increasingly hollow, Indira took the populist route, ordering a tightening of rules governing large businesses, which now needed permission to expand capacity,
invest in new equipment, or merge with other companies.

Darkness at Midnight

In 1974, India successfully tested a nuclear device in the Thar
Desert, making the country the world's sixth nuclear-armed
power. But if the intention was to win popular support, it
failed miserably. As the country's economic ills started to take
center stage, regional parties such as the Akali Dal and DMK,
communists, far-right Hindu nationalists, and her old foes in
Congress started to rally around the veteran Gandhian socialist Jaya Prakash Narayan (1902–1979). Worse was to come. In
June 1975, the Allahabad High Court ruled on a petition filed
four years earlier and found her guilty of electoral malpractice,
effectively annulling her election to parliament and barring
her from standing for office for six years.

Instead of resigning, Indira forced a compliant president
to proclaim a nationwide state of emergency starting at midnight on June 26, 1975. The Constitution was suspended, hundreds of opposition leaders were arrested, newspaper offices
found their power cut off, and organizations such as the Rash-
triya Swayamsevak Sangh (RSS) were banned. Most estimates
put the number of people detained without trial at around
110,000. Indira defended the state of emergency as being
necessary to "save the country from disruption and collapse."
Rather than an abrogation of democracy, it was an "effort to
safeguard it," she insisted. The opposite was true. The Thirty-
eighth and Thirty-ninth amendments to the Constitution
that were rushed through parliament barred judicial review

of the emergency and removed the Supreme Court's right to challenge the election of a prime minister.

The most egregious excesses of the state of emergency were engineered by Indira's son Sanjay (1946–1980), the leader of the youth wing of the party. Under Sanjay's orders, slums were bulldozed and more than six million people, mostly men, were subjected to a campaign of forced sterilization, fifteen times the number sterilized by the Nazis. Officials who didn't meet their quotas found themselves sacked from their jobs or evicted from their government housing. The campaign set back voluntary family planning efforts by a decade. Salman Rushdie would immortalize Sanjay's "civic beautification campaign" and "The Widow's" (Gandhi's) sterilization drive—as well as many of the upheavals that post-Independence India endured—in his book *Midnight's Children*.

In January 1977, Indira revoked the state of emergency just as abruptly and unexpectedly as it was called. Hubris, rather than any commitment to democracy, was behind the decision. She believed her victory in the upcoming national election was assured and her ruthless pattern of rule could continue under the cloak of democracy. The gamble backfired spectacularly. When the results of the election were announced, Congress had won just 154 seats, its worst performance to date. In the state of Uttar Pradesh, the party's heartland, it lost in every constituency. Her old foe Morarji Desai became prime minister and leader of the Janata Party alliance.

As India's first experiment in coalition government, the Janata alliance was an abject failure. Made up of parties representing socialists, right-wing groups, and farmers, it had no common purpose and soon degenerated into infighting. In late 1979, two of its members who had been sacked by Desai brought down the government in a no-confidence motion. Fresh elections were called for January 1980.

Aged sixty-two and accompanied for the most part by Sanjay, Indira chalked up nearly forty thousand miles in a grueling campaign, addressing two rallies a day and reaching an estimated one hundred million voters. In what would prove one of the most remarkable comebacks in Indian political history, she shook off the taint of the state of emergency and led Congress to a thumping victory, securing an outright majority of 351 in the 524-seat Lok Sabha. With his mother back in office, Sanjay was made Congress General Secretary, prompting speculation that he was being groomed to take over the prime ministership. But on June 23, 1980, shortly after taking off from Delhi's Safdarjung Airport, his new stunt plane crashed, killing him and his copilot instantly. Distraught and lonely, Indira turned to her eldest son, Rajiv, a commercial airline pilot with no experience or interest in politics, to fill the breach. In 1981, he was elected to the Lok Sabha from the family's traditional constituency of Amethi, in Uttar Pradesh.

During the final years of his life, Sanjay had been sponsoring Jarnail Singh Bhindranwale (1947–1984), an itinerant Sikh preacher, to undercut the Akali Dal, the main opposition party in the Punjab. Congress feared that the Akali Dal's demand for a Sikh state within the Indian union would encourage the Balkanization of India by inspiring other ethnoreligious groups to make similar demands. Indira's response was to split Punjab along linguistic lines by creating the Hindi speaking-majority state of Haryana. Rather than pacifying the Akali Dal, the move encouraged hardline secessionists who wanted their own independent homeland.

Instead of being a Congress stooge, Bhindranwale developed a taste for power and became the champion of the demand for a puritanical Sikh state to be known as Khalistan. Inspired by his preachings, Sikh extremists turned against Hindus, murdering innocent civilians as well as members of the security services. Moderate members of the Akali Dal also found themselves targets of Bhindranwale's henchmen. In May 1984, the Sikh preacher and hundreds of his followers barricaded themselves in Amritsar's Golden Temple, Sikhdom's holiest shrine, and began fortifying the sprawling complex with weapons. On June 4, the Indian Army launched Operation Bluestar, sending tanks into the temple compound. After twenty-four hours of fighting, Bhindranwale was dead, as were some five hundred Sikh extremists. The complex was badly damaged and many irreplaceable Sikh scriptures were destroyed.

Threats of reprisals against Indira followed swiftly, mostly from large Sikh communities in Britain, the United States, and Canada. But when a proposal came to remove Sikh bodyguards from her security, she wrote "Aren't we secular?" on the file. On the morning of October 31, 1984, two Sikh officers who had been recently reinstated as her personal bodyguards shot her at point-blank range.

Within forty minutes of All India Radio's announcement that Indira was dead, Rajiv Gandhi was sworn in as prime minister of the largest democracy in the world. His unpreparedness for the job was immediately apparent. Indira's assassination unleashed the worst communal violence since partition as Hindus turned against Sikhs in cities across northern India. In most cases, the police either looked on and refused to intervene or disarmed Sikh-majority neighborhoods to allow mobs to take revenge. Instead of going out into the streets to quell the rioters, some Congress Party leaders encouraged and led the mobs. The state-sponsored violence raged for three days, leaving up to three thousand Sikhs dead, property destroyed, and trust shattered. It would take two weeks for Rajiv to finally acknowledge the bloodshed.

In the December 1984 elections, Congress secured 415 out of 543 seats—the largest mandate of any party in the Republic's history. Asked by a journalist to explain why the party he led had won so convincingly, Rajiv responded, "Mainly because of my mother's death . . . Nobody knew anything about me, so they'd projected on to me. I became the symbol of their hopes."

The Coming of "Mr. Clean"

Courteous and self-effacing, Rajiv started public life as "Mr. Clean," but he lacked his mother's aura. Keeping himself out of the public eye while living a life of privilege had removed him from the real India. One of his favorite slogans, "A computer in every school by the twenty-first century," ignored the fact that most villages were not even connected to electricity. Although he abolished licensing in around thirty industries, the economy barely exceeded the "Hindu rate of growth." Under his mother's leadership, "briefcase politics"—the paying of bribes by businessmen disguised as party donations to secure contracts and permission to operate—had become endemic. As Rajiv admitted on the hundredth-anniversary celebration of the Congress Party in December 1985, "Corruption is not only tolerated but even regarded as the hallmark of our leadership."

Eighteen months later, his words came back to haunt him when Swedish media broke the news that massive kick-backs had been paid to Indian officials at the very top of the

Congress government who were involved in the purchase of Bofors guns from Sweden. The scandal led to the stalling of the reform process. With one eye on the upcoming election, Rajiv turned to populist policies that had worked so well in the past—increasing taxes on luxury goods and introducing a rural employment guarantee scheme.

Despite winning a huge mandate in the 1984 election and kickstarting the economic reform process, Rajiv Gandhi would be remembered for undermining India's secular fabric and failing to rein in corruption.

Rajiv's failure to curb corruption was not the only stain on his administration. More far-reaching was his betrayal of India's secular fabric. Nehru's determination to introduce a common civil code had the backing of Ambedkar, but never saw the light of day because of opposition from India's large Muslim minority. Legislation covering personal law in matters such as marriage secession, guardianship, and alimony was finally introduced for all communities except Muslims in the mid-1950s. In 1985, Muslim traditionalists were infuriated by a Supreme Court ruling that upheld the right of divorcee Shah Bano Begum to claim maintenance beyond the three months specified by Islamic law. But instead of welcoming the court's ruling, which in effect granted equality before the law to Muslim women, Rajiv bowed to hardliners who threatened to remove their community's support for Congress and rushed through a bill that liberated Muslim men from paying maintenance.

The backdown strengthened the hand of Hindu nationalists, who now had a political force that could articulate their voices—the Bharatiya Janata Party (BJP). The party was formed in 1980 as a repackaging of the Jana Sangh, the main post-independence right-wing grouping. In 1984, it won just two seats in the first election it contested, but the BJP was about to see its fortunes improve dramatically. In 1986, a local court approved a petition allowing Hindus to worship at the Babri Masjid (mosque), which was claimed to be the birthplace of the god Ram. When thousands of Muslim protesters took to the streets, Rajiv equivocated, leading the BJP to accuse Congress of using state-enforced secularism to appease Muslims. Stung by the accusations, Rajiv allowed Hindus to lay the foundations of a temple made from thousands of specially consecrated bricks brought from villages all over India inside the Babri Masjid compound.

By the time elections were called in 1989, India's electoral landscape had changed irrevocably. Political formations based on caste in the north and language in the south began attracting substantial support. Meanwhile, religious nationalists stepped into the void left by Congress, pledging to heal Hindu pride by renewing their promise to build the Ram temple. The strategy worked. In the 1989 election, the BJP stormed in with eighty-five seats. Congress saw its majority more than halved.

With no party obtaining an outright majority, a National Front coalition led by the Janata Dal under Vishwanath Pratap Singh (1931–2008) took office. The BJP stayed out of government, preferring instead to support it from the outside. Dependent on the political allegiance he received from so-called "backward castes," Singh decided to implement the Mandal Commission report. The report had been gathering dust for more than twenty years—its recommendation that 27 percent of all government jobs be reserved for "backward" castes, in addition to the 22.5 percent reserved for "scheduled castes and tribes," considered too controversial to touch. The prospect of being shut out of half of all government jobs sparked anger among middle and upper castes. Twelve people immolated themselves in protest, most of them students.

But it was the failure of V. P. Singh's government to work out a compromise over Ayodhya that proved his death knell. In 1990, BJP president L. K. Advani set out from the sacred temple of Somnath in Gujarat on a six-thousand-mile pilgrimage to Ayodhya in a truck decorated to look like Ram's mythical chariot. Fearing an eruption of communal violence, Advani was arrested on the orders of the chief minister of Bihar before he could reach the town. In protest, the BJP withdrew its support for the government. After losing a no-confidence vote, Singh resigned. The door was open for Rajiv, as the head of the largest party in the Lok Sabha, to accept the president's offer and form a government. He refused, deciding instead to give outside support to a breakaway faction of the Janata Dal with only fifty-four members, led by the veteran politician Chandrashekhar (1927–2007). Like its predecessor, this experiment in coalition government was doomed to fail. On March 13, 1991, Chandrashekhar resigned and parliament was dissolved, paving the way for a fatigued electorate to go to the polls for the second time in just fifteen months.

This time the main threat to Rajiv securing a third term in office came not from within India but from outside. In 1987, Sri Lanka's president, J. R. Jayewardene (1906–1996), asked Rajiv to help mediate in his country's long-running and brutal civil war against the Tamil Tigers, who were fighting for a separate

Tamil homeland in the north. Under an agreement brokered between Colombo and New Delhi, an Indian Peace Keeping Force would be sent to the island. Sri Lankan troops would return to their barracks and the Tigers would be persuaded to disarm. Opposed by Sinhalese and Tamil hardliners, the agreement never stood a chance. Rather than being welcomed as peacekeepers, the Indians were soon being viewed as an occupying force. Sri Lanka became India's Vietnam, a battleground that claimed the lives of more than a thousand Indian soldiers by the time Delhi pulled out its troops in early 1990.

The Tamil Tigers got their revenge on May 21, 1991, when a suicide bomber sent by the group assassinated Rajiv Gandhi as he was campaigning in Tamil Nadu. Once again, the question of succession weighed on Congress, whose natural tendency was to enlist Rajiv's grieving widow, Sonia. She emphatically turned down their requests. The party eventually settled on Narasimha Rao, a semi-retired politician from the southern state of Andhra Pradesh. The seventy-year-old Rao was seen as a neutral stopgap leader by Congress powerbrokers, who were already jockeying to step into his shoes as soon as the time was ripe. A pro-Congress sympathy wave allowed the party to scrape together 244 seats in the general election. That left the party about thirty short of a majority, forcing Rao to rely on the support of independents to form government. The BJP now had 120 seats, making it the main opposition party.

Instead of floundering in his new role, Rao surprised India and Congress by proving to be a decisive leader. His first move was to appoint Manmohan Singh (b. 1932), an Oxford-educated former professor of economics and a former governor of the Reserve Bank of India, as finance minister. The collapse of the Soviet Union had robbed India of its major trading partner, and the invasion of Kuwait saw thousands of Indian workers flee the Gulf, drying up the remittances that had sustained the country's foreign cash reserves. The war also caused a spike in oil prices, with the monthly bill for India's petroleum imports jumping 60 percent. Under pressure from the IMF, Rao devalued the rupee twice and announced a drastic austerity project. Singh tore down the "Licence Raj," deregulating industry, removing barriers to foreign investment in thirty-four sectors, including food processing and power generation, and providing tax concessions to private corporations. Tariffs were slashed from 300 to 50 percent. The effects were almost immediate, with industrial production and employment enjoying growth never seen before. By 1996, GDP was sprinting along at 6.2 percent. The Indian tiger had been unleashed, but it was still no match for China.

The Rise of Hindu Majoritarianism

As the leader of a minority government, Rao initially tried to court the BJP and seek a negotiated settlement to the Ayodhya dispute. But hardliners wanting decisive action prevailed. Responding to a call from Hindu leaders for the liberation of the mosque and the establishment of a Rama Rajya, or God's Kingdom, more than a hundred thousand *kar sevaks*, or volunteers, reached Ayodhya on December 6, 1992. Armed with tridents, bows and arrows, axes and hammers, thousands of Hindu fanatics scaled the walls around the Babri Masjid compound and, within hours, the mosque's three domes had been reduced to rubble. Rao responded by dismissing all four BJP state governments, banning Hindu organizations, and placing Advani under arrest once again. Hindu-Muslim riots broke out across India. The commercial capital, Mumbai,

The Babri Masjid was a symbol of the Indian government's determination to protect Muslims and uphold the tradition of the secular state.

suffered the worst of the violence, with at least nine hundred killed, the majority Muslims. Commenting on the destruction of the Babri Masjid, the author and journalist Kapil Komireddi wrote, "The barbarism in Ayodhya contained a self-empowering, even redemptive, message: an ancient civilisation had purged itself of the shame inflicted by history by razing the monument to its subjugation. The past, so many felt, had been avenged."

Rao's administration survived the Ayodhya crisis, but Congress was now well and truly past its peak as a political force. Muslims turned away from the party once it became apparent that the promise to rebuild the mosque would not be honored. Singh's economic reforms had increased inequality, and corruption was rife. The rural poor, traditionally the backbone of Congress support, bore the brunt of rising food prices and cuts in public investment and social programs. When the counting of votes finished in the 1996 election, Congress had suffered its worst defeat, holding on to just 140 seats, compared with the BJP's 160. Incapable of accepting the need to look for new blood, Congress stalwarts anointed Sonia Gandhi as the party's president.

Despite heading the largest grouping in the Lok Sabha, the BJP leader, Atal Bahari Vajpayee (1924–2018), failed to form a government—memories of Ayodhya were still too fresh for most parties to associate themselves with a Hindu nationalist–led administration. A coalition of regional parties calling itself the National Front clung to office for the next two years, until the midterm polls in 1998 saw the BJP boost its numbers sufficiently to attract enough allies to take office. Within weeks of coming to office, it flexed its muscles by detonating three nuclear devices under the Thar Desert in Rajasthan, prompting Pakistan to retaliate by testing five bombs beneath the mountains of Baluchistan a couple of weeks later. Although the BJP had proven its nationalist credentials, the coalition it headed survived for barely a year before a key regional party withdrew its support. The national election of 1999, the fifth in a decade, saw a further erosion of Congress support, with the party holding on to just 114 seats. This time, the BJP had the numbers to cobble together a coalition government that lasted for five years—with Vajpayee at the helm.

A skilled orator and a poet, Vajpayee represented the moderate face of Hindu nationalism. He put on ice three of the party's most contentious goals: building a Ram temple in Ayodhya, adopting a common civil code, and abolishing Kashmir's special status in the Constitution that gave it limited autonomy, a state flag, and certain rights relating to property and other matters. In February 1999, he visited Lahore to inaugurate a new bus service between the two countries. But hopes that the visit might lead to a long-term thaw in relations were dashed when Pakistani troops occupied the strategic heights near Kargil on the Srinagar-to-Leh highway, sparking a mini war. Then in December 2001, Pakistan-supported militants launched a brazen attack on Parliament House in New Delhi, raising tensions dangerously close to another open conflict between the now nuclear-armed nations.

Vajpayee's term as prime minister also saw an alarming spike in communal violence. On February 27, 2002, a train carrying Hindu pilgrims returning from Ayodhya was set on fire when it pulled into Godhra, a town in Gujarat. Fifty-eight people were killed. Despite there being no evidence as to the identity of the attackers or their motivation, Muslims in Godhra and in numerous towns in Gujarat were attacked, leaving an estimated three thousand people dead and more than a hundred thousand displaced.

The attack took place four months after the election of the BJP national secretary, Narendra Modi, as chief minister in Gujarat. The son of a *chai wallah* who made tea on a railway platform, Modi had become a full-time member of the RSS in 1971, a Hindu nationalist paramilitary volunteer organization. A decade and a half later, he joined the BJP, rising rapidly through its ranks and earning a reputation as a highly effective organizer and orator. In 2001, he was selected to replace Keshubhai Patel as the chief minister of Gujarat and to restore the party's declining fortunes in the state.

An investigative team appointed by the Supreme Court found no evidence of Modi's complicity in the violence. Yet critics blamed him for doing too little to stop the bloodshed, much of which was orchestrated by members of his party. According to a Human Rights Watch report, Hindu groups came armed with swords, *trishuls* (three-pronged spears), explosives, and gas cylinders. "They were guided by computer printouts listing the addresses of Muslim families and their properties, information obtained from the Ahmedabad municipal corporation among other sources, and embarked on a murderous rampage confident that the police was [*sic*] with them. In many cases, the police led the charge, using gunfire to kill Muslims who got in the mobs' way."

In the 2004 elections, the BJP's campaign slogan of "India Shining" had begun to look a little tarnished. A return to populist slogans of ending poverty and protecting minorities saw Congress scrape back into power, with former finance minister Manmohan Singh leading the United Progressive Alliance (UPA). Initially, Congress benefited from strong economic growth, averaging over 8 percent, which helped reduce poverty across all groups and regions. In 2007, India joined the trillion-dollar club, the same year as Russia. But the impressive numbers hid a distinctly mediocre story. India's per-capita income of $950 put it in 160th position among 197 countries. By 2010, four hundred million Indians still lived below the poverty line, while the top 1 percent owned half the national wealth. Nearly 45 percent of children under the age of five were malnourished. China's economy was seven times the size of India's and growing.

By the UPA's second term (2009–2014), its shine had also worn off. The coalition was still reeling from the botched response to the 2008 Mumbai terrorist attacks—a four-day-long killing spree by Pakistani militants that left 166 dead. In 2011, a seventy-four-year-old former army officer, Kisan

Baburao "Anna" Hazare, went on a hunger strike in New Delhi in an effort to convince the government to pass his party's anti-corruption bill. His grievances were embraced by millions of middle-class Indians. Instead of reining in "briefcase politics," Singh responded by putting the brakes on the economic reforms and retreating into a vast program of rural benefits and agricultural welfarism.

The Remaking of India

When Manmohan Singh declined to contest the 2014 election, Congress turned to Rajiv Gandhi's son, Rahul, a political novice who had remained all but invisible during his two terms in parliament and had even turned down the offer of a cabinet post. Modi ran a presidential-style campaign that targeted Rahul's privileged upbringing, while cultivating his own reputation for decisiveness and getting things done. Rajiv's failure to stem the anti-Sikh violence in 1984 deprived Rahul of a platform to criticize Modi for his handling of the Gujarat riots of 2002. Instead, Modi trumpeted the success of the "Gujarat model," supposedly based on good governance, rising incomes, and employment. Tapping into a yearning for change, he downplayed the BJP's Hindu nationalist agenda and instead projected the party's market-friendly and pro-liberalization credentials. The RSS mobilized the grassroots, while at the other end of the spectrum, big business started moving its support away from Congress. Among those publicly declaring their backing for Modi's authoritarian methods was Jagdish Bhagwati, professor of economics at Columbia University who told the *Financial Times*: "If people don't exercise authority, nothing gets done. You need someone who is providing a vision of somewhere where you can go."

*Narendra Modi mockingly called Rahul Gandhi a shahzada, or "princeling,"
while highlighting his lower-caste, working-class, self-made-man image.*

A poll of first-time voters in the eighteen-to-twenty-three
age bracket—a massive group of 120 million—found that 42
percent favored Modi. Only 17 percent supported Rahul, who
was twenty years younger than his rival, but as the acclaimed
journalist Rajdeep Sardesai noted, "appeared to speak the language of an older India—of handouts, of entitlements, even
vote banks." The BJP blitzed social media. Holograms of Modi
virtually addressed hundreds of rallies across the country. When
the results came in, the BJP had won 282 seats. All that Congress could muster was forty-four seats and 19.4 percent of the
vote. To add insult to injury, it was fifteen seats short of being
the number required to become official opposition.

The 2014 elections were a watershed moment for India. The
BJP became the first party in thirty years to achieve a parliamentary majority. Only a handful of Muslim candidates were nomi-
nated by the party, and for the first time in India's history there
were no Muslims in the ruling party's parliamentary group in the
Lok Sabha. When Rahul Gandhi tendered his resignation for his
dismal showing in the polls, the Congress old guard rejected it.

Once dismissed as a Brahmin-Bania party—a reference to its support among only high-caste Hindus and the merchant community—the BJP's base had crossed regional and caste boundaries. The only community that did not vote for the party was Muslims. Reflecting on the debacle, historian Ramachandra Guha declared, "The sometimes noble, sometimes ignoble 'structure of renown' erected by Motilal Nehru and his descendants is now merely a heap of rubble."

The 2019 elections saw further gains for the BJP, with its vote share rising from 31 percent to 37.4 percent and its tally of seats hitting 303 seats. This was despite an alarming rise in religiously motivated violence directed at minorities and shocking sexual crimes against women. Voters also shrugged off the economic hardship caused by the shock November 2016 decision to demonetize 500- and 1,000-rupee notes, rendering 86 percent of the country's currency in circulation worthless, ostensibly to crack down on corruption.

Armed with its strongest-ever mandate, the BJP went forward with implementing its long-standing commitment to revoke Article 370 of the Constitution that guaranteed a degree of autonomy for Jammu and Kashmir. The article allowed the state its own constitution, a separate flag, and its own penal code that included laws barring outsiders from purchasing land. The government also moved a bill dividing Jammu and Kashmir, with the Buddhist-majority Ladakh region becoming a separate union territory. Abrogating Article 370, the government argued, would help end violence and militancy and integrate Kashmir into the Indian mainstream by boosting the region's struggling economy through increased investment. Critics charged the BJP with acting unconstitutionally and wanting to change the demographic character of the Muslim-majority region. Protests in Kashmir against the abrogation led to a months-long communications blackout affecting phone and internet services.

No matter how the 2019 election is analyzed, there is no question that the BJP's rise to power is an aberration. Nearly twenty years of often rocky experiments with multiparty coalition government had come to an end. But the size of Modi's victory also raised fears of "democratic dictatorship" or a version of "bureaucratic authoritarianism" taking hold of the political landscape, particularly as it rested on a highly personalized leadership.

The Indian electorate's acceptance of a shift toward a more hegemonic style of politics is borne out by a 2017 Pew Research Center report, which found support for autocratic rule higher in India than in any other nation surveyed. A majority (55 percent) of Indians backed a governing system in which a strong leader can make decisions without interference from parliament or the courts, while 53 percent supported military rule. There was also majority support for experts,

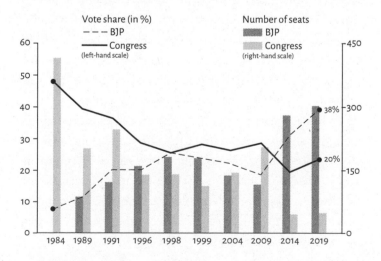

rather than elected officials, running the country on the basis of what they thought was best for the nation. In today's India, China is increasingly being seen as the model for countries wanting to lift themselves out of poverty and to become economic powerhouses thanks to the strong hand of their rulers.

The increasingly strident majoritarian tone of the BJP government is unsettling for many Indians, not just its vast Muslim minority. But democracy's gift to India has been a strong and resilient civil society and a safety valve that provides an outlet for frustration and anger. Indians take their democratic rights seriously, punishing governments that don't perform to expectations. The BJP has also lost all but a handful of state elections it has contested since 2017. In the winter of 2019–2020, thousands of people took part in a nationwide protest against the passing of the *Citizenship Amendment Act*. The Act provided a fast track to citizenship for refugees of all faiths fleeing to India from Afghanistan, Pakistan, and Bangladesh—except Muslims. A year later, an estimated 250 million people went on strike in support of farmers who had marched on the Indian capital in protest against government moves to deregulate the agricultural sector, making it the single largest protest in history. In November 2020, Modi bowed to the farmers' demands and repealed three contentious farm laws that would have removed agricultural subsidies and price regulation on crops.

India's economic reforms have unleashed expectations among young Indians aspiring to a better education, job security, access to affordable housing, and a safe environment in which to raise their families. While the reforms that began in the early 1990s are irreversible, the farmers' protest shows how difficult it will be to widen them progressively without unleashing widescale unrest.

CHAPTER 10

A "New India"?

When viewed against the almost five millennia that have elapsed since the beginnings of the Harappān civilization, India's existence as an independent nation is an insignificant blip. Even two centuries of colonial rule counts for little more than a footnote in this broad historical sweep. The Mauryan, Gupta, and Mughal empires still come out in front in longevity—some would even say in glory. No one can argue with India's achievements during these golden ages, whether in the fields of philosophy or literature, mathematics or medicine, architecture or the arts.

As India looks beyond the seventy-fifth anniversary of its independence in 2022, the burden of history and the desire to restore this past glory is weighing heavily on its politics and society. In the early 1700s, India was the world's largest economy. By the time the British left, India's share of global economic output had dropped to less than 4 percent. Newly independent India was synonymous with famine and deprivation. Despite the progress that has been made since then, India has yet to shake off these stereotypes or live up to its full potential.

For the first time in three hundred years, India's main strategic and economic rival, China, is tantalizingly close to turning the tables on the dominance of the West. India sees its rightful place as being alongside China in reasserting its own pre-colonial status. By certain measures, India is inching up the global rankings. Even considering the impact of the COVID-19 pandemic, it is on track to surpass Japan to become the world's third-largest economy before the end of the decade. In April 2023, it overtook China to become the world's most populous country. It is also expected to retain its third-place position for military spending. But by almost every calculation aside from population, China is far ahead, commanding around 15 percent of the thirty-two-trillion-dollar global trade in goods and services (2022 figures), compared to India's 2 percent, and attracting the bulk of foreign investment going into Asia. China has successfully deployed its Belt and Road Initiative in most of India's neighbors, projecting itself further into the Indian Ocean region and intruding into New Delhi's strongest sphere of influence.

With India's political landscape firmly dominated by the BJP, the discussion around righting the wrongs of the past is dominating the political narrative. Executive posts in once politically neutral institutions such as universities, scientific and cultural institutions are being filled with government appointees. Histories and school curriculums are being rewritten. Opposition to "love jihad," the claim that any marriage between a Muslim man and a Hindu woman is a form of forced conversion, has led to laws that outlaw intermarriage being introduced in states such as Uttar Pradesh, where the *Ghar Wapsi* or homecoming movement that seeks to reconvert Christians and Muslims to the Hindu fold is growing. Far worse has been the recent spate of lynching of Muslims on suspicion of consuming beef or for merely being in the wrong place at the wrong time, with beatings and abuse being aired on social media drawing little or no condemnation from the government.

Critics of the BJP, both domestic and foreign, are also firmly in the party's sights. In early 2023, income tax officials raided the offices of the BBC in New Delhi to investigate alleged financial irregularities. The raid came shortly after the broadcaster aired a documentary on Modi's involvement in the 2002 Gujarat violence. The documentary was banned in India and police raided campuses where students who defied the ban by watching it on their phones and at private screenings were arrested. Citing the "increasing harassment of journalists, nongovernmental organizations, and other government critics" under Modi and the ongoing social and economic marginalization of Muslims, untouchables, and tribal groups such as Freedom House scored India's democratic ranking as "partly free" for the third year in a row in 2023.

Although his party holds less than 10 percent of the seats in the Lok Sabha and continues to perform badly in state assembly elections, Rahul Gandhi has worked hard to revive the Congress Party's electoral fortunes ahead of the 2024 general election. In late 2022, he undertook a 2,218-mile trek from the southernmost tip of India to Srinagar, traversing a dozen states in an attempt to reengage with voters. He followed up his campaign with trenchant attacks on Modi's links with Gautam Adani. The Gujarati-born industrialist was ranked the world's third-richest person before 125 billion dollars were wiped off his net worth following a scathing January 2023 report by short-seller Hindenberg that accused his group of "brazen stock manipulation and accounting fraud." In what critics saw as a politically motivated court ruling, Rahul was shortly afterward stripped of his parliamentary seat after being convicted of defaming the prime minister in a 2019 campaign trail remark. Whether the ruling can be turned to Congress's advantage by galvanizing and uniting the disparate and badly divided opposition parties remains to be seen.

No other event in post-Independence India has thrown such a harsh light on India's failure of governance, the pitiful state of its health services, and the plight of workers in the informal sector as the COVID-19 pandemic. Prior to the pandemic, India took pride in being the largest supplier of generic medicines in the world. As countries scrambled to manufacture COVID-19 vaccines, India touted itself as the nation that would "save humanity from a big disaster." In February 2021, the BJP passed a resolution proclaiming that "the able, sensible, committed and visionary leadership of Prime Minister Modi" had defeated COVID-19. Two months later, India became the global epicenter of the virus. Mass gatherings at the Kumbh Mela religious festival in Haridwar and political rallies during state elections exploded into super-spreader events. Images of relatives begging for oxygen to save their loved ones, of funeral pyres being lit in parking lots as crematoriums ran out of space, and of the bloated bodies of COVID-19 victims floating down the Ganges will haunt the world's perceptions of India for many years to come.

More than anything, the pandemic highlighted the gap between government promises and performance. By one estimate, COVID-induced lockdowns saw an additional 230 million individuals fall below the national poverty line. Half of all women working in the formal and informal sectors lost their jobs. During the 2020/21 financial year, the economy shrank by 7.3 percent, the largest contraction in the country's history. Even Modi's staunchest supporters accused him of hubris and complacency. A once-compliant media stationed reporters outside hospitals and morgues and found evidence that rates of COVID-19 infections and deaths were up to ten times higher than revealed in official statistics. A concerted vaccination drive starting in the second half of 2021 helped stem the pandemic, but at the expense of other sectors of the country's creaking health system.

Devastating though its consequences have been, the COVID-19 pandemic is unlikely to stall the entrenched drift to the right in Indian politics. A Pew Research Center poll published in 2021 found that while a large majority of Indians viewed respect for other religions as an important part of being Indian, they displayed a high desire for religious segregation, especially when it came to marriage and accepting people of certain faiths as neighbors. This innate conservatism, combined with the lack of a coherent political opposition, will continue to work in favor of the BJP and its allies.

Monikers such as the "New India" and the "Second Republic" are entering mainstream discourse as decades of secular nationalism based on cultural pluralism are being replaced by cultural nationalism or Hindutva based on the majoritarian religion, Hinduism. But as political strategist Prasant Kishor points out, Modi would not be the most popular and powerful prime minister in recent memory by appealing to Hindutva alone. The two other planks of his success have been revitalizing India's welfare state and making nationalism central to his platform. Modi's pledge to restore India's rightful place in the world and make his supporters proud to be Indian has been central to his messaging since 2014.

India's refusal to condemn Russia's invasion of Ukraine reflects this more muscular nationalism, though there are other, more pragmatic factors at play, such as its dependency on Russian defense equipment and its appetite for cheap oil (in the twelve months following the invasion, imports of crude from Russia rose thirty-three times). India is also bargaining on the West's perception that it is indispensable in countering the rise of China, a strategy that has so far worked.

While the tensions between nuclear-armed India and Pakistan, aggravated by the Kashmir question and state sponsorship of terrorism, still give policymakers sleepless nights, it is the stand-off between New Delhi and Beijing that is now being labeled as the "most dangerous great-power relationship in the world." A toxic mix of nationalist tendencies, decades-long unresolved territorial disputes, misperceptions of each other's foreign policy goals, and mistrust as to their intentions are fueling dangerous new rivalries. In June 2020, at least twenty Indian soldiers died in hand-to-hand fighting in the Galwan Valley in eastern Ladakh. They were the first deaths on the Line of Actual Control, as the de-facto border between the two countries is known, in more than half a century. Had it not been for bilateral agreements that prohibit the use of weapons to resolve border disputes, the death toll could have been much higher. Following the clashes, both countries expanded their military deployments on the border, backing them up with new infrastructure to resupply and reinforce them.

What was viewed as Chinese aggression spurred a newfound enthusiasm on India's part to embrace the Quadrilateral Security Dialogue. Known as the Quad, it brings together India, the United States, Japan, and Australia in a joint effort to counterbalance Beijing's influence in the Indo-Pacific. So far, the other Quad members have tolerated India's swing to

Russia, hoping that Delhi can use its open channels of dialogue with Moscow to bring about an end to the war. India's awareness of the risks of aligning itself too closely with Russia has led to a greater focus on diversification and indigenization of its defense needs.

The postcolonial period may have been a mere postscript in India's long and eventful history, but it is one of which its people can be proud. In 1931, the average Indian could expect to live to the age of twenty-seven. The challenges of feeding its large population were such that Mahatma Gandhi once said, "If God were to appear in India, He would have to take the form of a loaf of bread." Since Independence, the rate of extreme poverty in India has fallen to 21 percent, and infant mortality has more than halved in the past two decades. In 2021, life expectancy was just shy of seventy years. According to the McKinsey Global Institute, the ranks of the middle class will have increased tenfold, from 50 million in 2005 to more than to 550 million in 2025. By the middle of the next decade, India will have more English speakers than the United States, giving it an enormous advantage in the global labor market.

Despite these achievements, the challenges for India, no matter where one looks, remain enormous. A 2020 UNICEF report found that 38.4 percent of children are stunted due to malnutrition, and only 42.5 percent in third grade can read a first-grade text. India is among the few countries in the world where the mortality rate among under-five-year-olds is worse for girls than boys, largely due to cultural factors that see males receiving better treatment. India's ratio of 914 girls born for every 1,000 boys is also one of the worst in the world. Despite laws against the use of prenatal diagnostic techniques for sex detection, the practice of gender-biased sex selection is widespread.

Based on demographic trends, India will need to generate a million jobs a year in the non-farm sector to absorb the sixty million new workers who will enter the economy by 2030. To get to the 8 to 8.5 percent growth per annum required to generate this level of employment, India will have to invest heavily in creating globally competitive manufacturing hubs, further capitalizing on its advantages in areas such as IT and digital services, medical and care-based products, and high-value tourism. But these service industries can only absorb a fraction of the working-age population. There is much-needed investment in manufacturing. Rather than taking advantage of the growing foreign investor disenchantment with China over its tough COVID-19 policies, growing political repression, and increasingly aggressive foreign policy, India is still perceived as a country where the government favors "national champions" such as the Adani Group and is prone to bowing to domestic pressures and changing policies that render investments unprofitable.

Most of the jobs needed will have to be generated in mushrooming urban conglomerates, where a lack of planning and investment has left millions lacking in basic amenities such as power, water, and sanitation. Seventeen of the twenty fastest-growing cities globally between 2019 and 2035 will be from India, according to an Oxford Economics Global Cities report. High levels of pollution and congestion have already made many of these cities almost unlivable. In 2020, India had twenty-one of the thirty most polluted cities in the world, with New Delhi topping the list. India is also home to several of the world's most polluted rivers, including the sacred Ganges. Up to 40 percent of the population may not have access to clean drinking water by 2030.

Yet India also has the world's largest tertiary-age (eighteen to twenty-two) population. This is projected to peak at 126 million in 2026, before stabilizing at 118 million by 2035. If quality educational opportunities can be found for these young adults, the pool of skilled workers will be enormous. The hurdles are significant: Indian enrollment in higher education (27 percent) lags far behind countries such as China (43 percent). A staggering seven hundred new universities will be needed to satisfy demand.

On the plus side, India's strongly federalist polity has allowed state governments to introduce their own reform agendas to attract investment and create jobs, with southern states such as Tamil Nadu, Karnataka, and Kerala leading the way. India still outflanks its competitors in outsourced offshore software development and there is little doubt that its global dominance will continue as outsourcing and AI becomes increasingly ubiquitous. Even in this sector, however, its performance is patchy. While Indian Institutes of Technology retain their Ivy League reputation, the rest of the IT education sector lags behind. About one third of Indians securing IT jobs are self-taught and a majority of graduates hired by tech companies need retraining. New Delhi also lags behind Beijing in research and development spending, investing just 1 percent of GDP in the sector compared with China's 2 percent.

Every Vote Still Counts

India's proudest achievement has been, without doubt, its almost unbroken record as a democracy. When India finally achieved independence in 1947, many foreign commentators believed that the country would not survive: linguistic and regional differences would make Balkanization inevitable; caste was alien to the concept of equality and therefore democracy, while high levels of illiteracy were at odds with political expression.

India's transition from colony to a modern functioning republic has not been perfect—continuing high levels of corruption, state repression in Kashmir, and growing inequality are some of its most glaring failures. Yet over more than seven decades it has successfully conducted seventeen general elections and hundreds of state polls, with participation rates that regularly outstrip that of the world's next largest democratic nation, the United States. A free and vibrant press and a strong civil society keep a check on the inevitable lapses of its political class. As the eminent writer Ved Mehta noted, India's democratic tradition has served as "a safety valve for every kind of national, religious, and caste rivalry." Among its more impressive outcomes was the election of an Untouchable woman, Mayawati, as chief minister of India's most populous state, Uttar Pradesh, on four occasions, most recently from 2007 to 2012.

But as the Indian-born economist and Nobel Laureate Amartya Sen warns:

> It is not enough to continue to have systematic elections, safeguard political liberties and civil rights, and guarantee free speech and an open media. Nor is it adequate to eliminate famine, or to reduce the lead of China on longevity and survival. A more vigorous—and vocal—use of democratic participation can do much more in India than it has already achieved.

Sen sees India deriving its strength from its ability to learn from elsewhere, transform ideas and make them its own. The ubiquity of the chili pepper, which was brought to India by the Portuguese and is now a fundamental part of Indian cooking, is an example. He also believes that India's "argumentative tradition," as he calls it, based on public reasoning, is the country's best defense against authoritarian tendencies and growing inequalities.

What India has lost, and what will be hardest to restore, is the state's commitment to secularism. When Lal Bahadur Shastri—India's second prime minister, serving from 1964 to 1966—was asked by a journalist to talk about his faith, he responded, "One should not discuss one's religion in public." He was partly taking his cue from Nehru, an avowed atheist. Today, Nehru's Congress Party, once the champion and protector of secularism, openly identifies itself with causes such as building a Ram temple in Ayodhya, to win back the voters it lost to the BJP juggernaut.

In recent decades, notions of India as a historical entity, a people, and a civilization have become highly politicized. Hindu nationalists refer to India as *Bharat Varsha*, the ancient Sanskrit name for a Hindu homeland that stretches from the "Indus to the Seas." The evidence for charting India's history is no longer found in the archaeological record or genetic DNA but in mythological epics such as the *Mahābhārata*. India's "real heritage" is contained in even older texts such as the Vedas. "The central battle in Indian civilization today is between those who acknowledge that, as a result of India's historical experience, our culture is as diverse as it is vast, and those who have presumptuously taken it upon themselves to define, in ever narrower terms, what and who is 'truly'

Indian," writes Indian author and Congress politician Shashi Tharoor. For all the talk of religious tolerance, members of the country's large Muslim minority remain conspicuously absent from senior positions in public institutions such as the armed forces, the police, courts, universities, and the media.

Despite the vast base the BJP can draw on through organizations such as the RSS, and the lack of viable political alternatives, there is nothing inevitable about India's drift toward majoritarianism. Democratic legitimacy is crucial to the party, and while its majoritarian impulses threaten liberalism, they have yet to undermine democracy. As the noted political scientist Sumit Ganguly argues:

> The sheer cultural, linguistic, and ethnic variety of the country will not be easily steamrolled. India's inherent diversity will stand in the way of forging a regime that embraces illiberalism. Indeed, it can be argued that India has endured as a working, if chaotic, state precisely because of its commitment (even if flawed and partial) to liberal democracy.

Ultimately, India's present and its future lie not in the hands of its politicians or its priests, but in those of its people: the rural poor who are prepared to save every rupee they can to invest in their children's education; the restless youth who aspire to a better quality of life; the vibrant middle class that is increasingly demanding accountability from elected officials; the dynamic diaspora that is showcasing India's talent to the world.

The Indian experiment is at once inspirational and flawed. But as a civilization, India has shown remarkable resilience, tackling challenges such as growing inequality and authoritarianism and providing a model to the world. Visionary leaders and thinkers will emerge who can unite their country's diverse communities and ensure that the benefits of social and economic progress are spread equitably and sustainably. India has produced such individuals in the past, from Aśoka to Gandhi, Kauṭilya to Tagore. As the world's oldest continuous civilization, India has much to draw on, and even more to offer the world. If its billion-plus citizens are given the chance to achieve their full potential, its greatest moments are yet to come.

Further Reading

Almost as difficult as condensing India's history into nine short chapters is the task of selecting a list of further reading. For introductory texts on India's history, it's hard to go past the two volumes of *The Wonder That Was India* (Picador, 1954); A. L. Basham covers pre-Muslim India up to 1200, while S. A. A. Rizvi surveys the period from 1200 to 1700. John Keay's highly readable *India: A History* (Grove Press, 2010) encompasses the entire span of Indian history until the 1990s. Other worthwhile introductory texts include Thomas R. Trautmann's *India: Brief History of a Civilization* (Oxford University Press, 2011) and Jawaharlal Nehru's *The Discovery of India* (Penguin Modern Classics, 2004), which was written while he was in jail. Though out of print, R. C. Majumdar's eleven-volume *The History and Culture of the Indian People* (Bharatiya Vidya Bhavan, 1977) is outstanding in its detail. Sunil Khilnani's *Incarnations: A History of India in Fifty Lives* (Farrar, Straus and Giroux, 2016) examines the broad sweep of Indian history though biographical sketches of key individuals. *The Argumentative Indian: Writings on Indian History, Culture and Identity* by Nobel Prize–winning economist Amartya Sen (Picador, 2006) narrates how history has shaped India's cultural identity.

The chapter "Lost Civilizations" draws on Romila Thapar's *The Penguin History of Early India: From the Origins to AD 1300* (Penguin Books India, 2003), Tony Joseph's *Early Indians: The Story of Our Ancestors and Where We Came From* (Juggernaut Books, 2018), and Neil MacGregor's *A History of the World in 100 Objects* (Penguin Books, 2010). *The Indus Civilization* by Mortimer Wheeler (Cambridge University Press, 1953) remains a classic on the Harappān period. Sources for Vedic India include Wendy Doniger's *The Hindus: An Alternative History* (Penguin, 2009)—a controversial but accessible overview of Hinduism—as well as Diana L. Eck's *India: A Sacred Geography* (Three Rivers Press, 2012) and René Grousset's *The Civilizations of the East:*

India (Knopf, 1931). Primary source texts include Kautilya's *Arthashas-tra*, composed between the third century BCE and the third century CE.

The chapter "Religious Revolutionaries" cites material from Andrew Skilton's *A Concise History of Buddhism* (Windhorse Publications, 1994), A. L. Basham's *A Cultural History of India* (Clarendon Press, 1975), and Jeffrey D. Long's *Jainism: An Introduction* (I.B. Tauris, 2009). Michael Wood's *In the Footsteps of Alexander the Great: A Journey from Greece to Asia* (University of California Press, 1997) provides a general introduction to the Hellenistic period in India.

Vincent A. Smith's classic work *The Early History of India* (third edition; Atlantic Publishers & Dist., 1999) and D. D. Kosambi's *An Introduction to the Study of Indian History* (Popular Prakashan, 1956) are invaluable sources for the Gupta period and subsequent ruling dynasties covered in the chapter "The Classical Age."

"The Coming of Islam" draws on a wealth of primary source material that has been reprinted in several books including Alberuni's *Book of India* (1910) and Sir Henry Miers Elliot's eight-volume *The History of India, as Told by Its Own Historians* (1867–77). The observations on how the caste system was a contributing factor in facilitating the Muslim invasions are from Arnold J. Toynbee, *A Study of History: Abridgement of Volumes I–VII by D. C. Somervell* (Oxford University Press, 1987). Further recommended readings include André Wink's *Al-Hind: The Making of the Indo-Islamic World* (Brill Academic Publishers, 1990), Abraham Eraly's *The Age of Wrath: A History of the Delhi Sultanate* (Penguin Books, 2014), and Richard M. Eaton's *India in the Persianate Age* (Penguin Books, 2019), which forensically covers the Islamic period up to the eighteenth century.

Scholars studying the Mughal period can avail a wealth of autobiographies and court-related records as well as accounts by European travelers. This chapter draws several of these, including *The Baburnama: Memoirs of Babur, Prince and Emperor* (Modern Library Classics, 2002) and the sixteenth-century texts *A'in-i-Akbari*, or "Constitution of Akbar," and *Akbarnama*, or "History of Akbar." Accounts by Europeans include François Bernier's *Travels in the Mogul Empire AD 1656–1668* (Atlantic Publishers & Dist., 1990; originally published in 1671) and Jean-Baptiste Tavernier's two-volume *Travels in India* (1676). Among the outstanding works on Mughal India are Abraham Eraly's *Emperors of the Peacock Throne: The Saga of the Great Mughals* (Penguin Books, 1997), Bamber Gascoigne's *The Great Moghuls* (Harper & Row, 1971),

Harbans Mukhia's *The Mughals of India* (Wiley-Blackwell, 2004), and John F. Richards's *Power, Administration, and Finance in Mughal India* (Routledge, 1993). The last of the great Mughals features in Audrey Truschke's *Aurangzeb: The Life and Legacy of India's Most Controversial King* (Stanford University Press, 2017). Truschke's *Culture of Encounters: Sanskrit at the Mughal Court* (Columbia University Press, 2016) is also outstanding. Robert Sewell's *A Forgotten Empire: Vijayanagar* (1900) remains the standard source on this dynasty more than a century after its first publication.

The chapter "Merchants and Mercenaries" draws on several notable works, including William Dalrymple's *White Moghuls: Love and Betrayal in Eighteenth-Century India* (Penguin Books, 2002); *The Anarchy: The East India Company, Corporate Violence, and the Pillage of an Empire* (Bloomsbury, 2019); and *Return of a King: The Battle for Afghanistan, 1839–42* (Vintage, 2013)—the latter documenting the disastrous First Anglo-Afghan War. Also recommended for students of the East India Company's rise and fall are Nick Robins's *The Corporation That Changed the World: How the East India Company Shaped the Modern Multinational* (Pluto Press, 2012) and Nicholas B. Dirks's *The Scandal of Empire: India and the Creation of Imperial Britain* (Belknap Press, 2008). *Late Victorian Holocausts: El Niño Famines and the Making of the Third World* by Mike Davis (Verso, 2000) provides socioeconomic perspective of nineteenth-century India. *Inglorious Empire: What the British Did to India* by Shashi Tharoor (C. Hurst & Co., 2017) is a polemical treatise on the cost of colonialism. David Gilmour's *The British in India: A Social History of the Raj* (Farrar, Straus and Giroux, 2018) and Charles Allen's *Plain Tales from the Raj* (Futura Publications, 1974) detail European society in the colonial period.

Few periods of Indian history have been covered as comprehensively as the Rebellion of 1857. "The Lighting of the Fuse" draws on several classics, including Saul David's *The Indian Mutiny: 1857* (Viking, 2002), Christopher Hibbert's *Great Mutiny: India 1857* (Penguin Books, 1980), and William Dalrymple's *The Last Mughal: The Fall of a Dynasty: Delhi, 1857* (Vintage, 2008). The period preceding the Mutiny draws on Subrata Dasgupta's *Awakening: The Story of the Bengal Renaissance* (Random House India, 2010), while the infamous "Minute on Education" can be found in Thomas Babington Macaulay's *Essays, Critical and Miscellaneous* (1841). For an Indian analysis written shortly after the rebellion, see *From Sepoy to Subedar: Being the Life and*

Adventures of Subedar Sita Ram, a Native Officer of the Bengal Army, Written and Related by Himself (Routledge, 2018).

Biographies of individuals associated with India's struggle for independence include Ramachandra Guha's *Gandhi Before India* (Knopf, 2013) as well as Stanley Wolpert's *Nehru: A Tryst with Destiny* (Oxford University Press, 1996) and *Gandhi's Passion: The Life and Legacy of Mahatma* (Oxford University Press, 2001). Other works on India's best-known historical figure include Judith M. Brown's *Gandhi: Prisoner of Hope* (Yale University Press, 1989) and Gandhi's own autobiography, *The Story of My Experiments with Truth* (Dover Publications, 1983; originally published in 1927). Recommended books on the transfer of power include *Indian Summer: The Secret History of the End of an Empire* by Alex von Tunzleman (Henry Holt & Co., 2008) and *Freedom at Midnight: The Epic Drama of India's Struggle for Independence* by Larry Collins and Dominique Lapierre (second edition; HarperCollins, 1997). Khushwant Singh's *Train to Pakistan* (Grove Press, 1956) remains the best historical novel on the period.

For an overview of independent India, it is impossible to ignore Ramachandra Guha's *India After Gandhi: The History of the World's Largest Democracy* (HarperCollins, 2007). Christophe Jaffrelot is an authority on the rise of Hindu nationalism; his books include *Modi's India: Hindu Nationalism and the Rise of Ethnic Democracy* (Princeton University Press, 2021) and *Majoritarian State: How Hindu Nationalism Is Changing India* (Oxford University Press, 2019). Katherine Frank's *Indira: The Life of Indira Nehru Gandhi* (revised edition; Houghton Mifflin Co., 2002) is a compelling biography of the world's second elected female leader, while Coomi Kapoor's *The Emergency: A Personal History* (Penguin Books, 2016) details Gandhi's suspension of democracy. Books on the Indian economy include Edward Luce's *In Spite of the Gods* (Anchor Books, 2008), John Elliott's *Implosion: India's Tryst with Reality* (HarperCollins, 2014), and James Crabtree's *The Billionaire Raj: A Journey Through India's New Gilded Age* (Tim Duggan Books, 2018). K. S. Komireddi's *Malevolent Republic: A Short History of the New India* (C. Hurst & Co., 2019) is a stinging critique of contemporary politics. Katherine Boo's *Behind the Beautiful Forevers: Life, Death, and Hope in a Mumbai Undercity* (Random House, 2012) and Sonia Faleiro's *The Good Girls: An Ordinary Killing* (Grove Press, 2021) provide forensic insights into the lives of India's urban and rural poor with a particular focus on the plight of women.

Image Credits

etching by François Balthazar Solvyns, 1799, CC BY 4.0; p. 154: Benjamin West—British Library, Public domain, via Wikipedia Commons; p. 159: Victoria and Albert Museum, CC BY-SA 3.0; p. 166: Copyright unknown, "Charmers of Serpents," *The Penny Magazine*, February 9, 1833, 49, via reynolds-news.com/2021/07/18/victorian-snakes/#_ ftnref13; p. 168: India Post, Government of India—[1] [2], GODL-India, via Wikipedia Commons; p. 172: Elizabeth Thompson, Scanned copy of the painting in the Tate Gallery, Public domain, via Wikipedia Commons; p. 178: Artist unknown, via amarchitrakatha.com; p. 185: Willoughby Wallace Hooper, pictured dated 1876–78, Wellcome Library Image Catalogue, WW Hooper Group of Emaciated Young Men, India Famine 1876–78, Public domain, via Wikipedia Commons; p. 190: George Grantham Bain Collection (Library of Congress). This image is available from the United States Library of Congress's Prints and Photographs division under the digital ID ggbain.16113, Public domain, via Wikipedia Commons; p. 198: Kanu Gandhi—gandhiserve.org, Public domain, via Wikipedia Commons; p. 203: Unknown author—[1] [2], a very similar image published in Muhammad Ali Jinnah: *A Political Study by Matlubul Hassan Saiyid* (Lahore: Shaikh Muhammad Ashraf, 1945), frontispiece. Copyright expired 1995. First Time People in Pakistan, Public domain, via Wikipedia Commons; p. 204: Yann (talk), Scanned by Yann (talk), Public domain, via Wikipedia Commons; p. 207: Royroydeb, Anonymous, Public domain, via Wikipedia Commons; p. 224: Unknown author, outlookindia.com/printarticle. aspx?290562, Public domain, via Wikipedia Commons; p. 227: By Tatiraju.rishabh at English Wikipedia, CC BY 3.0; p. 231: U.S. News & World Report photographer Warren K. Leffler. This image is available from the United States Library of Congress's Prints and Photographs division under the digital ID cph.3c34157, Public domain, via Wikipedia Commons; p. 239: Bart Molendijk / Anefo, Nationaal Archief, CC BY-SA 3.0 nl; p. 244: Ayman Aumi, CC BY-SA 4.0; p. 249: Naveenpf—File:ABD 0165.JPG, File:Rahul Gandhi in Ernakulam, Kerala.jpg, CC BY-SA 3.0.

Acknowledgments

I can vividly recall the moment an email from publisher Chris Feik landed in my inbox back in 2019 asking if writing *The Shortest History of India* would appeal to me. I was staying in Mumbai at the house of a Parsi friend who had regaled me with stories of schoolboy pranks with Salman Rushdie while attending Cathedral School at Breach Candy just down the road. From my window I could just glimpse Antilia, the unsightly two-billion-dollar residence of Mukesh Ambani, India's richest "Bollygarch." I was in Mumbai to research a book on the fabulously dysfunctional royal family of Jaipur and to pen a magazine feature on a rogue diamond trader with a penchant for ostrich-skin jackets. India had been an obsession for decades. How could I say no to the chance to write the ultimate backgrounder to all this and more.

This book owes its genesis to two of the greatest historians of their day, who taught me when I was an undergraduate. A. L. Basham and S. A. A. Rizvi—coauthors of the two-volume *The Wonder That Was India*—gave purpose to my passion and, together with my Hindi teachers Richard Barz and Yogendra Yadav, provided me with the skills I needed to spend many years working in India and then pass on my knowledge to students and readers.

Over the decades, numerous organizations and individuals have encouraged and nurtured my passages to India. They include Asialink, the Australia Council, the Australia India Council, the Australia India Institute, the Australian High Commission in New Delhi, and the Australian Consulates and their staff in Mumbai, Kolkata, and Chennai. Kama Maclean, Robin Jeffrey, Jim Masselos, Assa Doron, and Mark Allon are among the members of a sadly shrinking alumni of South Asia–literate scholars in Australia who have provided much-needed encouragement over the years.

It has been a great pleasure and privilege to work with the terrific team at The Experiment, including the wonderfully patient and thoughtful editor-at-large, Anna Bliss. My thanks also go to Black Inc. in Melbourne for including me in their Shortest History series. My gratitude, as always, to my superb agent, Fiona Inglis at Curtis Brown, and to Benjamin Paz for his work in expanding the reach of the book to a worldwide audience.

To my partner, April Fonti, thank you for always being there to share my passion for India, and for your patience, inspiration, and understanding when I needed it most. Finally, I am indebted to my children Adele, Alexander, Jonathon, and Nicolas for the infectious enthusiasm with which they have supported this and the other literary journeys I have embarked on.

Index

Brydon, William, 172, *172*, 177
Buddhism: Ambedkar's revival of, 37–40,
   40; Bamiyan destruction, 61; Buddha
   (Siddhārtha Gautama), 14, 36–38, 41–43,
   45, 56–61, 68–70; in Classical Age, 62,
   67, 69, 73; Enlightenment, 40–45, *41,
   43*; Hūṇas' violence toward, 72; Jātaka
   tales, 56–57; and Kaniṣka, 59–61, *60*;
   stupas of, 68; Untouchables and Buddhist
   conversion, 224, *224*
Bukka (Vijayanagara ruler), 103
Buland Darwaza, *122*
Burke, Edmund, 156
Butler, Elizabeth, *172*

Calcutta (Kolkata): Black Hole of, 148–52;
   East India Company (EIC) in, 143–45,
   144, 148–55; Great Calcutta Killings, 214
Caliphate in India, 82–105; and Arab trade,
   85–89; Delhi Sultanate dynasties, 89–102,
   91, 92, 97; elephants in warfare, *88*; events
   leading to, 82–86; Ghaznavid dynasty,
   84–88; Ghurid dynasty, 87–89; and Hindu
   caste system, 71; Vijayanagara Empire,
   102–5, *103*
Candragupta Maurya, 47–52, *49*, 56, 58
Canning, Lord, 175
Casey, R. G., 215
cave paintings, *68*
Ceras (southern kingdom), 75, 78
Charnock, Job, 143
Chelmsford, Lord, *192*, 194
chess, 65
Child, Josiah (London governor), 143
Child (EIC official), 143
China: economy of, 7, 252, 253–54, 256;
   Great Wall of, 58; India's foreign relations
   with, 229, 258; Kuśāṇas, 13; population
   statistics, 8, 10
Cholas (southern kingdom), 75–80
Christian missionaries, 107, 123, 130, 166,
   166, 170–71
Churchill, Winston, 199, 205, 210, 212, 213
Citizenship Amendment Act (2019), 252
class and caste system: Brahmins, 25–32,
   34–39, 59, 65, 72–74, 86, 99, 175, 250; Dāsa,
   28, 30, 31, 34, 35; and early migration,
   20–21; Gandhi on, 196; and INC support,
   244–45; in India under British rule,
   182–83; *jātis* (occupation groups), 70–71;
   and mutiny of 1857, 167–71, 173, 175; and
   Raj, 189; social disruption by, 84–85;
   Sufism on, 100–101; Untouchables, 37–40,
   71, 72, 224, *224*, 226, 262; varṇas, 34–36;
   zamindars, 157, 167
Classical Age, 62–81; and age of invaders,
   71–75; empires of the South, *75*, 75–81, *78,
   81*; during Gupta Empire, 62–72, *67, 68*

Collected Works (Gandhi), 195
Cornwallis, Lord, 156–57, 159, 165
COVID-19 pandemic, 256–57
Cripps, Stafford, 210
Cunningham, Alexander, 15
Curzon, George Nathaniel, 188–93, *190, 192, 193*

Dalhousie, Lord, 173–74, 175
Dalrymple, William, 175
Dara Shukoh (Mughal emperor), 130, 132–33
Darius I (ruler of Persia), 54
Darius III (ruler of Achaemenids), 45
Dāsa, 28, 30, 31, 34, 35
Defence of India Act (1915), 194–95
Delhi Durbar, 191–92
Delhi Sultanate dynasties, *89*, 89–102, *91,
   92, 97*, 109–11, 113–17
Desai, Morarji, 231, 232, 235
Deva Rayā II (Vijayanagara ruler), 104
al-Din, Ghiyath, 96
The Discovery of India (Nehru), 6, 118, 224
Disraeli, Benjamin, 183
dodo bird, *126*, 126–27
Dost Mohammad (Afghan ruler), 171–72
Drake, Roger, 150
Dravidian civilization, 53, 54, 75
Dufferin, Lord, 187
Duleep Singh (Sikh maharaja), 172–73
Dupleix, Joseph-François, 145–47
Dyer, Reginald, 198–200

East India Company (EIC), 138–52. *See
   also* mutiny of 1857; and Anglo-Maratha
   Wars, 157, 159–62; and Anglo-Mysore
   Wars, 157–60; automaton (tiger eating
   British soldier), *159*; and Battle of Buxar,
   153–55, 157; and Battle of Plassey, 151–53; in
   Calcutta (Kolkata), 143–45, *144*, 148–55;
   and Charles II, 141; and Clive, 138–39, *139*,
   145–54, *154*, 160; and Ellenborough, 82,
   84; end of rule by, 164–66, 170–71, 174,
   180; and French Compagnie des Indes,
   140, 145–47; and India's naming, 9; and
   Regulating Act, 155–57; and Roe, 127–29,
   137, 141, 143; seventeenth-century growth
   of, 139–43; shipping tonnage, *142*
economy and trade. *See also* East India
   Company (EIC): Arab trade, 85–89;
   China's modern-day economy, 7, 252,
   253–54, 256; cloth as currency, 142;
   coinage and monetary systems, 55, 57–58,
   59–60, 63, 65, 80, 87, 93, 97, 116, 125, 153;
   of Harappān civilization, 19; of India,
   growth trajectory, 8, 10, 253–54, 256;
   of India, post-independence, 220–21, 224–
   34, 227, 238, 247; of India vs. Pakistan and
   South Korea, 228; infrastructure under
   British rule, 173, 183–84;

About the Author

John Zubrzycki is an Australian author who has been studying Indian history for more than forty years. He has worked in India as a diplomat and foreign correspondent, taught Indian studies, and written extensively on Indian society, culture, and politics. He is the author of four books—*The House of Jaipur: The Inside Story of India's Most Glamorous Royal Family*; *Empire of Enchantment: The Story of Indian Magic*; *The Mysterious Mr Jacob: Diamond Merchant, Magician and Spy*; and *The Last Nizam: The Rise and Fall of India's Greatest Princely State*. He majored in South Asian history and Hindi at the Australian National University and has a PhD in Indian history from the University of New South Wales. John was the deputy foreign editor at *The Australian* before becoming a full-time writer.

Also available in the Shortest History series

Trade Paperback Originals • $16.95 US | $21.95 CAN

978-1-61519-569-5

978-1-61519-820-7

978-1-61519-814-6

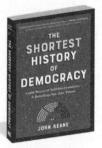

978-1-61519-896-2

978-1-61519-930-3

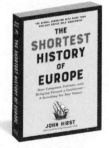

978-1-61519-914-3

978-1-61519-948-8

978-1-61519-950-1

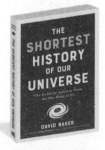

978-1-61519-973-0